D1286176

The Moral Dimensions of Empathy

The Moral Dimensions of Empathy

Limits and Applications in Ethical Theory and Practice

Julinna C. Oxley
Assistant Professor of Philosophy, Coastal Carolina University, USA

palgrave
macmillan

First published 2011 by
PALGRAVE MACMILLAN

Palgrave Macmillan in the UK is an imprint of Macmillan Publishers Limited, registered in England, company number 785998, of Houndmills, Basingstoke, Hampshire RG21 6XS.

Palgrave Macmillan in the US is a division of St Martin's Press LLC, 175 Fifth Avenue, New York, NY 10010.

Palgrave Macmillan is the global academic imprint of the above companies and has companies and representatives throughout the world.

Palgrave® and Macmillan® are registered trademarks in the United States, the United Kingdom, Europe and other countries

ISBN 978-0-230-27656-7   hardback

This book is printed on paper suitable for recycling and made from fully managed and sustained forest sources. Logging, pulping and manufacturing processes are expected to conform to the environmental regulations of the country of origin.

A catalogue record for this book is available from the British Library.

Library of Congress Cataloging-in-Publication Data

Oxley, Julinna C.
   The moral dimension of empathy : limits and applications in ethical theory and practice / Julinna C. Oxley.
      p. cm.
   Includes index.
   ISBN 978-0-230-27656-7 (alk. paper)
   1. Empathy. 2. Ethics. I. Title.

   BJ1475.O95 2011
   177'.7–dc23   2011021115

10   9   8   7   6   5   4   3   2   1
20   19   18   17   16   15   14   13   12   11

Printed and bound in the United States of America

In memory of Adam "Dean" Lutz
Go Ahead

Contents

Acknowledgments

I owe a great debt of gratitude to many people for making this book possible. My parents, Paul and Beverly Oxley, taught me the importance of empathy early on in life and I am deeply appreciative of their influence. I am grateful especially to my mother, a psychologist, for the conversations on moral development and child psychology that gave me much to think about as a philosopher. Her encouragement over the years is inestimable. My husband, Philip Whalen, has been my rock. He encouraged me day after day, and his unending support motivated me to keep working.

I am especially grateful to Jerry Gaus, who pressed me for many years to clarify my ideas on empathy. I am deeply grateful for his encouragement in writing this book. His comments on earlier drafts of the chapters have been invaluable and his influence on my thinking will be evident to anyone familiar with his work. I am also grateful to Linda Zagzebski, who encouraged me to publish my ideas on empathy. This book would not be in print had she not suggested it. Eric Mack and Bruce Brower were also extremely helpful to me and I am deeply grateful for their critical feedback on earlier drafts of the chapters.

Many of the ideas in this book have been influenced by my "family" of friends in New Orleans. I am especially grateful to Tisere Thomas, who initially got me thinking about empathy rather than sympathy. I also had memorable and formative conversations with Sherri Hutton, Isabelle Henderson, Jennifer Gaines, Tierney Kelly, Michael Bradley, Lucas Davenport, and Dean Lutz. Thank you for your friendship and patience during the ten years I have been thinking about empathy.

I owe special thanks to my friends and colleagues who read chapters of this book at various stages. Jonny Anomaly, Deb Breede, Amanda Brian, Dennis Earl, Denise Forrest, Holley Tankersley, Karsten Stueber, Nathan Nobis, Beverly Oxley, Kate Oestreich, Cynthia Port, Renee Smith, Jon Trerise, Keira Williams, and Philip Whalen provided much-needed feedback and editorial suggestions.

This book would not have been possible without friends and family to help care for my daughter Marigny, who was born in the middle of this book project. I am deeply grateful to Cristina Egloff for providing daycare for Marigny for 18 months while I put the book together. She gave me the peace of mind needed to focus on the book daily. I am also thankful to my sister Andeena Oxley, Beverly Oxley and Philip Whalen for providing additional care for Marigny on weekends so that I could finish this book. This book is for Marigny.

Part I
Why Empathy?

1
The Empathy-Morality Connection

In recent years, empathy has received significant popular attention from scholars and pundits who believe it is the basis of the moral life, and who suggest that developing empathy will be the solution to our moral failings. When Phoebe Prince, a 15-year old from South Hadley, Massachusetts, committed suicide after being bullied by her schoolmates, TIME magazine ran a story stating that research in empathy suggests that it is a "key, if not *the* key, to all human social interaction and morality."[1] Psychologists and moral educators interviewed for the article argued that to prevent severe bullying in schools, students needed to be taught how to "put themselves in another person's shoes," so that they can consider others' feelings and stop abusing their peers. In a similar vein, political advisor and activist Jeremy Rifkin states in *The Empathic Civilization* that empathy is the "social glue" that keeps society functioning as a cohesive whole. "Without empathy it would be impossible to even imagine a social life and the organization of society...Society requires being social and being social requires empathic extension."[2]

Does empathy really make people nice to others and keep us together as a society? If so, how does it do this? Over the last several decades, psychologists have investigated the relationship between empathy and prosocial behavior, and have concluded that the more one identifies with another person or is similar to that person, the more likely she is to empathize with her and be altruistically motivated toward her.[3] Although this sounds good, the problem is that empathy is also biased. People tend to empathize to a greater degree with family members, members of their primary group, close friends, and people whose personal needs and concerns are similar to their own. They also tend to empathize more with victims in an immediate situation—in other words, with those who are

3

present, rather than those who are absent.[4] If this is the case, an ethics built on empathy in the way that Rifkin suggests cannot, at least without correction from moral principles and concerns, be the "social glue" that keeps society functioning together as a cohesive whole. It is certainly not the sole basis for morality. Many of our emotions, such as resentment, indignation, and guilt play a central role in providing a motivation and interest in morality. In addition, fear of others and concern for our own self-interest motivate us to cooperate with others and set limits regarding our interactions with others, so that our social engagements are more stable. Empathy is certainly part of the story of morality, but by no means the whole of it.

The view that I will articulate in this book is that empathy is essential to the moral life, and is instrumental to developing a wide range of moral capabilities as they are defined by a variety of ethical theories. Empathy has the potential to enrich and strengthen moral deliberation, action and moral justification to others. But empathy is not intrinsically moral and does not always lead to moral thought or action. An empathizer that is simply motivated to act *pro-socially* in favor of the person with whom she empathizes does not necessarily act *morally* or prudently. To support this thesis, I examine empirical psychological studies on empathy, theories of empathy in the philosophy of mind, normative ethical theories of right action, and contractual ethical theories of moral deliberation and justification, to show how empathy can be ethically "educated" or informed by moral principles and criteria to be useful in moral judgment and deliberation. But before I elaborate, let me put my thesis in the context by examining how other moral philosophers have viewed the role of empathy in the moral life.

1.1 Empathy and ethics

Moral philosophers have always been interested in the role of emotions in ethics, but empathy is different from emotions like guilt, fear, anger, joy or sorrow. Our colloquial usage of the term empathy suggests that it involves "feeling another's pain" or "stepping into another person's shoes," but the original definition of empathy suggested that it involved "feeling with" another person. The term empathy was introduced into the English language by Edward Titchener in 1909 as a translation of the word *Einfuhlung*, which was originally specified by the German psychologist Lipps to describe "feeling one's way into another" or resonating with another person.[5] Titchener views empathy as feeling one's way into another's perceptions or imagination.[6] This makes possible the transfer of emotion from one person to another.[7] For now, let us suppose that empathy can involve any of these ideas— taking up another's perspective, feeling another's emotion, or feeling *into* another's emotion and perceptions.

So what is the connection between empathy and ethics? Perhaps the most obvious connection between empathy and ethics is "golden rule-style" reasoning, which involves figuring out what to do in a situation by imagining what you would want done if you were in the other person's position. On this view, moral deliberation involves imagining the other person's perspective and what it would be like to be in that position, or feeling the emotion they feel in that situation, determining what you would like to happen in if you were in that position, and then performing that action. But it is not at all clear that this kind of empathetic perspective-taking would be moral. Suppose for example that a student makes a bad grade on a test, and comes to the professor's office crying and requesting to do extra work to improve the grade. The professor empathizes with the student and feels her distress about the bad grade, and determines that, if she were in the student's position, she would want the professor to offer an opportunity to change the grade, or to do extra credit to change the grade. But should the professor change the grade, or offer the student an opportunity to do extra work? Most people think that she should not, because it would be unfair to the other students who also did poorly on the exam. In this situation, empathy and the golden rule do not generate the correct moral answer.

But this does not mean that empathy is inappropriate in all moral deliberation. The view I will endorse in this book is that empathy should figure centrally in moral deliberation, reflection, motivation, and action, but that empathy *alone* is insufficient as a moral guide. While empathy is instrumental to moral action, it must be used in tandem with specific moral principles and directives to generate a moral response. My argument here is that empathy ought to play an *instrumental* role in defining and motivating normative moral principles and obligations, and it can plausibly do this in many ethical theories, even rationalist ones. I will maintain that empathy is instrumental to bringing about the motives, actions, and virtues that are advocated by a variety of moral theories because it performs a number of *epistemic* functions that enable us to reflect on our beliefs about others in a new way. These epistemological processes and products are distinct from altruistic cognition, motivation or behavior,[8] and are evident in the more cognitively developed kinds of empathy. Empathy enables people to understand how others see the world, helps them to appreciate others' perspectives and connect with them emotionally, eliminates the perception of conflict between oneself and others, and makes possible the perception of similarity between oneself and others.

Focusing on empathy's epistemic dimension is an approach that has the resources for explaining how empathy and empathic thinking are relevant to ethical reflection, deliberation, and justification. Empathy understood in this way is instrumental to finding opportunities to act on the moral law, justifying moral principles, justifying oneself to others by showing that certain principles and practices are reasonable to others, and taking up the "moral point of view." These are tasks required by several ethical theories, including Kantian ethics, utilitarian ethics, and contractarian ethics, and not just ethical theories that emphasize care and altruism. Since empathy's most important functions are epistemic, empathy alone is insufficient and undesirable as a sole moral criterion; empathy is a psychological experience, not a normative principle. Thus, it cannot serve as a criterion of morally good action.

This view regarding empathy's contribution to ethics is distinct from others made regarding the normative role of empathy in the moral life. For example, care theorist Michael Slote argues for the centrality of empathy to care ethics, and claims that "empathy plays a crucial enabling role in the development of genuinely altruistic concern or caring for others."[9] Empathy should be the basis for the ethics of care, for in his view, empathy generates empathic caring, and empathic caring can be used as "a plausible criterion of moral evaluation."[10] I discuss Slote's view in greater depth in Chapter 4, but essentially, he argues that empathy should serve a *constitutive* role in defining normative moral principles and obligations. In the ethics of care, empathy does not need "correction" by more objective, systematic, or principled moral concerns, or even by general care principles.[11] Empathic bias is not a limitation of empathy, but a source of justification of care ethical principles. The degree of "natural" empathetic engagement with others corresponds to our obligations to them; differences in the strength of empathy for others correspond to "differences of intuitive moral evaluation, and that fact...will allow an ethics of caring that brings in empathy—an ethics of empathic caring—to give a fairly general account of both public/political and private/individual morality."[12] This position is difficult to defend, because it seems intuitive that empathy's biases need correction by considerations that are external to the empathetic experience.

My position regarding empathy and its epistemic functions is also distinct from feminist philosopher Diana Meyers' moral theory.[13] Meyers puts forward a normative theory of moral deliberation called "empathic thought," which involves imagining the other person and her situation in order to produce sensitive understanding and recognition of the other, oneself, and the relationship; this will determine the values and goals that are important and relevant in the situation.[14] The moral agent then uses her own personal moral ideals and commitments, rather than utilitarian or Kantian principles, to make a moral judgment. I examine her view in greater detail in Chapter 5, but for now let me state that while Meyers' theory of moral deliberation is compatible with my thesis that empathy is instrumental to performing a number of tasks in normative moral deliberation, her main argument, that empathic thought should supplant "impartial reason," understood as universalizable reasoning that does not recognize differences between individuals and is applied systematically, without recognition of difference and cultural prejudice, is not.[15] I agree with Meyers that our perception of others frames the terms and conditions of moral deliberation, and that we ought to advocate for empathy, since empathy with others reframes our understanding of them, and enables us to understand them in relation to ourselves. But I will make the case that traditional moral theories that construe moral subjects as rational deliberators are not the main problem; using empathy, these theories can be corrected so that they do not sustain systematic cultural prejudices.

1.2   Defining empathy

Before elaborating my thesis further, it is necessary to define empathy more carefully and explicitly. There are many definitions of empathy, and the plausibility of any claim regarding empathy's relationship to morality depends entirely on how it is defined. There is no one accepted definition of empathy in the academic literature, and this is likely due to the fact that empathy has been researched from a variety of disciplines—social psychology, experimental psychology, personality theory, counseling theory, moral theory, cognitive neuroscience, primatology, and philosophy of mind—so that there is no one definition that suits the needs of the specialists who study it. Psychologist C. Daniel Batson distinguishes eight different uses of the term empathy that have emerged in the psychological, philosophical, and neuroscientific literature:

1. Knowing Another Person's Internal State, Including His or Her Thoughts and Feelings

2. Adopting the Posture or Matching the Neural Responses of an Observed Other
3. Coming to Feel as Another Person Feels
4. Intuiting or Projecting Oneself into Another's Situation
5. Imagining How Another Is Thinking and Feeling
6. Imagining How One Would Think and Feel in the Other's Place
7. Feeling Distress at Witnessing Another Person's Suffering
8. Feeling for Another Person Who is Suffering[16]

These phenomena are all identified as empathy by different types of researchers. But there is no agreement that they are all *really* empathy; in fact, most philosophers would describe concepts 7 and 8 above as *sympathy*, which involves feeling care or concern for someone's well-being, or feeling sorrow, or sorry, for another. Sympathy is different in that it involves direct concern for another person as a subject, and is motivated by an interest in the other person and her well-being; empathy does not require this kind of concern.

Since there are so many definitions of empathy, it will be useful for me to give an overview of how other disciplines view the relationship between empathy and morality. This will clarify how my investigation of empathy and the development of moral capabilities connect—or do not connect—with other fields of research. I briefly describe the empirical studies of empathy that relate to behavior, and then state whether I will use this information (a) to elaborate a philosophical understanding of empathy, (b) to develop my thesis regarding the role of empathy in normative ethics, or (c) not at all.

One of the most interesting areas of research on empathy is in cognitive neuroscience, where researchers investigate the biological and neurological bases of empathy, understood as (2) adopting the posture or matching the neural responses of an observed other. To do this, scientists first used functional magnetic resonance imaging (fMRI) in rhesus monkeys to determine which parts of the brain are activated when observing another's emotional state.[17] The resulting discovery was of "mirror neurons" that fire when a monkey performs an action, as well as when they observe another being perform that same action. Similar mirror neuronal systems have been found in humans; groups of neurons are stimulated during both the performance of certain actions and the mere observation of those actions in other beings.[18] The claim by researchers is that mirror neurons contribute to our ability to (1) know and understand another person's internal state, including his or her thoughts and feelings, and (3) feel the emotions that other people feel. While mirror neurons may contribute to social cognition, this research is better used to investigate the biological bases of our interest in and concern for others.[19] I am interested in developing an ethical theory that takes the perspective-taking features of empathy as central to moral deliberation (concepts (4)–(7)), and since neuroscientists focus on concepts (1)–(3), this literature will not figure prominently in my work here.

Epistemologists and philosophers of mind interested in social cognition and our knowledge of other minds also study empathy. "Simulation" theorists such as Alvin Goldman first expressed an interest in empathy and defined it as simulation of another's point of view.[20] Empathy in this context is defined as (5) imagining how another is thinking and feeling, or (6) imagining how one would think and feel in the other's place. Although Goldman and philosopher Robert Gordon are in favor of using empathy in moral deliberation, they imply that moral deliberation involves simulation of what you would like to happen if you were in another's situation, and acting accordingly.[21] I have already suggested that this is an inadequate view of how empathy should function in normative ethics, and will substantiate my view in Chapters 4 and 5. More relevant to my project here is philosopher Karsten Stueber's defense of empathy as (4) intuiting or projecting oneself into another's situation, as the primary way that we get information about others.[22] I build on Stueber's defense of folk psychological views of knowing others in Chapter 3, and articulate the view that empathy has specific epistemic functions that are relevant to ethical deliberation.

Finally, the field of psychology boasts a century's worth of research on empathy—in social psychology, experimental psychology, personality theory, and counseling theory. Psychologists in the first half of the 20th century saw empathy as a capacity to feel another's emotion, to feel one's way into another's life and perspective, and as such, it is a skill that one can develop over time. Sigmund Freud described empathy as when "we take the producing person's psychical state into consideration, put ourselves into it and try to understand it by comparing it with our own" and "that which plays the largest part in our understanding of what is inherently foreign to our ego in other people."[23] And the psychoanalyst Heinz Kohut says that in empathetic experience, "we think ourselves into his place" and take by "vicarious introspection," or empathy, the experience of another "as if it were our own and thus revive inner experiences" in order to arrive at "an appreciation of the meaning."[24] This definition of empathy is important to Karsten Stueber's defense of empathy as a method of getting knowledge about others in the social sciences, and is appropriate for a context in which one has a motive to get knowledge about another for the purposes of historical research or social science. It was also important to clinician Carl Rogers, who believed empathy played a central role in counseling theory: "To sense the client's inner world of private, personal meanings as if it were your own, but without ever losing the 'as if' quality, this is empathy."[25] Since both the social scientist's relation to her subject and the therapist-client relationship are unique, and based on the therapist's (or researcher's) desire and interest in understanding the client's (or subject's) "inner world," this definition of empathy will be less relevant to my purposes here.

More recent psychological research on empathy will figure prominently in my work here. Research on empathy's role in social cognition, how we match emotions, and perspective-taking and its consequences are relevant to my thesis regarding empathy's role in moral development, and I discuss it throughout the book. Specifically, I employ contemporary moral psychologist's Martin Hoffman's distinctions of five modes of empathic arousal to show how the cognitively advanced types of empathy have both an epistemological function and a normative one.[26] In addition, I use social psychologist Daniel Batson's empirical studies regarding the relationship between empathy and altruistic action to show that some modes of perspective-taking are more effective than others in eliciting different kinds of "moral" responses, and that these differences in perspective-taking should be taken into account when teaching empathy.[27]

Psychological research on empathy in different populations of people, such as those with autism or psychopathology, has also gained significant attention from philosophers interested in meta-ethical issues such as the nature of moral agency and the nature of moral judgments (as rational or sentimental).[28] Philosophers are interested in this research because they believe empathy involves both emotion recognition and emotion matching, and that its affective dimension contributes to moral judgment; thus, those who lack empathy will lack the ability to make moral judgments, and this should tell us something about moral agency and whether morality is ultimately grounded in affect or reason.[29] Although these are important philosophical issues that have implications for normative ethics, I will only address them insofar as they are relevant to my thesis regarding empathy's role in moral deliberation. While I do believe empathy is very important to moral deliberation and judgment, I agree with Martin Hoffman that being incapable of empathy does not "doom one to manipulating or killing others."[30]

Those who lack empathic abilities may use other methods to learn people's emotions and understand their point of view, if they are interested in doing so.

1.3   Moral dimensions of empathy

With this overview of the different connections between empathy and ethical concerns, I now turn to clarifying what I will do in this book. My interest is in the normative role of empathy in ethics, or the appropriate role for empathy in moral deliberation and action. Since my focus is on how empathy impacts moral evaluation, and since empathy is not an emotion *per se*, I will not address the relationship between emotions and moral evaluation in general. The central issue I will examine is empathy's role in making a moral decision. My thesis is that empathy should play a supporting role, i.e. an instrumental role in making a moral decision or in moral judgment, but that it cannot be the sole basis for moral judgment.

Chapter 2 begins by defining empathy. This chapter is a rather technical analysis of the philosophical definitions of empathy, because as we have seen, many distinct but closely-related phenomena are identified as empathy. Some philosophers, especially philosophers of mind, have equated empathy with simulation, and I show that while the most cognitively-advanced kinds of empathy may include simulation, simulation is neither necessary nor sufficient for empathy. In light of ordinary language usage that suggests empathy is in some way emotional, I make the case that some kind of "affect" should be included in the philosophical definition of empathy, which could include, for example, one's sharing another's emotion. The reason this addition is crucial is that otherwise, a sadist's "simulation" of another's state could be considered "empathy," and this goes contrary to the way people commonly use the term empathy. Then, I articulate a multi-dimensional *functional* account of empathy that can serve as a broad framework for how to define empathy in philosophical studies. The functional account defines empathy as the correspondence between various inputs (empathy's "triggers"), processes (what it means to experience empathy), and outputs (empathy's epistemic and behavioral consequences). The advantage of this definition is that it allows for a variety of phenomena to be considered "empathy" but also allows for the identification and specification of one particular type of empathy.[31]

Part II explores the kind of experience empathy involves—what empathy does and what it doesn't do. Chapter 3 examines what empathy does, the kind of attitude that is involved in empathy, and how these features relate to moral judgment and deliberation. The central question I address is whether empathy involves strong "approval" of another's emotion, or whether it is the kind of experience that can be used to learn about another's emotion. I contend that certain kinds of empathy, namely, the cognitively-advanced types of empathy[32] do not require strong approval—they require what I will call "prima facie" approval of another's emotion—and that the most important function of empathy is epistemic: empathy can be used to acquire justified beliefs about others' mental and emotional states. The cognitively advanced types of empathy have the requisite cognitive content needed to impact one's beliefs and thus have epistemic functions. These include information gathering and understanding others. Most importantly, the knowledge gained through empathy is different from knowledge gained about others with theories or in a strictly rational way. Knowledge gained with empathy is framed in reference to oneself, and this is why it is important for moral deliberation: empathy can transform one's view of others, one's view of what is valuable, and one's view of what matters, both to others and to oneself.

After describing empathy's positive dimensions, Chapter 4 discusses empathy's limitations or negative qualities, and explains why, given these limitations, empathy cannot be the sole basis of moral judgment. To support this thesis, I make two arguments: first, that the research showing that empathy motivates altruism is limited to a certain range of situations (such as clinical settings), and so we cannot conclude that empathy *generally* generates altruistic outcomes. Second, I claim that, given empathy's tendency to bias and prejudice, as suggested by the empirical studies, it cannot be an appropriate *foundation* for morality; it should be understood as playing an *instrumental* role in moral deliberation and judgment. My line of argumentation in this chapter will examine and rebut Michael Slote's view that empathy's purported connection to altruism recommends a *constitutive* role for empathy in defining normative moral principles and obligations.

Chapter 5 lays out my view of the appropriate normative role of perspective-taking empathy in moral deliberation and judgment. To support my thesis that empathy cannot be the sole basis of morality, I assert that what makes empathy relevant to moral deliberation is its *salience effect:* empathy makes salient another's particular emotions, concerns, reasons, interests, and considerations in such a way that they are relevant and important to the empathizer, so that she is motivated to respond to these considerations. When empathy's salience effect is at work, it can generate *empathetic deliberation*, which involves acquiring a sensitive appreciation of another's feelings, reasons, beliefs, and point of view. But empathetic deliberation is not tantamount to moral deliberation, unless it is informed by moral principles, reasons, or commitments. *Empathetic* deliberation is *moral* deliberation when these concerns are taken into account in combination with personal moral commitments, or an impartial decision procedure. Empathetic deliberation is not simply hypothetical deliberation, and theories that incorporate empathy should allow empathy's salience effect to play a significant role in the deliberative process.

After describing how empathy can contribute to moral deliberation as it is defined from a wide range of ethical theories, Chapter 6 examines the role of empathy in *contractual* ethical theories in particular. Contractual ethical theories are distinct from other normative ethical theories because they are based on the idea of rational agreement and seek the public justification of moral principles. My thesis is that the philosophical contract theories of John Rawls, John Harsanyi and David Gauthier seek to provide grounds of agreement for points of view that are thought to be irreconcilable, and they do this by engaging in interpersonal justification and providing deliberation that *models* different types of empathy. This is a rather surprising thesis, given that these contract theories are supposed to be grounded in rationality or reasonableness; nevertheless, I show that the reasoning modeled in three social contracts is *empathetic*, insofar as it involves thinking about, imagining, or reflecting on another person's feelings, reasons, and responses in a certain situation to discover their reasons for supporting different principles. There are different ways of imagining oneself in the perspective of others, and these differences are captured and expressed in different kinds of contractual reasoning. Ultimately, the contractual method's goal of public justification is best understood as interpersonal justification, a process of justification that seeks to take into account all points of view and perspectives.

Once empathy's contribution to moral deliberation and justification has been articulated, I explain how this contribution can be enhanced when empathy is *taught*. Chapter 7 examines the different kinds of empathy that can be taught, the methods of teaching empathy (rationally, through induction, through interaction with a baby), and the purposes for which empathy can be taught (for the purposes of generating care, for cultivating understanding and diversity, or for developing the skill of reading others' emotions). I contend that these differences in method and context are important because the moral context of empathy varies from one program to another, so teachers of empathy, including parents, need awareness of what they are asking students to do when they "empathize" with others. Citing empirical evidence, I conclude that the cultivation of empathy must begin early in life in order for people to be inclined to use empathy in making a moral decision.

Chapter 8 reflects on the implications of my argument regarding the normative role of empathy in moral deliberation and judgment for feminist ethics in particular. I argue that the goals of feminist ethics would be well-served by focusing more attention on empathy, but simply because a theory implements empathy does not mean it automatically satisfies the goals of a feminist ethic. I also examine the idea that empathy is "gendered"—that is, the claim that women are more empathetic than men—and show that while women may have better *expressions* of empathy than men, women are not necessarily more empathetic than men. Moreover, gendered stereotypes of empathy should not recommend disparate moral expectations for men and women. I briefly explain how empathy can be used to teach a variety of virtues, such as respect for difference, diversity, tolerance, and non-violence, and suggest that these could be integrated into a framework of social virtues that could promote social cooperation.

This concludes my summary of the arguments that are to come. Ultimately, my aim here has been to persuade the reader that empathy should be at the center of our reflection on ethics. Empathy enables us to more accurately perceive and appreciate others' emotions, feelings, and situations, and such experiences facilitate our understanding of others and their needs. Since empathy has attributes associated with both "thinking" and "feeling," it is a unique experience that can make a powerful epistemic contribution to moral judgment. Nevertheless, this contribution should not be overstated. Empathy is not a cure for the human condition. But the more we can understand it, apply it, and teach it, the more we can improve human interaction.

2
What is Empathy?

The previous chapter mentioned eight different ways that empathy has been defined in philosophy, psychology, and neuroscience. How should empathy be defined in philosophy and normative ethics in particular? Several proposals have been made. Ethicist Justin D'Arms defines empathy as both an act *and* a capacity: empathy involves responding "to the perceived feelings of another with vicarious emotional reactions of one's own, and empathy is the capacity for, or the occurrence of, such a vicarious experience."[1] This definition captures the idea that empathy involves responding to another's emotion by acquiring a similar emotion, and focuses on the "feeling another's emotion" aspect of empathy.

On the other hand, philosophers of mind Peter Goldie and Robert Gordon emphasize the imaginative or simulative aspect of empathy. Goldie defines empathy as "a process or procedure by which a person *centrally imagines* the thoughts, feelings, and emotions (what I will call the *narrative*) of another person."[2] And Gordon says that an empathetic simulation involves an "imaginative shift in the reference of indexicals' where the imaginer 'recenters his egocentric map.'"[3] While Goldie and Gordon's definitions are plausible, they fail to include the affective dimension of empathy—arousing feelings or transferring emotion—which D'Arms includes, and which developmental psychologists, cognitive neuroscientists, and laypersons take to be characteristic of empathy. Goldie and Gordon imply that empathy involves "stepping into another's shoes," but does not require feeling a resulting, congruent emotion.

Excluding the affective dimension of empathy is a mistake, and my goal here is to explain why definitions of empathy should include the idea that empathy involves experiencing a *congruent* emotion in regard to another's perceived state, but not necessarily the other's *exact* emotion.[4]

Although this feature may seem unimportant, if empathy is understood to be mere simulation, then it is possible to interpret a sadist's simulation or imagination of her victim's pain as "empathy." But this interpretation goes contrary to common usage of the term empathy; what is different in this case is that the sadist does not really "feel" her victim's pain. Psychologists who study empathy recognize that this type of simulation is not empathy as we usually think of it, and thus define empathy in a way that involves an affective dimension.[5] Philosophers ought to do the same, and so my goal is to clarify the concept of empathy by defending a *functional* account of empathy that has already been adopted by a number of psychologists. This definition outlines the features required for empathy, and at the same time allows for a wide range of experiences to be called empathy. The functional account defines empathy as a multidimensional process involving (a) mental events such as imitation, projection or pictorial representation, (b) affective components, and (c) epistemic or behavioral outputs.

To articulate this view of empathy, I explain the difference between empathy and sympathy, describe the philosophical roots of the idea of empathy, and differentiate the two dominant conceptions of empathy, *emotional contagion* (which involves the spontaneous transfer of emotion) and *imaginative perspective-taking* (which involves perspective-swapping or role-taking). Then I distinguish three main types of perspective-taking empathy: *other-focused empathy, self-focused empathy,* and *dual-perspective empathy*. Next I describe the importance of shared emotional response, and explain why empathy should be understood as including an emotional response of *matching* another's emotion. Finally, I articulate the functional definition of empathy and outline the advantages of using this definition in the philosophical study of ethics.

2.1   Empathy as emotional contagion

Although the term empathy did not emerge into the English language until the 20th century, both Adam Smith's and David Hume's discussions of sympathy mention qualities that are now considered to be empathy.[6] Thus, the two dominant approaches empathy outlined at the beginning of the chapter can be traced to Smith and Hume. The first conception of empathy—an affective response to another person's feeling, namely, feeling the other's emotion—can be traced to David Hume's definition of sympathy: a capacity of human nature to "receive by communication" the "inclinations and sentiments" of others, "however different from, or even contrary to our own."[7] This is why Hume describes sympathy (our concept of empathy) as a capacity for communicating emotions; the point of empathy is to "take us so far out of ourselves, as to give us the same pleasure or uneasiness in the characters of others."[8] Hume's discussion of the *transmission of emotion* provides conceptual roots for empathy understood as an affective transfer of emotion, even though other features of his concept of sympathy do not apply to empathy.

Before clarifying this view of empathy further, let me briefly describe how contemporary thinkers view the difference between empathy and sympathy. Sympathy involves care or concern for the other, and is often described as "feeling sorry for" the other.[9] Stephen Darwall usefully defines sympathy as "a feeling or emotion that responds to some apparent threat or obstacle to an individual's good and involves concern for him, and thus for his well-being, for his sake."[10] This definition captures what is distinctive of sympathy, namely, that it involves feeling *concern* for someone's well-being, or feeling sorrow, or sorry, for another, while empathy involves the transfer of emotion, and in some cases, perspective-taking that is absent in sympathy.[11] Most importantly, sympathy involves direct concern for another person as a subject distinct from oneself, in a way that empathy does not. In principle, it is possible to feel sympathy without empathy and vice versa.[12]

So how are emotions transferred from one person to another, according to Hume? He argues that when one person observes another's passions, "the idea is presently converted into an impression, and acquires such a degree of force and vivacity, as to become the very passion itself, and produce an equal emotion, as any original affection."[13] For example, Amy's impression of Zack's affective state is immediately or non-inferentially converted into a copy of Zack's feeling, without inference or conscious cognition. In this experience, Amy comes to feel Zack's emotion spontaneously, non-cognitively, and in virtue of her having an idea of Zack's experience, so that the passion arises "in conformity to the images we form of them."[14] Though Hume's argument here is philosophically complex, the model he proposes suggests that the observer's (Amy's) own ideas of the other's (Zack's) experiences are duplicated into affective experiences that reflect her observation by force of the imagination.[15] Hume's theory serves as the basis of the modern view of empathy as *emotional contagion*, where one person non-inferentially "catches" another's feeling simply in virtue of perceiving it.[16]

Empirical research has been conducted on young infants and toddlers, and these studies suggest that it is plausible for emotions to be transmitted in this way, in that certain types of empathic arousal occur via a sort of trigger-response. In these studies, 10- to 14-months old infants responded to the distress expressions of others with crying, and seemed to imitate the distress cues of the other as if they were "trying on" their emotional expressions.[17] Studies show that young children "catch" the emotions of others by performing a kind of *motor mimicry* of the other agent, and by mimicking the facial expressions of adults.[18] In fact, it seems more likely that emotional contagion would occur in infants and toddlers who lack sophisticated linguistic skills and a robust concept of "self," since infants (usually up to age two) cannot yet distinguish their own experiences from the experiences of others. Thus, their empathetic responses are plausibly described as non-cognitive and non-inferential. These responses are evidence for the "triggering" of an emotion in a non-inferential, immediate way, via perceptions or Humean conversion of ideas into impressions.

Recent research in neurobiology suggests that there is another explanation for this type of emotional contagion—mirror neurons. Cognitive scientists have recently been touting the "mirroring" capacity in both animal and human minds.[19] This capacity is of some neurons to activate during both the performance of certain actions and the mere observation of those actions. These neurons replicate the neural stimulation of actual action during the observation of those actions, and they also fire when we feel affective sensations or observe such affective sensations in others. Essentially, when Amy observes Zack crying, the stimulated regions of Amy's brain and the signal patterns of those regions are similar to Zack's regions and patterns. The theory is that merely observing emotions can trigger neurobiological responses that are a primitive kind of empathy like emotional contagion. Since these responses trigger an emotion via perception or direct representation, they should not be interpreted as equivalent to *understanding* another's emotions, as Remy Debes maintains.[20] The mirror neurons that fire when we observe emotions cannot account for the more robust mental content needed for the more cognitively advanced kinds of empathy that involve a transfer of emotion in virtue of Amy finding Zack's emotion intelligible and appropriate.[21]

2.2 Empathy as imaginative perspective-taking

The second way of defining empathy is traced to Adam Smith's view of sympathy. According to Smith, we come to feel the emotions of others not merely by perceiving what they are feeling, but by imagining ourselves in their position and simulating their experiences.

Smith's discussion, like Hume's, is technically on *sympathy*, but his writings on the topic are widely recognized by philosophers and psychologists alike to refer to our modern term empathy. Smith says that when, for example, we observe someone balanced on a tightrope:

> By the imagination we place ourselves in his situation, we conceive ourselves enduring all the same torments, we enter as it were into his body, and become in some measure the same person with him, and thence form some idea of his sensations, and even feel something which, though weaker in degree, is not altogether unlike them.[22]

By imaginatively projecting oneself into the perspective of others, one imagines, simulates, and feels what it would be like in that situation, and as a result, experiences in some degree the emotion the other person feels. Smith argues that the transmission of emotion is a result of the imaginative experience of the other's internal states, because by entering into another's perspective and imagining how he views the world, one can understand how he views the world at least momentarily.

Smith's description of empathy—like Hume's—implies that physical proximity to the other person augments empathy, for direct observation or physical closeness makes salient the other person's emotions and experiences in a way that motivates the imaginative experience. Physical proximity and interaction with the other is indeed crucial for empathy.[23] What distinguishes Smith's accounts of empathy from Hume's is its emphasis on a conscious awareness of the other's internal states, and imagination of the other's internal perspective; thus, it is thought to be a more "cognitive" account of empathy. The primary difference between empathy as *imaginative simulation* and empathy as *emotional contagion* is that the former requires conscious cognition of the other person's internal states and the latter does not. Since there are a variety of ways one might take up another's perspective, I now distinguish the ways one can simulate another's perspective.[24]

2.2.2   Self-focused imagination[25]

There are at least two ways to take up another's perspective: (a) imagining *oneself* in another person's situation and circumstances, or (b) imagining what it is like to be *someone else* in his situation and circumstances. Philosophers of mind have different terms for these kinds of imagination, some of which are called empathy, but the terms I use to describe these two kinds are *self-focused imagination* and *other-focused imagination*. Once

I have distinguished these two imaginative viewpoints, I will explain how they relate to empathy.

Self-focused imagination involves imagining *oneself* in another person's position. For example, Amy imagines being in Zack's circumstances (but doesn't think about being Zack himself), and imagines *herself* in *his* situation. This way of imagining situations is quite common. People sometimes ask for advice, and the response is, "Well, if I were in your situation, I would...." In this case, we imagine ourselves in the *circumstances* of another person's position, but use our own desires, beliefs, psychology, and personality to guide the imaginative process and determine a response. Self-focused imagination is illustrated in an oft-cited experiment performed by Kahneman and Tversky. In this experiment, they asked respondents to answer questions about people's emotional responses in a hypothetical case of "missed flights."[26] The situation people are told in the experiment is the following: Mr. Crane and Mr. Tees both arrive at an airport 30 minutes late. Upon arrival, Mr. Tees learns that his flight left on time, so he missed it by 30 minutes. But Mr. Crane learns that his flight was delayed, and he missed it by only five minutes. The respondents are then asked who would be most upset about missing the flight. Consider for a moment how you might respond. If you answered that Mr. Crane would be more upset than Mr. Tees, then your response is in line with 96 per cent of the respondents.

This experiment has some interesting implications. Kahneman and Tversky originally thought the experiment was important because it showed that people had *the same* response to a hypothetical situation, and were frustrated by the same kinds of scenarios. But Peter Goldie notes that what is interesting is that people answered the question about Mr. Crane and Mr. Tees not based on what *the two men* would feel, but on what *they* would feel. The respondents were not given any special information about Mr. Crane and Mr. Tees, like whether either of them was unusually patient or extremely irascible. Thus, when faced with a hypothetical situation, they imaginatively projected themselves into the situation and answered based on what *they* would feel in the situation. Goldie argues that since the respondents didn't have any information about the two men, this cannot be an example of simulation or "in his shoes" imagining. And yet, this kind of self-focused imagination *can* be a forerunner of empathy.[27] In fact, when people do not have much information about another but observe someone in distress, they often project themselves into another's situation, draw on their own experiences to predict the other's emotion, and respond. Whether they *accurately* predict or feel what the other person is feeling is another question.[28]

2.2.3 Other-focused imagination

The second way of imagining oneself in another's perspective is what I call *other-focused imagination*. Here, Amy focuses on Zack's psychological features and imagines "what it is like" to be Zack, with Zack's beliefs, desires, and concerns. She doesn't judge Zack's mental states, but imagines them from his internal, first-person perspective. She imagines how he is thinking and feeling. This sort of imagination requires that Amy have some relevant information about Zack, which she uses to imagine being Zack. This could include perceptual information regarding Zack's situation, such as observing him win a race or fall from a bicycle, first-hand knowledge of Zack and his situation, i.e. that Zack's mother has died, or third-hand information about Zack and his own situation, such as through literature or media. No matter which case, Amy imagines the situation of Zack, and imagines being Zack in that situation. The accuracy of Amy's imagination largely depends on how much information she has about Zack and the extent to which she aims to genuinely imagine being him.

Suppose, for example, that Amy has a friend Ginger, and Ginger's mother has died. Amy imagines how Ginger must feel in this situation, and imagines being Ginger. To do this accurately, she will need to take into account the fact that Ginger has (had) a horrible relationship with her mother, and so when she imagines what it is like to be Ginger, she simulates having Ginger's beliefs (that her mother is a bad person) and attitudes (disdain for her). Amy concludes that Ginger might plausibly be glad of her mother's death. Now if Amy doesn't have the relevant information about Ginger and her mother, then other-focused imagination will be difficult to accomplish. Amy needs some knowledge of Ginger's beliefs, attitudes and other emotions that could provide the content needed for other-focused imagination.

Of course, even if one has information about another person, she can never *really* know whether other-focused imagination will accurately reflect the exact emotions and feelings of that other person. Suppose that Amy imagines herself in the situation Dr. Martin Luther King, Jr. Though Amy doesn't know Dr. King, she has read about him in books, seen pictures of him in various types of media, and has a lot of information about his beliefs, family relationships, and what he desired with regard to the civil rights movement. Supposing that Amy has a substantial amount of information about Dr. King, she can imagine being him and campaigning for social justice across the South, going to jail, preaching, and befriending fellow civil rights workers. But there is so much information that Amy does not have—knowledge of his personal life and how he acted in outside the public eye—that her other-focused imagination will be limited. In this case, there is information that she does not have—knowledge of what it was like to be a black man in the Jim Crow South—and which a (non-Black) woman could not get. Although imagination can transport one's awareness to another's perspective so that she sees herself "as" another, there is no guarantee that one really sees things "as" the other sees them.[29] This is one of the limits of other-focused imagination, but as I explain later, its goal is to focus one's attention on the *other* and not oneself.

2.2.4   Dual-perspective imagination (combination mode)

A third kind of imaginative perspective-taking is called *dual-perspective imagination,* and it involves taking up the other's perspective, but still seeing things from one's own perspective.[30] Dual-perspective imagination is when Amy imagines being in Zack's circumstances, and sees things from both her own and Zack's perspective; she switches back and forth from her own perspective to his, and in this regard, it is inherently the recognition of two (different) perspectives. Dual-perspective imagination is achieved by acknowledging the other's emotion, while retaining one's own perspective in the situation. Philosopher John Deigh captures this type of perspective-taking when he describes *mature* empathy: "taking another's perspective and imaginatively participating in this other person's life...without forgetting oneself." He says that "to empathize with another...one must recognize him as separate from oneself, a distinct person with a mind of his own, and such recognition requires that one retain a sense of oneself even as one takes up the other's perspective and imaginatively participates in his life."[31] I will dub this dual-perspective *empathy.*

Dual-perspective *imagination* is the kind of imagination used in role-taking, or putting oneself in another person's perspective or "shoes."[32] The personality theorist Jean Piaget emphasized role-taking, because it teaches people to learn how to "decenter" and abandon one's own perspective. This, he notes, is an integral part of social development.[33] In this process, the idea is to take up another perspective while at the same time remembering one's own. Returning to the example of Ginger whose mother has died, when Amy uses dual-perspective imagination, she imagines having Ginger's evaluative response to her situation, which may involve feeling relief, satisfaction, and a kind of gladness. But Amy can at the same time acknowledge that she herself does not share Ginger's feelings and that she has a different evaluation of the situation. Role-taking and dual-perspective imagination reveal evaluative differences in people's perspectives, and the role-taker sees the conflict between the viewpoints. Psychologists suggest that role-taking is useful because as one takes the other's role, she can at the same time evaluate what it is like to be the other person, and thus develops understanding and social intelligence.

2.3 From imaginative perspective-taking to empathy

The foregoing discussion clarifies the variety of ways that a person can simulate or imagine another's perspective. But this is not tantamount to empathy, for we generally use the term empathy to describe feeling an emotion that is congruent with the other person's emotion. Thus, a definition of empathy that includes some sort of simulation, imitation, role-taking, or perspective-swapping *and* the transfer of emotion is superior to the conceptions of empathy as mere simulation.

Are there any *philosophical* theories of empathy that satisfy both of these criteria? Both Alvin Goldman and Stephen Darwall offer views of empathy that include (a) shared emotions and (b) some kind of imaginative perspective-swapping. Goldman argues that what distinguishes empathy from perspective-taking is that "the output states are affective or emotional states rather than purely cognitive or conative states like believing or desiring" and the empathizer "is aware of his or her vicarious affects and emotions as representatives of the emotions or affects of the target agent."[34] Stephen Darwall agrees when he maintains, "empathy consists in feeling what one imagines *he* feels, or perhaps should feel (fear, say), or in some imagined copy of these feelings."[35] He argues that this is "genuine" empathy, and is distinct from *self-focused* empathy, where "we simulate others' emotions by placing ourselves in their situation and working out what we would think, want, and do, if we were they."[36] Darwall here is drawing a distinction between self-focused and other-focused empathy, and only the latter counts as empathy for him. While Darwall is right to think that empathy must involve considering the other person's specific attributes, self-focused empathy is still, on my view, "genuine" empathy, since it involves "thinking oneself into another's perspective," and then feeling an emotion that is congruent to the other's.[37]

While these philosophers believe that empathy requires the affective transmission of emotion, it is important to distinguish clearly the three ways of perspective-taking. There are three main kinds of simulative or perspective-taking empathy: **self-focused empathy**, **other-focused empathy**, and **dual-perspective empathy**. These distinctions reflect the epistemological "focus" of the empathy. In **self-focused empathy**, Amy acquires Zack's emotion because she simulates being in Zack's circumstances, and responds by feeling an emotion similar to his. This transmission of emotion occurs even though the content of her simulation reflects her own psychology. In **other-focused empathy**, Amy imagines or simulates having Zack's beliefs and psychology in Zack's circumstances, so that she acquires an emotion that is congruent with Zack's. She imagines having Zack's evaluative stance, and comes to feel an emotion congruent to his. In **dual-perspective empathy**, Amy simulates Zack's beliefs and psychology, sees the differences between those and her own, acquires an emotion that is congruent to Zack's, and works back and forth between her perspective and Zack's. These definitions of empathy are superior to the definitions of empathy as mere simulation, for they include the transfer of emotion that is characteristic of empathy.

Although theorists do not agree on *how* similar the emotional experience of the empathizer and the target should be, presumably there should be a correspondence between the two emotional states. For example, if Amy feels indignant when Zack feels angry, this could count as empathy because the emotions are somewhat similar. Most theorists believe that an exact match of emotion is not required, and say that experiencing similar emotions as a result of responding to another's emotional state is sufficient for empathy.[38] In general, psychologists suppose that what William Ickes calls "accurate cognitive assessment of another's feelings" is central to empathy.[39] This is correct, because similar emotions are those that have roughly the same cognitive content and affective states, and the difference is in the degree of the emotion experienced, such as in the case of being "afraid" and being "mortified." While we may not *know* whether one's emotion matches the other, these epistemic worries are secondary; the defining feature of empathy is that one person feels an emotion that is congruent or similar to another, as a way of responding to that person. The ability to feel a congruent emotion depends on the empathizer's understanding of the other's situation and emotion, and I discuss this in greater detail in the following chapter.

Empathy needs to be defined in terms of "congruent emotions" because if empathy is defined as mere simulation, then it appears that a sadist's imaginative perspective-swapping with her victim can be considered "empathy," and this goes contrary to everyday parlance. It is a mistake to call the sadist's simulative imagination "empathy," because the sadist does not experience a congruent emotion. This point is worth emphasizing because a number of philosophers have supposed that empathy is tantamount to simulation or perspective-taking.[40] John Deigh argues that the sadist's imaginative perspective-swapping is empathy but not "mature empathy" because she doesn't *respect* the one experiencing pain and doesn't appreciate the other's autonomy and assessment that the pain is bad. Mature empathy requires "seeing that *from that person's perspective* that his purposes are worthwhile."[41] But this seems like a stronger requirement than is necessary for empathy, and closer to a requirement for sympathy.

Likewise, Martha Nussbaum suggests that a torturer "may be acutely aware of the suffering of the victim, and able to enjoy the imagining of it," in a way that is empathetic.[42] But this goes contrary to our common usage of the term empathy, and doesn't capture the way that empathy includes the transfer of a *similar* emotion. Sadistic simulation lacks the transfer of a similar emotion. This is a crucial point, for most psychological accounts of empathy, as well as our everyday usage of the term empathy, indicate that there is a "match," broadly understood, between emotional states.[43]

To see the difference between empathy and mere imaginative simulation, let me briefly describe how empathy works using a cognitive theory of emotion. The question of whether emotions are cognitive or non-cognitive is a central issue in emotion studies, and I am not claiming here that the cognitive theory of emotion is correct.[44] My point is that the cognitive theory of emotion clearly depicts why the sadist's emotion should not be considered empathy: his emotion doesn't match his target's either in terms of (a) cognitive content or (b) emotional feeling.

Although there are a variety of cognitive theories of emotion, the one I adopt here is that an emotion is *an intentional stance* or propositional attitude *toward some state* or belief.[45] Cognitive theories of emotion suppose that emotions are not just feelings, but neither are they merely beliefs; rather, emotions are an *affective* response or attitude toward some state with cognitive content. This theory is useful because it treats emotions as intentional stances with rationally evaluable content that are affective in that they involve physical "feelings."[46] This approach is particularly useful for examining the perspective-taking empathy, since it enables breaking down the cognitive content of the emotion.[47]

To represent an emotion as an intentional stance toward some state, the cognitive aspect of the emotional state can be represented in the following way: someone's loving Michael is represented as

X(*Love*)[Michael] (with affect/feeling)

It is even possible for someone to have the emotion:

X(*Fear*){I love Michael} (with affect/feeling)

Although the representation here suggests that the emotion is just an evaluative attitude, it is important to remember that the affective part of emotions, namely, the feelings that we have when we experience emotions, are central to the definition of an emotion. The representation is just a useful way of depicting the cognitive attitudes and how they are directed toward a particular state of affairs or beliefs.[48]

Using this scheme, perspective-taking empathy can be described as a situation in which Amy imagines or simulates Zack's emotion by imagining having Zack's attitude toward a particular state. For example, suppose:

Zack(*Fear*)[Walking on Tightropes]

For Amy to empathize with Zack, she takes up Zack's perspective and sees things and feels things affectively as he does. This can be done quickly, and without conscious effort, but it will involve some kind of simulation. Using the distinctions in kinds of empathy described in the previous section, Amy could do this in three ways:

Self-focused Empathy: **Amy imagines {being Amy**(*Fear*)[Walking on Tightropes]}

Other-focused Empathy: **Amy imagines {being Zack**(*Fear*)[Walking on Tightropes]}

Dual-perspective empathy: **Amy imagines {being both Amy & Zack** (*Fear*)[Walking on Tightropes]}

If Amy's imagining or simulating Zack's situation produces an emotion that is congruent to Zack's fear, then Amy can be said to empathize. If there is no resulting similar emotion, then Amy does not empathize.

Though this is a simplified account of empathy, it shows how imagining being in Zack's situation and acquiring a congruent emotion is at the core of empathy. On this account, the sadist doesn't empathize because she doesn't feel an emotion similar to the object of her imagination. This is primarily because the sadist doesn't have the same thoughts or intentional states as her target, and so her imaginative musings don't count as empathy. This can be shown by using the theory of emotion proposed above. Let us represent the non-sadist's feelings about torture as follows:

Non-sadist Zack(*Boo*)[Lying on the Rack]

Let us now represent the sadist's imaginative musings, where she simulates Zack's position. This means she would need to imagine Zack's perspective in one of the following ways:

Empathizer: Amy imagines {Amy, Zack, or Amy & Zack(*Boo*) [Lying on the Rack]}

But the sadist *does not imagine from the other's perspective in this way, period*. Zack dislikes pain, and for the sadist to take up his perspective, she must imagine disliking pain. This makes it possible for the sadist to feel what her victim feels. But the sadist *enjoys* Zack's pain and doesn't replicate the same attitude. Without the replication of the same attitude, there can be no transfer of a similar emotion. Instead, the sadist Amy has a yea- or pro-attitude toward Zack's boo-attitude:

Sadist: Amy(yea) imagines{Non-Sadist Zack [(*Boo*)(Lying on the Rack)]}

In this case, the sadist Amy does not see (or feel) things as Zack sees and feels them; she maintains a yea-attitude toward Zack's boo-attitude, and does not take up the perspective of Zack, or simulate his boo-attitude.[49] This theory of an emotion shows why the sadist's imaginative musings don't count as empathy and distinguishes Deigh's view from my own. His view is that while the sadist might *rationally acknowledge* that Zack has a boo-attitude toward pain, she doesn't respect that he has his own ends and desires to not have the pain. But on my view, the sadist doesn't empathize because she doesn't have the same thoughts, beliefs, or intentional attitudes that Zack does. This suggests that there is a difference *in kind* between the sadist's imaginative simulation and empathy, and not just a difference *in degree* of emotion involved in empathy versus imaginative simulation. The sadist enjoys imagining Zack's pain but does not have the same attitude or intentional state that he does. This is the simplest explanation for why the sadist doesn't empathize: the sadist's pleasure judgment regarding her victim's pain prevent her from empathizing with him.[50]

For present purposes, it is unnecessary to state whether emotions are cognitive or non-cognitive, or whether all instances of empathy are cognitive or non-cognitive. Given what we have surveyed regarding the two main paradigms of empathy, it is likely that some kinds of empathy, especially the empathy of infants and very young children is non-cognitive, and is a result of impressions or perceptions of other emotions. But as we mature, our empathy and our other emotions become more sophisticated. This is likely due to the development of language. In fact, in his studies of the different kinds of empathy, Martin Hoffman shows that there are developmental changes in cognitive processing capabilities. He shows that certain kinds of empathic arousal, namely role-taking or simulative empathy, require an advanced level of cognitive processing.[51] Perspective-taking empathy requires an ability to focus on another's inner states, and this kind of empathy doesn't appear until later in development.[52] I argue in this book that the more cognitively advanced kinds of empathy are relevant to moral deliberation and ethical reasoning; while a baby's contagious cries or laughter may effect moral development, the more advanced kinds of empathy include cognitions that can be instrumental to moral deliberation, reflection, motivation and reasoning.

2.4   A functional account of empathy

Highlighting the difference between empathy as "contagion" and empathy as "simulation" suggests that there are significant differences in what researchers and laypersons alike call empathy. While contagion and simulation are the most widespread conceptions of empathy, they share a common phenomenon—the transmission of an emotion from one person to another—but these are not the only ways that an emotion could be transmitted. Justin D'Arms suggests that simulation and contagion are "mechanisms of empathy" rather than explanations of the transfer of emotion,[53] and I agree that there are many *modes* of transmitting an emotion with empathy. The difference, roughly, is in the causal direction of the transmission. In contagion, Zack's feeling an emotion is causally efficacious in bringing about an emotion in (the receptive observer) Amy that is congruent to his own. And in simulation, Amy's imagining Zack's feelings produces the transmission; Zack is merely the "target" of Amy's imagination and her emotional reaction. Thus, empathy in general should be understood as *responding to another's emotion with a congruent emotion, in virtue perceiving the other's emotion with some mental process (such as taking up the other's point of view or simple motor mimicry).*

Based on what psychologists have surmised about empathy, empathetic transmissions can result from a variety of processes: cognitive representations, simulation, inner imitation, theoretical beliefs, and even non-linguistic pictorial cognitions. Thus, it is useful to have a broad conception of empathy that is agnostic with regard to the *kinds* of cognitions that comprise the empathizer's mental states. The psychologist Martin Hoffman was the first to recommend a definition of empathy that embraced the various modes of mental states and transmissions.[54] Several psychologists have followed his lead, and have defined empathy as the transmission of emotion from one person to another via some causal process with both intrapersonal and interpersonal outcomes.[55] The following figure is an adapted version of the model of empathy proposed by the psychologist Mark Davis, and describes the empathic process as

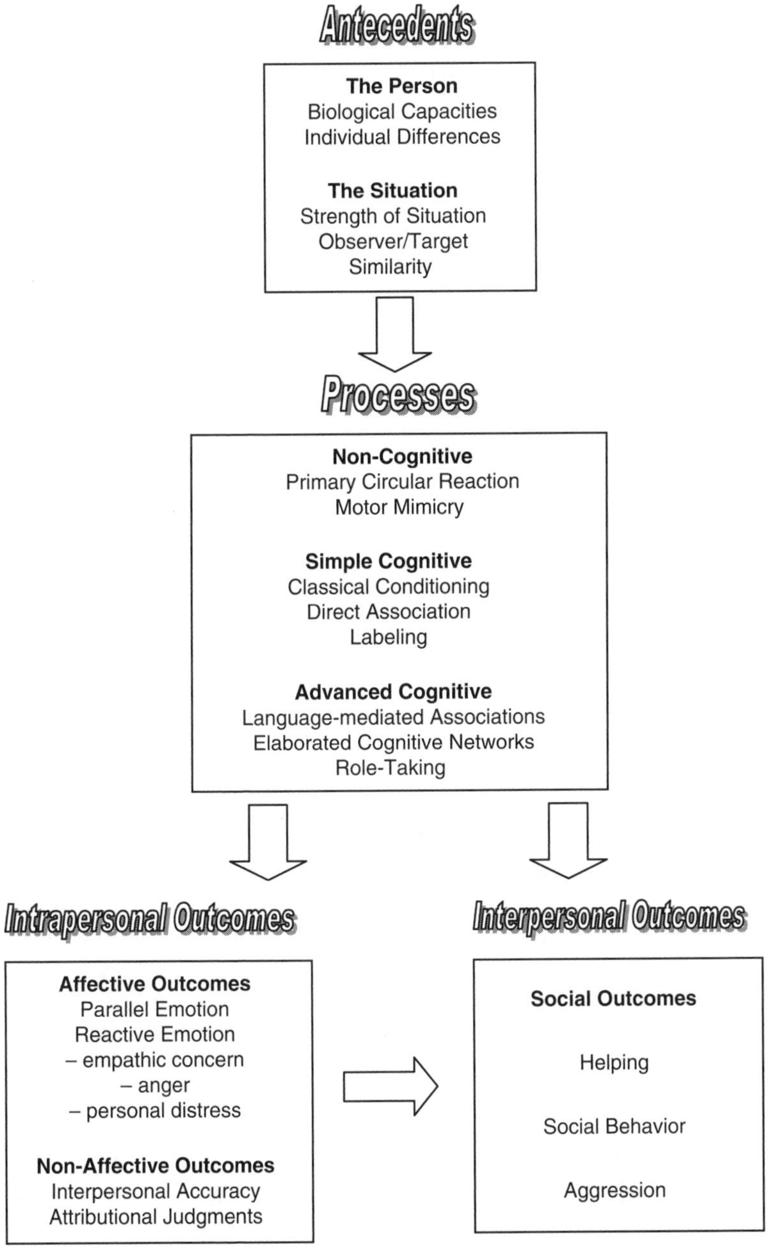
Antecedents
The Person
Biological Capacities
Individual Differences
The Situation
Strength of Situation
Observer/Target
Similarity
Processes
Non-Cognitive
Primary Circular Reaction
Motor Mimicry
Simple Cognitive
Classical Conditioning
Direct Association
Labeling
Advanced Cognitive
Language-mediated Associations
Elaborated Cognitive Networks
Role-Taking
Intrapersonal Outcomes
Affective Outcomes
Parallel Emotion
Reactive Emotion
– empathic concern
– anger
– personal distress
Non-Affective Outcomes
Interpersonal Accuracy
Attributional Judgments
Interpersonal Outcomes
Social Outcomes
Helping
Social Behavior
Aggression

Figure 2.1 A Functional Account of Empathy

consisting in antecedents, processes, intrapersonal outcomes, and inter-personal outcomes.[56] I call this a *functional* account of empathy because it takes empathy to be a function of certain inputs, processes, and outputs.[57]

This account of empathy supposes that there are a variety of ways of describing the mental states in empathetic transmission, and suggests that empathy can include both non-cognitive transfers of emotion and cognitively sophisticated understanding. This definition of empathy is much broader and more useful than philosopher Elliot Sober and biologist David Sloan Wilson's stringent definition of empathy as: "S empathizes with O's experience of emotion E if and only if O feels E, S believes that O feels E, and this causes S to feel E for O."[58] Psychologists research trans-missions of empathy, such as motor mimicry, that may not include beliefs but which still involve the transmission of similar emotion, and the functional account of empathy is a broad definition that allows more specific definitions of empathy to be distinguished and studied.[59] The advantage of this approach is that it is agnostic with regard to the *kinds* of cognitions that comprise the empathizer's mental states (described under "Processes"). A variety of factors may trigger empathetic responses: mimicry, primitive response reactions, classical conditioning, simulation, or association with one's personal experience.

Philosophers who debate the nature of these processes will be inter-ested in examining whether empathetic cognitions run via "off-line" simulation, "on-line" simulation, whether they implement "theories" of others' minds, or whether they are essentially pictorial or linguistic representations of another's phenomenal experience. This, for example, is the topic of Karsten Stueber's examination of the place of empathy in understanding others within the "folk-psychological" framework, which supposes that the mental concepts used by ordinary people ought to be used to understand others as minded creatures.[60] But for the purposes of evaluating empathy's role in *moral* matters, endorsing a particular theory of mind is unnecessary. All that is needed is to accept the idea that *empathy involves feeling another's congruent emotion in virtue of perceiving the other's mental and emotional state.* I take it that there is sufficient evidence for the plausibility of this definition of empathy, for it has been defended by a number of leading psychologists and philo-sophers of mind.[61]

The functional account of empathy has four advantages. First, it high-lights the fact that the *causes* of empathy and the *effects* of empathy are distinct. Empathy's effects are not necessarily pro-social or altruistic, but can be cognitive and/or affective; and its processes and outcomes can be epistemic (having to do with our beliefs) and/or behavioral (having to do with our actions). Second, the functional account of empathy can accommodate the three main types of simulative empathy mentioned previously: *self-focused empathy, other-focused empathy,* and *dual-perspective empathy*. Since the functional account depicts the way that empathy involves two distinct perspectives, it can accommodate the ways those perspectives interact. Third, the functional definition of empathy allows for different types: non-cognitive, simple cognitive, and advanced cognition.

Fourth, the functional account has the resources for examining empathy's epistemological function, or role in acquiring justified beliefs about others' mental and emotional states.[62] Since empathy is a response to another's feelings, beliefs, and attitudes in virtue of acquiring a similar emotion, it is possible to learn more information about others from such an experience, primarily when empathy includes cognitive processes. These processes are present when: (a) the empathic experience has some cognitive content in that it involves higher-order cognitions, or (b) when the empathy does not involve cognitive mediation at the time it is experienced, it has the resources for being cognitively reflected on in that the empathic transmission of emotion can be assessed using higher-order cognition. In these cases, empathy has the requisite cognitive content needed to impact one's beliefs.[63]

Let me say clearly that my reason for endorsing the functional account of empathy is that it can serve as a broad framework for how to define empathy in philosophical studies. Ideally, philosophical definitions of empathy will fit the functional model of empathy in that they will include antecedents, processes, an emotional match, and various outcomes. I am *not* arguing that the functional account of empathy should replace the eight distinctions of empathy that I discussed in the previous chapter. Rather, my main point has been to say that the kinds of empathy that I will discuss as playing a role in ethics and morality will fit the functional model.

While some philosophers might reject the argument that philosophical discussions of empathy should include some reference to feeling another's emotion, it is crucial that empathy be understood as including emotion *matching* because empathy involves understanding and appreciating another's feeling and not just imagining it. This is what distinguishes empathy from mindreading or simulation. (Of course, in cases where an individual may understand and appreciate another's emotion, but only feel the other's emotion to a small degree, there may be a difference *in degree* between imaginative appreciation and empathy.) My point is that everyday usage of the term empathy implies that it includes having some degree of similar affective states and most other theorists recognize this. Philosophers should, too.

2.5 Conclusion

We now have in hand a working definition of empathy understood as *feeling a congruent emotion with another person, in virtue of perceiving her emotion with some mental process such as imitation, simulation, projection, or imagination.* Since empathy is a response to others, as opposed to ignoring them, it is indeed an expression of our social nature and what makes it useful to ethics. Let me conclude by considering an objection to the use of empathy in ethics, namely, that it can be an unjustified assertion of knowledge of another's inner life.

Lorraine Code argues that "responsible empathetic knowing can never be assumed," otherwise it is "declared empathy" where, instead of seeking to understand the other's emotions, one *tells* the other how she feels.[64] I agree with Code that *certain* kinds of empathy, especially self-focused empathy, can be problematic in that they involve projecting one's own beliefs about others onto them, and these beliefs can be mistaken. The worry is that someone might merely *project* her own beliefs and thoughts onto others instead of correctly understanding the other's emotion. Based on what I have said here, other-focused empathy and dual-perspective empathy will be more reliable forms of empathy because they seek to be grounded in true beliefs about others. By imaginatively participating in another's life in a way that one resonates with her emotions, she becomes aware of another's situation, emotions, beliefs, and desires in a way that is responsible rather than self-focused.

Our capacity to share the feelings of others is a way of coming to share another's evaluation of the world, and, as I will show in the following chapter, enables us to "see" or appreciate previously unrecognized evaluative features of our social circumstances. I turn now to investigating the epistemological dimensions of empathy, so as to learn how it can contribute to moral deliberation and moral judgment.

Part II

The Moral Dimensions of Empathy

3
The Epistemic Functions of Empathy

The previous chapter provided a working definition of empathy that was broad enough to include different phenomena called empathy, but specific enough to allow identification of different kinds of empathy. Although my proposed definition, *feeling a congruent emotion with another person, in virtue of perceiving her emotion with some mental process such as imitation, simulation, projection, or imagination*, does not necessarily resolve the debate on how to define empathy, it provides a framework for how to interpret and understand the variety of phenomena called empathy. But from this point forward, my discussion of empathy will identify a particular type of empathy, one that fits the functional account of empathy, and examine it in detail. My goal in the book is to examine the role of empathy in moral deliberation and judgment, and I have already suggested that empathy alone is insufficient for moral judgment. My argument to this conclusion is laid out in this chapter. By examining different kinds of empathy and their corresponding functions, I show that feeling empathy alone does not express a moral judgment.

To understand empathy's contribution to moral judgment and deliberation, we must first examine what empathy with another person expresses or implies. Regarding this issue, philosophers have made one of two claims: empathy expresses understanding and appreciation of that other person, or empathy implies *approval* of the other's emotion. Philosophers in the former vein have argued that empathy serves primarily an *epistemic* function: we can use it to acquire additional knowledge of others' minds, states, and emotions. For example, philosopher Karsten Stueber argues that empathy is the "epistemically central, default method for understanding other agents," the primary way we gain "knowledge of the minds of other individual agents."[1] Stueber's central point is that empathy is one of the most important ways that we get knowledge of other minds and his thesis is framed in answer to the question of how we get knowledge of other minds, others' beliefs and desires, and what others are thinking and feeling.[2] Essentially, empathy can generate new beliefs about others, or transform existing beliefs about others, and the knowledge acquired through empathy is different in kind from knowledge acquired from theories or sources outside oneself, such as through books or media.

Philosophers implying that empathy expresses *approval* of the other's emotion have suggested that empathy has a *normative* function and is itself a kind of judgment. On this view, empathy involves affirmation of another's emotion as appropriate given the situation. Stephen Darwall argues, for example, that "when we projectively mirror others' feelings, we not only show them how they feel, we also show them that we agree with them about how *to* feel."[3] Darwall's idea is that when we project ourselves into another's situation, imagine that person's feelings and come to feel the way she does, then we come to feel her emotion only by validating it and approving of it. Remy Debes more explicitly argues in favor of the normative role of empathy when he claims that that empathy, or coming to feel the same emotion as another person, can only happen when someone judges that another's emotion is appropriate by comparing the other's feelings (given the context and the situation) to his own feelings and understanding of the situation. When one comes to feel the same emotion as another, empathy is performing a normative role because one approves of the other's emotion.[4]

Which of these two claims is correct? Is it possible for one experience of empathy to have both functions, or is there some tension between the idea that empathy is a kind of normative judgment and the idea that empathy can be used to gather information about others? The answer that I will articulate here is that empathy primarily serves an epistemic function, in giving us knowledge and understanding of others, but empathy does require *prima facie* approval of another's emotion in order for it to have this function, and in this sense, empathy is normative. Let me say quickly, though, that this thesis only applies to certain types of empathy, those that require advanced cognition. Moreover, the most important contribution that cognitively-advanced empathy can make to the moral life is that it performs epistemic functions and can thus contribute to our knowledge and understanding of others. Empathy makes salient others' emotions and situations, and is thus a way to gain information about them. The implication of this thesis is empathy is not merely a way of passing judgment on another's emotion; it can transform the empathizer and her view of others and the world by bringing her attention to features of another's situation that enable her to expand her range of beliefs and values.

3.1   Illustration of the epistemic and normative dimensions of empathy

Since the idea that empathy has an epistemic function seems vague, let me briefly illustrate how perspective-taking empathy serves the epistemic functions of gathering information about others and understanding them. Medical doctor Jodi Halpern describes a situation where she had a patient, Mr. Smith, who was a successful executive, when a sudden neurological disorder left him paralyzed from the neck down. She was gentle and kind in her interaction with Mr. Smith, but this made him frustrated and uncooperative. She assumed that this was because he felt despondent and afraid. She tried to talk more softly, to be more calm, and more concerned, but he remained frustrated and uninterested in cooperating with her. Because he was unable to articulate his emotions, or explain why he was refusing her help, she had a hard time knowing what strategy to take.

To help her figure out a new strategy, Dr. Halpern imagined the situation from Mr. Smith's perspective—"what it would like to be a powerful older man, suddenly enfeebled, handled by one doctor after the next,"[5]—and realized that this would be frustrating, and that he would feel impatient, rage, and then, a sense of shame. By emotionally resonating with Mr. Smith and using her imagination to unify the details of his life, she was able to have an accurate affective experience of Mr. Smith's feelings.[6] This served the epistemic purpose of helping her to get information about his emotions and understand their complexity. By imagining the situation from his point of view, and learning and feeling his emotions and his beliefs, she gained information that allowed her to envision alternative, more productive, methods of interaction with Mr. Smith.

This example briefly illustrates empathy's epistemic function and the way it can be used to acquire information about others' emotions and beliefs. Since people are different, and do not always experience the same emotions in the same situations, empathy is a useful way to learn about others' emotions. By entering into Smith's perspective and seeing the situation from his point of view, Dr. Halpern was able to appreciate his perspective and see why he would feel certain emotions. Without empathy, she could not have understood her patient's frustration and irritability as a product of his feeling emasculated and embarrassed. In this regard, empathy is more than merely judging another's emotion; empathy enables us to learn more about others as well. This is not to say, though, that approval played no part in Dr. Halpern's empathy. Two elements or phases are involved in empathy's performing an epistemic function, and one of these involves approval. The first phase involves finding the other's perspective, feelings, reasons, and beliefs *intelligible*,[7] and the second involves approving of the other's emotion by taking it to be *appropriate* in the situation (in light of the circumstances, etc.). Let me explain.

When an emotion is *intelligible* to another, the emotion, what it is about, its causes, and its context are understood by the observer, either in the empathic experience itself, or upon reflection. If an observer does not find another's emotion intelligible, she will not resonate emotionally because she does not understand why the other is experiencing the emotion. The importance of the emotion would be lost. On the other hand, intelligibility is not enough for empathy. An observer must also approve of that person's emotion, not in the sense that *she* would have the same emotion if she were in the other's situation, but because she takes it to be *prima facie* plausible given the person's situation, circumstances and point of view. Empathy is not merely a way of judging the other's emotion as correct or good, but is a way of judging it to be plausible.

With this basic illustration of the epistemic function of empathy in hand, I now explain how empathy's epistemic function has a normative dimension. The two conditions needed for empathy to have an epistemic function include (1) *intelligibility* of another's emotion, or learning another's internal beliefs, thoughts or emotions, and (2) *prima facie* approval of another's emotion. And yet, these dimensions interact: empathy's normative dimension limits its epistemic function, and empathy's epistemic function broadens the potential range of objects of approval; in other words, empathy can expand people's horizons because the knowledge gained is relative to the individual and in this regard personalized.

3.2   Modes of empathic arousal

In order to learn empathy's epistemic functions, it is first necessary to distinguish different types of empathy, such as emotional contagion and imaginative simulation. And yet, these categories are still too broad. Psychologists have used finer distinctions in their research on types of empathy, and so I use psychologist Martin Hoffman's differentiation of the *modes* of empathic arousal, or types of mental events that trigger an empathic emotional response. These modes are useful for distinguishing the kinds of empathy that have an epistemic function. Hoffman identifies five modes, three of which are "primitive" in that they are automatic and involuntary. These are best understood as types of emotional contagion. The other two modes involve greater mental cognition and effort, and thus can be considered kinds of imaginative simulation.[8]

Hoffman's first mode is **mimicry**, which is an involuntary response to another's expression of emotion. He argues that there are two steps in mimicry: first, the observer Amy automatically imitates Zack's facial expression, voice and posture; this triggers afferent feedback, in which Amy's physical response (i.e. facial expressions) produces feelings in Zack that match Amy's feelings. For example, newborns imitate the emotional expressions of people around them by imitating facial gestures and expressions of joy and sadness, and this display of expression makes the adults feel happy and the baby feels happy.[9] The "mirroring" of emotion described by cognitive neuroscientists may amount to a kind of mimicry in the neuronal structures.

The second mode of arousal for empathy is **classical conditioning**, which is evident especially in the preverbal years of early childhood. In classical conditioned empathy, young children acquire empathic feelings as a conditioned response when they observe someone experiencing an emotion. For example, when a baby is being held by its mother, securely, affectionately, and with a smile, the baby feels good and the mother's smile is associated with the baby's feeling; the result is that the smile can function as a stimulus to make the baby feel good. This is empathy because the baby is "catching" the emotion of happiness as a conditioned response to the mother's expression emotion.[10] The difference between classical conditioning and mimicry is that mimicry is an *imitation* of another's emotion, whereas classical conditioning is more of a *learned response* to a situation, not just a direct copying of the person with the emotion.

The third mode of empathic arousal is **direct association**, where Zack's situation reminds Amy of similar experiences in her own past, and this evokes feelings in Amy that fit Zack's situation. For example, if Amy has had feelings of pain and discomfort, and she observes Zack in a situation that evokes memories of this past experience, it can cause the same feelings to arise in Amy as a response to his situation. In this case, Amy empathizes with Zack in virtue of the fact that she had a similar experience to Zack in the past.

Fourth is **mediated association**, where Zack's emotion is communicated through language, and Amy responds to him by feeling his emotion. This is a more complex mode of arousal because it requires semantic processing and interpretation on the part of the listener. Narrative empathy involves listening to others and coming to feel what they feel. This is one type of mediated association empathy, for in mediated association, language is the "link between the model's feeling and the observer's experience."[11] Mediated association also includes written language; empathy can be the result of reading a novel, news story, poem, biography, etc. In both hearing and reading, an observer or reader knows the context or situation and learns about the events that cause an individual to feel a certain way; if she comes to feel the emotion that the character or individual feels, it is because she understands what the emotion is about, appreciates it, takes it to be appropriate, and shares in the other's evaluation, thus allowing her to share the other's emotion.

The fifth mode of empathic arousal is **role-taking** and is also called perspective-taking or imaginative simulation. It involves putting oneself in another's place and imagining how she or he feels. Hoffman distinguishes three types of role-taking: **self-focused role-taking, others-focused role-taking and a combination mode**.[12] *Self-focused role-taking* is when Amy observes Zack and imagines how she would feel in the same situation; *other-focused role-taking* is when Amy focuses directly on Zack and imagines being him, so that the result is Amy's feeling something like what Zack feels. In these cases, role-taking involves intentionally simulating the other's situation and/or imagining being that person, and trying to understand that person. Halpern's imagining being her patient and feeling his emotions in that situation is an example of others-focused role-taking. When an observer shifts back and forth between other-focused and self-focused role-taking, then she imagines herself in the other's position, but also imagines being the other person. This is the *combination mode*. Hoffman explains that taking up another's point of view or considering another's emotions and her situation is an ability acquired later in life, although children as early as nine years old can role-take.[13]

Although all five modes evoke empathy in that they bring about a shared emotion, only the last two modes have sufficient cognitive content to be able to impact our beliefs about others. Imitation and classical conditioning do not have the requisite cognitive content to elicit epistemic products. (They may, of course, be the first of a multi-step process that includes the modes that require greater cognition.) Although one might argue that imitation empathy or conditioned empathy, such as a baby's responding to a mother's smile with a smile, involves understanding another's emotion, this is better described as "trivial understanding" of another's emotion,[14] since it is the *recognition* of another's emotion and not genuine *understanding* of it. Karsten Stueber calls these modes "basic empathy" because they enable *recognition* of an emotion, not understanding of it: basic empathy is the "theoretically unmediated quasi-perceptual ability to recognize other creatures directly as minded creatures and to recognize them implicitly as creatures that are fundamentally like us."[15] Basic empathy allows one to recognize, for example, *that* someone is angry, but does not help her know *why* he is angry.

The higher-order forms of empathy, mediated empathy and role-taking empathy, involve greater cognition and contribute to the complex ability to figure out *why* someone is angry. They require recognition of another's emotion, awareness of her situation, and the ability to piece together information about that person. Stueber calls this "reenactive empathy" and it involves using our deliberative capacities to reenact or imitate in our own minds the thought processes of the other person, so that we conceive of another person's social behavior "as the behavior of a rational agent who acts for a reason."[16] By empathetically representing another's mental state to oneself, one can imagine and feel another person's beliefs, reasons, and worldview and draw conclusions regarding his or her values, responses, or preferences. I now explain how these types of empathy can perform epistemic functions.

3.3 Empathy's epistemic functions

Psychologists have long argued that one of the most important functions of cognitively developed empathy is to gather information about others;[17] empathy brings about awareness of another's state and makes information about the other person salient to the empathizer. (I describe this *salience effect* and its importance in moral deliberation in Chapter 5.[18]) Of course, the information one gets from empathy depends on what one is interested in. One might get new information about another's emotions, her beliefs about herself or the world around her, her desires for herself and the world around her, her preferences, or how she might respond to another's actions. It all depends on the focus of the person who uses empathy, and as I explain in section 3.6, this is one of the ways that empathy's epistemic function is limited as a method of gaining information about others. Since studies show that perspective-taking, in particular, is more conducive to getting accurate information about others, I will describe this mode's epistemic functions. (Note that mediated empathy, which requires processing emotions with language, works the same way.)

The process of acquiring knowledge about others that I describe here is based on Karsten Stueber's theory of empathy, which is modeled on Alvin Goldman's simulation theory of the mind.[19] Stueber says empathy proceeds in three phases:[20]

(1) *The matching phase*—when one entertains different beliefs and adopts a different conative relation to the world in order to recreate the other's perspective on the world.
(2) *The simulation phase*—having adopted the other's perspective, one starts thinking about the world from that perspective and entertaining reasons for possible actions and thoughts.
(3) *The attribution phase*—after completing the simulation phase, one ceases to entertain the other's perspective and bases her interpretation of the other's action (or expression) on her knowledge of what happened during the simulation phase.

In the first and third phases, propositional knowledge, or "external" knowledge about another person, is allowed, but in the simulation phase, one thinks about the world from the other's point of view and gets new beliefs and knowledge, in virtue of the simulation. Otherwise the simulation would be superfluous—such knowledge could be generated without empathy. The idea is that our mental structure makes it possible to use empathy to learn about another's choices, beliefs and desires by using antecedent information about them as hypothetical inputs. My argument—and Stueber's—is that empathy can generate such knowledge without implementing theories of others, and that empathy is crucial to gaining a personal understanding of others (if not the only way to gain knowledge of others).[21] I explain this more in the final section.

3.3.1   First function: Gathering information about the other person

Let me now illustrate how the different types of perspective-taking are used to perform the epistemic function of information-gathering. In 2004, Israel's justice minister, Yosef Lapid, saw a picture on television of an old Palestinian woman in her ruined home looking under the tiles for medicine. The picture reminded him of his own grandmother, and so he spontaneously took up the perspective of the woman's imaginary Palestinian grandson and asked himself, "What would I say if this were my Grandmother?"[22] By taking up the perspective of the (imaginary) Palestinian grandson, he was able to get information about the way he, and presumably other Palestinians, would view Israel's actions. Namely, he learned that someone in such a situation would be very frustrated and dissatisfied with Israel's plan to demolish homes, such as ones belonging to the old woman, in Gaza.

Since Lapid took up the perspective of an imaginary person, he was engaged in **self-focused perspective-taking empathy**, which involves imagining *oneself* in another person's situation. In this case, Lapid imagined himself in the situation of the Palestinian woman's grandson. And in turn, he got information about how such a person would view the world from that perspective. Implementing Stueber's analysis, we could say that Lapid:

(1) *recreated the other's perspective of the world* by imagining himself as a young Palestinian man watching his grandmother search through the rubble of her home for medicine,

(2) *imagined the world from that perspective* by resenting the people who caused the damage, and

(3) *attributed beliefs and feelings to the other based on what happened during the simulation phase* by reaching the conclusion that the young man would disapprove of Israel's plan to destroy additional homes in Gaza in the future.

Since Lapid was engaged in self-focused empathy—imagining himself as the grandson of the Palestinian woman—his conclusion is only as accurate as his knowledge of Palestinians and their feelings about having their homes destroyed.

Since self-focused empathy involves projecting oneself into another's situation, and thus projecting one's own beliefs and values into the situation, it runs the risk of gaining inaccurate information.[23] This does not mean that information about others cannot be acquired with self-focused empathy, it just means that it may not be accurate. If the observer and the target are similar with regard to their emotional responses, or what Goldman describes as "psychological homologies or similarities" between the empathizer and her target,[24] then the empathizer can get accurate information. Or if the empathizer has a good deal of information about the target, then he can more accurately simulate the other. Given Lapid's knowledge of Palestinians, and the presumption that people dislike having their homes destroyed, Lapid was right to conclude that

Palestinians disapproved of Israel's plan to destroy homes in the Gaza strip. But the conclusion of this type of empathy is not *always* accurate because it is based on imagining oneself in another's position.

It is appropriate to conclude, then, that since empathy can generate conjectures that cannot be verified, and the kind of knowledge generated by empathy is limited to the observer's understanding of the situation, it cannot be the only method by which we learn about others. In fact, imaginative empathy should *not* be a substitute for *actual conversations* with others, where people reveal their beliefs, emotions, thoughts, and desires in a straightforward manner. Personal interaction with those who are different from ourselves brings about the possibility of learning about others and experiencing empathy when we may not expect to. Empathy, nevertheless, is often a reliable way to get information about others when one has no other method of gathering information about them.

Dual-perspective empathy can also yield information about another person and the way they view the world. The combination mode of empathy involves a cognitive attempt to ascertain how the individual's beliefs, desires, and feelings about her own life connect together and translate into her responses. It includes an affective understanding of how the other feels, and reverting to one's own perspective in order to make sense of that person's emotion and situation, by comparing that person's emotion to one's own. Consider the example of Dr. Jodi Halpern, which I used at the beginning of the chapter. Her patient, Mr. Smith, was a successful executive, when a sudden neurological disorder left him paralyzed from the neck down. She was gentle and kind in her interaction with Mr. Smith, but this made him frustrated and uncooperative. So she imagined what it would like to be a powerful older man, suddenly enfeebled, handled by one doctor after the next, and realized that he was ashamed of his situation.[25] Implementing Stueber's analysis, Halpern:

(1) *recreated her patient's perspective of the world* by imagining herself as the enfeebled man. She says the affective part of empathy provides a context for understanding the other's point of view: "the experiencing emotion guides what one imagines about another's experience, and thus provides a direction and context for learning."[26]

(2) *imagined the world from his perspective* by learning not only how he feels and the emotions he is experiencing, but about his related desires, preferences, and what he values.

(3) *attributed beliefs and feelings to the man based on what happened during the simulation phase* by reaching the conclusion that he feels ashamed

and emasculated, and does not want to be coddled. She does this by switching back and forth between her own perspective and his.

In this case, Halpern used antecedent, theoretical information about her patient, that he was once powerful but now enfeebled, to recreate his perspective. Once she created his perspective, she focused on her patient's personality and beliefs, became aware of the relevant facts about his situation, and then pieced together this information to figure out the emotions he was experiencing. This process required Halpern to not project emotions onto her patient; she had to imagine the situation from his unique point of view. Once she did this, she came to the conclusion that he had different emotions than the ones she had been attributing to him. Once she realized that he felt ashamed and emasculated, she switched to her own point of view in order to draw conclusions about how he wanted to be treated and how she could best relate to him.

Before moving on to empathy's second epistemic function, it is important to state that the simulation model that I've been using to illustrate empathy's information gathering function can be interpreted broadly as an affective process as well. Although Stueber's simulation model suggests that empathy is a kind of information-processing capacity, Halpern believes that it is the emotional resonance with Mr. Smith (rather than the cognitive dimension of the empathy) that allowed her to unify the details of Mr. Smith's life, and have an accurate affective experience of his feelings. On her view, the affective dimension of empathy provides a context for understanding the other's point of view: "the experiencing emotion guides what one imagines about another's experience, and thus provides a direction and context for learning."[27] How can this be accounted for in the simulation model? Can the affective dimension of empathy be part of the simulation model? Halpern believes that it can, and argues that the emotions involved in the simulation are an organizing context for the cognitions and other inputs that one will use to imaginatively empathize and get new or different information about others. As she explains, "the use of resonance in the service of imagining another's emotional meanings transforms states of resonance into complex emotional dispositions that provide a context for the imagined experience."[28] Her point is that the emotion as it is experienced by the empathizer yields knowledge about the other person that she did not have before the empathetic experience.

While Halpern's view of empathy's epistemic function involves information-processing with a predominantly affective experience of empathy, her model is not terribly different than Stueber's, insofar as it involves antecedent knowledge, hypothesizing another's emotion, and feeling a resulting emotion. By implementing the knowledge that she had about her patient, and hypothesizing about his feelings and desires based on that knowledge, she was able to affectively feel how he was being treated. Halpern merely takes the affective dimension rather than the cognitive to be what makes the epistemic contribution possible. The information-processing model of empathy that I am using here can thus accommodate this insight and include affects. On the view I am proposing, the three phases of empathy can be viewed as a process of using antecedent information to affectively and/or cognitively get additional information about another person or their worldview, and attributing certain beliefs and feelings to that person.

3.3.2   Second function: Understanding others

The second epistemic function of empathy is that it contributes to *understanding others*, which involves grasping the way that the other's feelings, desires, and social situation work together to explain how life is for another, thinking about her as a whole person, and connecting one's own experiences to the other's. Someone who empathizes "sees" things from the point of view of the other, with sensitivity to the other's feelings and desires, and understands and appreciates that person and how life is for her. The empathy needed to understand others in this way involves more than just spontaneous feeling with others or simulation of their feelings or situation. It requires a cognitive attempt to ascertain how the individual's beliefs, desires, and feelings about her own life connect together and translate into her responses, as well as an affective understanding of how the other feels.

To see how empathy can lead to understanding others in a deeper way, consider, for example, Anna, who is angry about the way Michael has been treating her at work. He talks graphically about sex around her, comments on her appearance using sexual language, publicly discusses the body parts and appearance of other women in the workplace, brags about his own sexual prowess, and describes departmental meetings as a "men's club." Now suppose, one day, after a particularly humiliating comment, Anna gets angry and yells at Michael. She tells him that she is sick of his sexist comments and the harassment she feels in the workplace. She explains why his comments have enraged her, and says she wants his berating her to stop. In essence, she attempts to make her anger intelligible to Michael explaining how the comments seem from her perspective, using details that will make him see that, while he might be trying to be funny, his language is not entertaining to her.

Michael's empathy is contingent on his ability to grasp her reasons for her frustration as appropriate reasons for being irritated and his ability to see them from her point of view (where a reason is understood as "a consideration that counts in favor" of the other's emotion, belief, or action).[29] If he takes up her perspective and finds it intelligible, then he will see Anna's reasons as *reasons* and not, as Christine Korsgaard says, as mere noise.[30] Once he does this then it is *possible* for him to approve of Anna's emotion—presumably he does *not* approve of it or judge it appropriate just yet.[31] Let us suppose that, while listening to Anna, although he is shocked, he is able to take the first step in Stueber's process; Michael

(1) *recreates Anna's perspective of the world* by adopting a different conative relation to the world. To recreate her perspective, he must take the reasons for her emotion as logical and appropriately related to her emotion. Perhaps he says, "I feel you. I hear what you're saying."

(2) *imagines the world from her perspective* and simulates her point of view by thinking about the world from her perspective and appreciating the reasons for her emotion. He sees that his speech and actions towards her are disrespectful, when seen from her point of view.

(3) *attributes* feelings, beliefs and thoughts to her based on the simulation and reaches the conclusion that his comments and behavior are indeed offensive and, from her point of view, inappropriate.

By taking up Anna's perspective and hearing his own remarks from her point of view, he is able to take the situational antecedents of her emotion as logically and appropriately related to her emotion. Michael recognizes that she does not enjoy hearing his words and that she does not appreciate being viewed merely as a sexual object. In fact, Michael can only feel Anna's emotion by focusing exclusively on her point of view. If he reverts to his own point of view, he will likely be unable to see how his remarks are problematic.[32]

To summarize, empathy is not the only way to gather information about others and to understand them in a deeper way. We often use books, magazines, and other forms of media to learn about other people, their culture, and their history. Nevertheless, empathy is particularly well-suited to appreciating and understanding others' emotions, because empathy involves an affective and emotional response on the part of the observer, and this provides additional insight into the other's emotion. This is not to say that empathy is always reliable. As I have suggested above, others-focused empathy is more reliable than self-focused empathy because in this type of empathy, one tends to attribute beliefs to others rather than deduce them from one's own.[33]

3.4   Conditions on empathy's epistemic function

We now have in hand an understanding of empathy's two epistemic functions, information-gathering and understanding others. But as I suggested earlier, for empathy to perform these epistemic functions, certain conditions must be met. The *necessary* but not *sufficient* conditions on empathy's having an epistemic function in any given situation are having (1) *intelligibility* of the other's emotion, and (2) *prima facie* approval of the other's emotion. The analysis of empathy presented here will explain how empathy can perform an epistemic function and at the same time express a normative judgment.

In order to feel as the other person does, one must find that the other's perspective, feelings, reasons, and beliefs make sense. This is *intelligibility*. Essentially, an observer should find another's emotion, what it is about, its causes, and its context understandable, either in the empathic experience itself or upon reflection. In empathy, one appreciates and shares the other's emotion, not simply because she "approves" of the emotion in the sense that she would have the same emotion if she were in his situation, but she approves of it in the sense that she takes it to be intelligible in light of the circumstances, etc. If she did not find the other's emotions intelligible, she would not resonate with him because she would not understand why he was experiencing that emotion. Since empathy is a *response* to another's emotion, one must find the other's emotion and its content intelligible so that one is motivated to respond to it.

Psychologists who studied empathy in the first half of the 20th century recognized that intelligibility is crucial to empathy's performing epistemic functions. Psychotherapist Carl Rogers was perhaps the most influential in claiming that empathy is a way to make an emotion intelligible: he argued that when we perceive or imagine the phenomenal experiences of another person as if they were our own, by bracketing our own judgment of the other person, it is possible for their emotions make sense to us.[34] He emphasizes role-taking, and says that it enables one to make new links between moods and beliefs and is an organizing context for the cognitions and other inputs that one will use to imaginatively empathize. Clinicians such as Sigmund Freud, Carl Rogers and Heinz Kohut claim that if an emotion is unintelligible to the observer, one can empathize proactively (namely, by imagining that person's perspective, their life situation, and their response) and make it intelligible by feeling the emotion and seeking to understand how that person's values and interests connect.[35] To do this, one needs some minimal antecedent knowledge or understanding of another person (their values, needs and desires) in order to feel their emotion and in order to respond empathically. This is why these psychologists believed empathy was relevant to psychological theories of intelligence, social interaction, and personality.

Although intelligibility is relevant to perspective-taking empathy, it is also required for mediated association empathy—the linguistic or pictorial representation of an emotion through conversations, letters, books, or films. In this mode, one makes another's expression of emotion intelligible by learning its cognitive content linguistically.[36] Justin D'Arms' example of empathy illustrates this. In his anecdote, Mara and Sam have two different emotional responses to the same event: Tracy's standing them up for dinner. Sam feels that Tracy's doing so is understandable, and he is not terribly irritated. But Mara is angry and irritated. In his description of the episode, D'Arms says that Mara's emotional responses "arrive as invitations (with sketchy directions) to see the matter as she does."[37] Although they have two different evaluations of the situation, as Sam listens to Mara, he comes to see her view of things, and insofar as he thinks her emotions appropriate, comes to think that Tracy treated them badly and also feels angry about Tracy's standing them up for dinner.

D'Arms concludes that since Sam did not take up Mara's perspective and see things from her point of view, the empathy was the product of *emotional contagion*. But this is not the case. Sam did not immediately "catch" Mara's emotion simply by observing it, as in imitation empathy or classically conditioned empathy. In imitation empathy and classical conditioned empathy, perception of the other's emotion is sufficient for empathy, because those kinds of transfers of emotion merely require perception of an emotion and not a rich understanding of it. Rather, Sam "caught" Mara's emotion because he came to *understand* her emotion and its causes, because he found her emotion to be intelligible—a process that occurred using language and cognition. If Sam had not found Mara's response intelligible, he could not have come to feel her emotion.

And yet, intelligibility is not enough for empathy to have an epistemic function. Empathy involves not just making another's beliefs and point of view intelligible to oneself, but also accepting those beliefs, reasons, and desires as appropriately related to the emotion. In order to feel the other's emotion, an observer must *approve* of the other's emotion in that she takes it to be appropriate in the situation. The modes of empathic arousal (mediated association and role-taking) that require intelligibility also thus involve approval, affirmation, or validation of another's emotion as appropriate in the situation.[38] Martha Nussbaum's claim that disapproval of another person or her emotion prevents one from feeling *compassion* for another person also applies to empathy; disapproval of another's emotion will prevent empathy, because if one does not validate another's emotion or take it to be appropriate, then she will not be able to feel it.[39] Approval of another's emotion as appropriate in the situation is required for empathy to perform the epistemic functions because it involves not just seeing that someone is angry but agreeing with them that anger is appropriate in the situation. This allows one to feel the other's anger. There may be situations in which we disapprove of our own emotions, and in these cases, it is possible to "empathize" with someone in the same situation who is having the emotion that we disapproved of in ourselves.[40] But the empathy in this case is more akin to intellectualized understanding rather than feeling the other's emotion. It is difficult to feel another's emotion when one disapproves of it, although it is possible for one to understand another's emotion while disapproving of it.

What does it mean to approve of another's emotion? Essentially, it means that one views it as appropriate in the circumstances; the emotion makes sense when considering the person who has the emotion and the situation in which she expresses it. But this is *not* approval in the sense that the person's emotion is judged to be morally correct, all things considered. Empathy requires merely *prima facie* approval of the other's emotion, or initial acceptance of the other's emotion given the context and situation, in order for it to have an epistemic function. If someone tells a story or expresses her emotions in a way that makes sense to the listener and is appropriate in the listener's perspective, then the listener will empathize provided that she finds the story and emotion intelligible and approves of the person's response as appropriate given the situation.

Although empathy requires *prima facie* approval of the other's emotions and attitudes, it does not require full resonance with the other's emotion, though some, such as Adam Smith, suggest that this is required to share another's emotion. Smith says that "to approve of the passions of another...is the same thing as to observe that we entirely sympathize with them; and not to approve of them as such, is the same thing as to observe that we do not entirely sympathize with them."[41] Smith suggests that one must approve of all aspects of another's emotions to empathize. But emotions are complex, and when a variety of emotions are experienced at once, an observer (or listener or reader) can approve of some aspect of another's emotions but not fully approve of the emotion. To see this, consider a situation in which a co-worker, Mary, comes to Jenna's office after being verbally chastised by her boss for making a big mistake on a project. Mary begins crying and explains how she is embarrassed about making the mistake, and is genuinely sorry for it and frustrated with herself for making it, but is also angry because she believes the boss was too hard on her. I take this to be a typical expression of emotion that involves anger, disappointment, sadness, and general frustration.

If we use Stueber's three-phase model of empathy to see how empathy performs the epistemic function, we'll see that empathy does not require Jenna's *complete* resonance of Mary's range of emotions. In phase one, Jenna entertains different beliefs and adopt a different conative relation to the world, and finds Mary's sadness and frustration intelligible. She adopts Mary's perspective and sees in the second phase of empathy reasons for Mary's anger at the boss, and finds them to be intelligible, appropriate reasons her judgment in the situation. Jenna approves of her emotion as appropriate in the situation, in order to feel Mary's emotion and to empathize with her. But, if, in the third phase, Jenna finds that, while she feels Mary's frustration, she does not feel her anger, as she believes the boss's treatment was appropriate, then she seems to have partially empathized. While Jenna empathizes with Mary when she quarantines her own judgment (which is equivalent to finding her emotion intelligible from another's perspective), she does not believe Mary's anger is objectively justified, which she realizes when she reverts to her own perspective.

This situation suggests that while empathy expresses approval of another's emotion, it is better to view this expression as a *prima facie* approval of the knowledge and feelings required to engage in the empathic process, rather than *full* approval of Mary's emotion. Approval, in this scenario, is merely an appreciation of or acceptance of another person's reasons, and does not necessarily imply *moral* approval (or all things considered approval) of another's emotions. Moreover, it is possible to empathize with someone, and feel some parts of her emotion, and yet disapprove of other aspects of the person's emotion and the *actions* that follow from it. To use the previous example, it is possible for Jenna to fully empathize with

Mary, and to feel Mary's anger. But this does not mean, for example, that Jenna would approve of Mary's actions that follow from her anger, such as slandering the boss or engaging in acts of violence against him. Emotions are complex, and we may not fully approve of or feel all aspects of someone's emotional experiences.

This conclusion regarding the idea that empathy involves only *prima facie* approval of another's emotion suggests that the epistemic function of empathy and the normative nature of empathy go hand in hand. Just as imitation and classical conditioning empathy do not have an epistemic function, neither do they have a normative function: imitation and classical conditioning do not express "approval" of another's emotion. Just as a baby does not understand her mother's emotion (she loves her baby and is happy to see him) in the sense that he knows what it is about and the situation that gives rise to it, nor does he "approve" of his mother's emotion. Although mimicry or classical conditioning could be considered a kind of affirmation or validation of another's emotion, the baby does not take the mother's emotion to be an *appropriate* response given the situation in the way that is required for approval. The empathy of mimicry or "mirroring" another's emotion, or feeling a somatic and affective sensation via a direct representation of another's expression of emotion in the way described by cognitive neuroscientists lacks a judgment of approval, and thus it does not have the normative function.[42]

3.5   Normative and epistemic functions limit each other

Empathy's epistemic function correlates to normative approval in a deeper way as well. In the same way that empathy is limited by the individual's approval of the other's emotion, empathy's epistemic dimension broadens the scope of the normative so that one's evaluative perspective can be expanded. That is, empathy is not merely an expression of approval of another's emotion; one's views regarding what one approves of can be influenced by the emotional displays of the other person. Finding another's emotions intelligible makes possible empathy with another when she did not expect to do so, when she did not initially approve of the other's emotion or actions. In these cases, as one listens to or observes the other person, she somehow makes the other's situation and emotions intelligible by comparing them with her own understanding. This can happen in many ways, and as Donald Davidson says, "the process of making the beliefs and other propositional attitudes of others intelligible to ourselves necessarily involves our fitting others into our own scheme to some degree."[43] One may *perceive* similarity between oneself and others, *suppose* that there are similarities between oneself and others, or *conceive* of others' interests and emotions like her own. A co-worker, for example, may be able to see that her co-worker's anxiety about finances is *like* her anxiety about getting tenure. A child may see that another child's hurt feelings *are like* her own hurt feelings. Even if there is little similarity between oneself and another, such as when the other is from a different culture, social group, or age group, one can come to see that others' experiences are like one's own when she makes an effort.

But can one empathize with another's emotion if she believes that his actions and emotions are morally wrong? People do seem to empathize with others' emotions and yet at the same time disapprove of their actions. Juries are a classic example, and attorneys often try to choose juries who will empathize with their clients, even though they likely disapprove of the person's actions. Research regarding juror empathy for defendants and victims has shown that empathy for the victim and the defendant highly influences jury perceptions of the criminal, the selection of verdict, and the choice of sentence. A study of mock juries found a correlation between the displays of emotion on the part of the victim and the criminal (the case was one in which the individual confessed), and the punishment selected.[44] The basic hypothesis was that the emotions of those on the jury would be evoked by displays of emotion on the part of the criminal and victim. The study showed that the amount of emotion displayed by the victim as he took the stand and explained his actions significantly influenced empathy for the criminal. (Since the mock juror's judgment required recommending a sentence for the criminal, and not a punishment directly affecting the victim, the mock juror may have been more focused on the criminal.) The study concludes that observing another's display of emotion is crucial in enabling the jury member to identify with the other, for an observer's own emotions are evoked when another person displays emotion:

> The results of this study further establish the importance of the empathy variable in understanding the relationship between the social actor and the observer. An observer makes decisions/judgments based on perceptions of the social actors' emotion displays and identities. As affect control theory studies have shown, the emotions of the actor and object of behavior are significant factors in identity perceptions and judgments. An individual observing another individual's emotion

display, which may be an emotion of distress, will also have his/her own emotions influenced by these emotion displays.[45]

When someone shows emotion, the observer has an opportunity to think of the other's situation, values and feelings as that person does, from an internal perspective, and in so doing, the observer comes to appreciate the other's values and emotions in a way that he otherwise could not. By seeing things from the other's perspective, his understanding and perception of the situation and his beliefs about the other person may change. The capacity to share the feelings of others is a way of coming to share another's evaluation of the world and it enables one to "see" or appreciate previously unrecognized features of the other's life, emotion, and social circumstances. In essence, the affective nature of empathy makes one sensitive to another's experience in a way that mere belief cannot accomplish. The affective dimension of empathy explains why it is possible to empathize with people and emotions with whom one would not normally engage. Empathy is guided and limited by the extent of the resonance with another's emotion; if one does not resonate completely, it is likely because he does not believe the emotion is justified.

And yet, studies show that empathy is less likely to be evoked if one does not identify with the other person; empathy is constrained by the individual's ability and willingness to see similarities between another person's interests, concerns, and situation, and her own. Studies have shown, in fact, that jurors are more likely to empathize with those of their own race, and many attorneys suspect that racial bias in trial outcomes is related to empathy.[46] Douglas Linder even goes so far as to say that, "not only will race continue to matter in jury selection, in many cases it will decide trial outcomes."[47] He attributes the persistence of racial bias to, among other factors, empathy: people vicariously identify with another's feelings when that person's experiences, values, and appearance are similar to one's own. So long as race is an important part of identity, says Linder, empathetic reactions will be more common and more intense between members of the same racial group than between members of different racial groups.[48]

Despite the fact that people identify most strongly with those with whom they identify—whether due to race, experience, beliefs or values—empathy can nevertheless *transform* people and thus transform their perceptions of others.[49] This is why Linder suggests that empathy should not be banished from the courtroom: in proper measure, empathy can be the enemy of prejudice, and juries that acquitted, for example, Emmett Till, the murderer of civil rights worker Viola Liuzzo, lacked the empathy that was needed to render a just verdict.[50] In fact, philosopher Nancy Sherman explains that empathy has "a transformative element—to know what it is like to be someone else, where this knowledge is different from merely observing others."[51] Feeling another's emotion enables one to think about and feel the experiences of others, and this is why it plays a role in the "epistemology of value," to use Justin D'Arms' term.[52] Since empathy contributes to our understanding of how others see the world, it can help us move beyond a limited evaluative perspective to one that is "more fully responsive to the values of things." D'Arms suggests that we have a scarcity of resources for transcending our own perspectives, and this is why empathy is extremely valuable in providing an opportunity to learn something new.[53] But as the previous discussion implies, the possibility of transformation is ultimately constrained by one's normative beliefs and commitments, so it remains true that the epistemic function of empathy is limited by the normative dimension, which involves approving of another's emotion or beliefs.

Empathy's most important epistemic contribution to knowledge of others is that it enables one to grasp what is important to people different from oneself, by examining those things in a new way, from the other's point of view. The information gained from empathy can be evaluated in tandem with her own personal moral commitments, ideals, and concerns to generate moral deliberation. Our moral commitments can change over time, and this is what makes possible the change in an empathizer's beliefs. Empathy can be a reliable way to acquire true beliefs about others, which happens as a result of feeling something new and thus seeing things differently, and this can take place independent from belief-based theorizing. These new beliefs or changed beliefs may take time to root, for it is possible that, if one's emotions are not congruent with her cognitive states or beliefs—such as if one feels a murderer's sadness and remorse, but still believes that his actions were wrong—she experiences cognitive dissonance.[54] Following such an experience, the empathizer must determine how to make sense of her emotions and beliefs and decide how to respond.

3.6 The personal nature of empathetic knowledge

Empathy yields knowledge about others and facilitates understanding of others, not by acquiring more information about the other person theoretically, but by having an experience that yields insight into the other's life. This is why the knowledge gained from empathy yields information about others that is *different in kind* from information gained from learning about others externally or theoretically.[55] The central difference between knowledge acquired through empathy and knowledge acquired theoretically is that empathetic knowledge is framed in the context of the other person and oneself—subjectively and egocentrically—but with the result of knowing more about the other than one did prior to empathy.

Karsten Stueber illustrates the difference between empathy and other forms of information-gathering by comparing methods of gathering information: we could learn how tall someone is by using a measuring stick (an external method) or by comparing that person to oneself (a subjective, internal method).[56] This distinction can be applied also to the emotions: one can learn by reading books on sexual harassment that women dislike being spoken to in certain ways in the workplace; or one could observe a colleague's expression of anger or frustration at being treated a certain way by her boss and listen to her own personal testimony. Using this method, one is able to feel her colleague's humiliation, frustration and anger towards the boss, and appreciate *why* she dislikes being treated that way by her boss.

To see how the knowledge yielded by empathy is unique in that it is personal, imagine a government official engaged in foreign affairs who is responsible for negotiating with officials from other countries. This person reads books and newspapers to learn more about the people who live there, and interacts with the foreign officials through letters and face-to-face conversation. Now it is possible for this official to learn about the people with whom he engages by approaching them "externally," by learning about their beliefs, desires, and values by reading books. But if he empathizes with these people, he looks at them differently. Instead of seeing them as alien others to whom he has no connection, he pays attention as he interacts with them and feels their emotions, so that he can consider their point of view "from the inside" and learn what the world is like from their point of view.

Robert S. McNamara, who was once U.S. Secretary of Defense, asserted that this is an appropriate use of empathy: it should be used for the purposes of strategizing in foreign affairs. He even recommended that political leaders "Empathize with your enemy."[57] McNamara implies that politicians should empathize to get accurate, sensitive information about how the enemy is thinking and reasoning about the situation, and especially to understand how they reason regarding achieving their own interests. He suggests that empathy involves suspending the attitude that the other is an enemy (in the sense that he is a rational maximizer with his own agenda), and conceiving of the other *non-*

instrumentally, as an agent with understandable emotional experiences. His point is that we need empathy in order to understand how an enemy would *instrumentally* reason about the situation from their perspective. We cannot get this kind of internal information about others by thinking about them externally, for we will have no appreciation of what they want to achieve and will be unable to identify mutual goals.

Because the observer must bring his own sensibility, imagination, and perspective to the empathetic experience, the knowledge that is generated in this situation will be unique in the sense that it is framed in terms of the empathizer's perspective. Empathy involves comparing another's internal states with one's own; when one finds these intelligible and approves of them, then one can learn more about that person and her worldview. This is what Yosef Lapid did when he saw the picture of the Palestinian woman in her ruined home looking under the tiles for medicine. He adopted her beliefs and a different conative relation to the world, and recreated the Palestinian perspective. He then began thinking about the world from that perspective, imagining her thoughts and reasons for her emotions and actions. And in doing so, he was able to attribute certain thoughts, feelings, and beliefs to her. Instead of merely observing the old woman's response as appropriate given the situation, he appreciated her emotions from her perspective. The result was that he got information about the way other Palestinians would view the Israeli military's actions.

3.7   Conclusion

Empathy plays an important epistemic function in enabling us to see others' reasons and emotions as valid concerns. This function is even recognized by those who lack empathy.[58] The high-functioning autistic Temple Grandin suggests that autistic people, who are often described as lacking both perspective-taking abilities and the ability to emotionally resonate with others, are unable to gain internal understanding of another person's perspective, and so they get information about other's emotions in more rudimentary ways, such as through sensory information rather than comparison with oneself.[59] Since autistic people recognize the *significance* of others' emotions, they can learn somewhat schematically how to respond to them and how to assess their relevance to a given situation. As Grandin says, such responses are "learned like acting in a play" so that they are a learned behavior rather than a natural or instinctive response.[60]

Grandin's statement suggests that empathy's epistemological function is central to cognitively transforming our understanding of others so that we can imagine alternative methods of relating to others, and those who lack empathic abilities must use more complicated—and less reliable—means of interacting with others and their emotions. And while the knowledge that empathy yields is limited and fallible, it is one of the *few* ways that we have of connecting with others' perspectives, emotions, and points of view. By using the beliefs and knowledge that we have about others to take up their point of view, we are able to get new beliefs about others and their view of the world with empathy. By forming new beliefs and feeling another's emotion, one can better understand that person's situation, desires, and reasons.

Empathy's epistemic function explains why it should play a significant part in moral deliberation and reasoning: empathy brings information to our attention and is one of the few ways that we have to connect with others' emotions and points of view. And yet, empathy alone does not provide information sufficient for moral guidance. I turn now to explaining empathy's limitations in order to better describe empathy's appropriate role in moral deliberation and judgment.

4
Empathy, Altruism and Normative Ethics

Empathy contributes to our knowledge of others, but empirical research on empathy also suggests that it tends to cause or motivate altruistic action. The empirical evidence suggests that when individuals empathetically take up the perspectives of others and feel others' emotions, they put the concerns and needs of those others ahead of their own. Such studies do not nullify the idea that empathy has epistemic functions, for it is entirely possible that certain types of empathy have epistemic functions *and* motivate altruism. This chapter will examine this possibility and investigate the relationship between the epistemic functions of empathy and the consequences of empathy. My suggestion is that the empirical research is important for understanding the psychological and moral effects of perspective-taking empathy in clinical settings, but it does not tell us about when people actually empathize in real life situations, when they ought to empathize, or how empathy relates to our moral duties and obligations to others. Moreover, while empirical research reveals the likely effects of empathy, it also shows that people tend to empathize with those who are most similar to themselves. Empathy appears to be biased in favor of those with whom one is most similar.

So how should these empirical studies be used in the study of ethics? Some philosophers have used this empirical research to support philosophical theses regarding our moral duties and obligations to others, and others have used it as evidence for their view of human nature. For example, care theorist Michael Slote rightfully asserts that, "empathy plays a crucial enabling role in the development of genuinely altruistic concern or caring for others,"[1] but he also implies that empathy is the *basis* of moral judgment: empathic caring can be used as "a plausible criterion of moral evaluation."[2] I disagree strongly with Slote's idea that empathy can ground our moral obligations given empathy's limitations. The empirical research showing that empathy is often biased suggests that empathy ought not be the sole experience from which we derive our moral duties. Empathy is unsuitable as a *criterion* of morality because it is an experience, not a normative principle. Although empathy may sometimes motivate altruism, this fact cannot be used to ground our moral duties and obligations to others. This connection may, of course, be used to argue that empathy should be emphasized in moral theories that emphasize altruism. But it is not the case that empathizing with others generates altruism that is always moral.

4.1   Empirical research on the consequences of empathy

The empirical psychological research suggesting a connection between empathy and altruism is primarily on *perspective-taking* empathy and *mimicry* empathy (using Hoffman's categories described in Chapter 3.1).[3] I focus here on perspective-taking empathy. Psychologist C. Daniel Batson's research on the connection between perspective-taking empathy and moral and pro-social consequences (including cognition and action) is especially important here, as it is widely cited as showing a connection between empathy and altruism.[4]

Batson researches people's empathic responses towards persons in distress and examines whether experiencing such empathy induces altruism, understood as behavior that benefits the other person and has no benefit to oneself; he concludes in his well-known "empathy-altruism hypothesis" that empathy tends to generate altruistic feelings and motivation that are ultimately directed toward the goal of increasing the welfare of the person in need.[5] Batson tests for several variables, including empathic distress, ease of escape conditions, similarity between the observer and the target, amount of need the person is in, etc., and his findings show that the more someone relates to another or is similar to the other, the greater the target's need, and the greater the observer's discomfort, the more likely the observer is to help or aid the other.[6] Batson also shows that while feeling empathy for a person in need evokes altruistic motivation to help another person, empathy can be "overridden by increased self-concern introduced by awareness of the high cost of helping."[7]

Most of Batson's experiments have researched the consequences of perspective-taking empathy, namely, by taking up the perspective of someone in distress. In these experiments, subjects are asked to take up the *objective* perspective (*no-imagine* perspective), the *imagine-self* perspective (imagining *oneself* in another's perspective), or the *imagine-other* perspective (imagining being the other person).[8] In one experiment, participants had the opportunity to assign themselves and another research participant to two different tasks, with one task clearly more desirable than the other.[9] One task had positive consequences (the chance to earn raffle tickets) and the other task had neutral consequences (no chance to earn raffle tickets) and was described as rather dull and boring. Participants were provided a coin to flip if they wished to decide that way, and Batson describes this as the "fair" or "moral" choice. The researchers assign one set of participants no perspective-taking instructions when deciding which tasks to assign (*no-imagine* condition). A second group of participants is asked to imagine their own thoughts and feelings were they in the place of the other participant before they made the task-assignment choice (*imagine-self* condition). And the third group is asked to imagine the other person's feelings and thoughts before they made the task-assignment choice (*imagine-other* condition).

The researchers hypothesized that imagining oneself in the other's perspective would stimulate a "moral" response, or the desire to be *fair*, or flipping the coin to decide the matter. (While Batson argues that flipping a coin is "moral" because flipping a coin is a type of procedural justice, rather than a choice on the basis of self-interest, this is not a very convincing interpretation of the choice to flip the coin. A participant may choose to flip the coin as a way to avoid responsibility in the situation, and this does not seem "moral" at all.) The researchers also predicted that imagining the *other* person's feelings would show increased partiality in favor of the other participant, and that this would not usually lead to more coin flipping, but to pursuing the altruistic action directly by simply assigning the other participant the positive-consequences task without flipping the coin. The results were not as predicted. The proportion of participants assigning the other participant to the positive consequences task was 0.25 in *both* the no-perspective and the imagine-self conditions. But for those in the imagine-other condition, 0.58 of the participants assigned the positive consequences task to the other participant. More importantly, in this condition, 15 (of 24) participants chose not to flip the coin, and 11 of these assigned the other person to the positive consequences. This proportion was significantly higher than the proportion of those in the no-perspective condition (0.33) and the imagine-self condition (0.11) who did not flip the coin and assigned the positive-consequences task.[10]

Batson and colleagues conclude, on the basis of what was found in this experiment, that "the imagine-other perspective evoked empathy-induced altruistic motivation directed toward the goal of increasing the other's welfare,"[11] but that imagining *oneself* in the other person's perspective does *not* lead to altruism. Nor did it lead to the "moral" choice of flipping a coin.[12] So in a second, related experiment, Batson tested whether the *imagine-self* condition (imagining oneself in the other's position) could induce making a "moral" choice defined as an egalitarian distribution of goods, and found that it did. In this experiment, participants were asked to accept an initial task assignment that would give them highly positive consequences (two raffle tickets for each correct answer on their task) and the other participant nothing, or change the assignment so that oneself and the other would receive moderately positive consequences (one raffle ticket each for each correct answer on the task).[13] When given the opportunity to change from asymmetrical consequences (unfair advantage) to symmetrical consequences (the same number of raffle tickets per correct answer), 0.38 of the participants in the no-perspective condition changed the distribution from unfair to fair, while 0.83 of those who imagined *themselves* in the other's position chose the egalitarian distribution.[14]

What do these studies imply about the consequences of perspective-taking empathy? Batson concludes that taking up the imagine-self perspective can stimulate judgments of justice (at least defined as choosing the distributive/egalitarian justice of having the same payoffs, and not as the procedural justice of coin-flipping), even if it does not motivate altruism. His conclusion is based on the fact that participants who made the choice without perspective-taking instructions tended to retain their position of advantage, while the participants who imagined themselves in the other person's situation were far more likely to give up their position of advantage in favor of an equal distribution. Another plausible conclusion to draw from this study is that different types of empathetic perspective-taking can induce different types of attitudes towards others. If perspective-taking empathy can motivate an interest in fairness and justice, then we must carefully distinguish between different kinds of perspective-taking and their likely consequences, especially when we "induce" empathy or ask someone to take up another's perspective, such as when we are teaching children to consider things from another's perspective, which I discuss in Chapter 7.

Interestingly, some of Batson's experiments are designed to show the limitations on people's altruistic inclinations. Several experiments use "similarity manipulation" to test whether people tend to be more altruistic towards people they are similar to, versus those they are not as similar to. In these experiments, subjects are *unknowingly* paired with a person in need who is highly similar to themselves, based on a questionnaire they filled out weeks prior to the experiment. Researchers compared the rate at which people helped the other based on low similarity/high similarity and in easy-escape/difficult-escape conditions. Results showed that in a low similarity/easy escape condition, only 0.18 of subjects helped the person in need. But in a high similarity/ easy escape condition, 0.91 of the subjects helped the person in need. (Subjects in difficult escape/low similarity helped at the rate of 0.64 and subjects in difficult escape/high similarity helped at the rate of 0.82). Batson concludes that similarity to the person in need of help is a significant motivation to help, even when escape is easy. People are more likely to be altruistic to those who are similar to themselves.[15]

4.2 Interpretation of the empirical data

There are two worries regarding Batson's empathy-altruism hypothesis and its potential use in normative ethics. First, Batson's experiments cannot contribute much to our understanding of the role empathy plays in actual moral reasoning and motivation. These experiments measure, as Batson says, "induced" empathy, where one group of participants is asked to focus on the other person's feelings and emotions. Since the subjects are *asked* (i.e. induced) to take up another perspective, those who take up the *imagine-other* perspective are given a *special* reason—by the researchers—to take the others' situation, concerns, and reasons into account. Similarly, those who take up the *imagine-self* perspective, are given a special reason to take their own reasons into account when deciding what to do. There is no control group in which participants are given no instructions at all. Thus, these experiments do not test whether people tend to *voluntarily* take up another's perspective or imagine themselves in another's perspective; nor do they tell whether people are naturally inclined to take up one perspective or another. Participants are simply instructed to take up a perspective and act, and this is different than self-motivated empathy. Involuntary or self-motivated empathy involves feeling another's emotion and taking her situation, concerns, and reasons into account, because she wants to or believes it is important. By asking the subjects to engage in different kinds of perspective-taking empathy, the researchers induce empathy and guide the reasoning process. Once subjects become aware of the other's feelings and situation, this knowledge is in the forefront of their minds, such that they think about the other's situation and not their own; this motivates altruism because the other person's needs are salient at the moment. This hypothesis uses empathy's epistemic function to explain how perspective-taking with someone in distress could contribute to a pro-social action.

It is appropriate to conclude, then, that these experiments do not tell us much about empathy as an involuntary and self-willed phenomenon. They were not designed to motivate people to empathize by taking up others' perspectives, or to track whether people instinctively take up others' perspectives when they are faced with the opportunity to help someone in need. Thus, it is not clear what contribution this research makes to moral philosophy; its usefulness in moral education, which might include teaching children or students to take up others' perspectives, is more readily apparent. If it is a goal is to make people more altruistic, then the research does have value insofar as it can recommend strategies for moral education; it is useful to know which kinds of inducements bring about the desired experiences and actions. But these studies do not measure whether people are likely to take up another's perspective, whether people can be taught to take up other's perspectives, or what motivates people to take up others' perspectives on their own. The empirical psychological research on empathy is limited in the information it yields regarding empathy and moral action, and so its connection to normative ethics is not readily apparent.

Moreover, psychologist Martin Hoffman concludes that Batson's experiments show that empathy is limited insofar as people are subject to "empathic over-arousal."[16] When an observer's empathic distress is so heightened that it becomes aversive, it can be transformed into a feeling of *personal* distress. This is empathic over-arousal. Batson is careful to track whether egoistic motivation is heightened in his experiments, and in experiments that involved viewing a subject receiving electric shocks, the motivation to reduce one's personal distress of viewing the subject's shocks increased significantly. Hoffman concludes that people are more likely to empathize, rather than act on the basis of personal distress, when they are in a relatively comfortable state, and not preoccupied with their own needs and concerns. If an observer's empathic distress becomes so painful and intolerable that it is transformed into an intense feeling of personal distress, the person may cease to empathize entirely. Batson's experiments confirm that this happens when the feeling of distress is particularly high.

Hoffman also concludes that Batson's experiments show that empathy is biased. Batson's experiments reveal two types of empathic bias: *familiarity bias* and *here-and-now bias*. "Familiarity bias" is where people tend to empathize to a greater degree with family members, members of their primary group, close friends, and people whose personal needs and concerns are similar to their own; "here-and-now bias" is where people tend to empathize the most with people (especially victims) in an immediate situation, with those who are present, versus with those who are absent.

Two types of similarities contribute to familiarity bias: *structural similarity* and *content-based similarity.* "Structural similarities in people's physiological and cognitive response systems" enable people with similar cognitive abilities to respond to events similarly, even if they do not produce *identical* feelings.[17] For example, "normal" adults (i.e., statistically average adults) empathize less with those with cognitive or intellectual disabilities, such as people with Down's syndrome, autism, or neurological damage, for "normal" adults do not understand their responses or read their minds well.[18] Presumably this is due to less *structural similarity* between the two groups.[19] *Content-based similarity* also contributes to familiarity bias: Hoffman cites a number of studies in which empathy is "greater between people in the same culture who live under similar conditions" than between people from different cultures who rarely interact.[20] People who are similar to each other culturally will have similar emotional responses, and this explains why people tend to empathize with their friends and those with whom they are familiar.[21]

Nevertheless, Hoffman suggests that these biases may benefit a moral agent in practical ways. For example, *empathic over-arousal* "can intensify one's dedication to help in existing relationships, especially those in which one is in the role of helper."[22] And *here-and-now bias* can become generalized and produce distress for other victims as a group, not just individuals.[23] In addition, here-and-now bias focuses our attention "selectively" so that we are not completely overwhelmed by our empathy. Hoffman concludes that over-arousal and empathic bias might be empathy's self-regulating mechanisms: "what keeps promiscuous empathy from becoming a significant problem for society are empathic bias and over-arousal and the powerful egoistic motive system that underlies them."[24] And yet, Hoffman implies that these biases limit empathy's usefulness in the derivation and justification of moral norms.[25] Since empathy is biased in these two ways, we have good reason to believe that it is not well-suited for playing a foundational role in ethics. Alone, empathy would produce moral judgments that are not equitable or fair, and are perhaps prejudiced.

It is worth noting that Batson's empathy-altruism hypothesis is disputed by psychologists and philosophers alike.[26] Not all psychologists agree that empathy yields altruistic behavior or cognition, and psychologist Nancy Eisenberg claims that "there is no reason to assume that perspective-taking invariably leads to altruistic cognitions or behaviors;"[27] most psychologists defend the weaker claim that empathy *tends* to induce pro-social behavior. Although Batson's "empathy-altruism" hypothesis is much stronger than most other psychologists', even he thinks that empathy can be overridden by self-interest, and that "increased potential for self-benefit can increase prosocial behavior."[28] Thus, even Batson recognizes that he cannot show that empathy produces *genuine* altruism, i.e. without any motive of self-interest. Since my interest is in the kind of empathy Batson researches and how it should figure in to normative ethics, and not whether empathy results in *genuine* altruism, I will not examine this claim further.

4.3   Problems with using this research in normative ethics

Now that we have a better idea of empathy's potentially positive contribution to moral action, we can ask, how should empathy figure in to normative ethical theories that prescribe moral rightness and wrongness? Ethical theorist Michael Slote uses Batson's research on empathy as the foundation for his version of care ethics, and assumes that Batson's conclusions are correct: "namely that empathy is a crucial source and sustainer of altruistic concern or caring about (the well-being of) others."[29] Slote's view is that "empathy plays a crucial enabling role in the development of genuinely altruistic concern or caring for others."[30] He claims that empathy generates empathic caring, which can be used as "a plausible criterion of moral evaluation."[31] According to this criterion, empathetic feeling toward others is morally required and persons ought "*not* to act from uncaring motives, *not* to act in ways that reflect a lack of empathic concern for others."[32] In order to avoid requiring that people act from particular motives, i.e., the motive of empathic care, Slote emphasizes the importance of *action* over and against attitudes and feelings. His criterion of moral rightness states that *actions* are "morally wrong and contrary to moral obligation if, and only if, they exhibit or express an absence (or lack) of fully developed empathic concern (or caring about) others on the part of the agent."[33]

Slote also derives moral obligations from empathy. He argues that the degree of "natural" empathetic engagement with others corresponds to our moral obligations to them; differences in the strength of empathy for others correspond to "differences of intuitive moral evaluation, and that fact...will allow an ethics of caring that brings in empathy—an ethics of empathic caring—to give a fairly general account of both public/ political and private/individual morality."[34] In other words, the more we empathize with someone, the greater our obligations to her, and the less we empathize, the less moral obligations we have to her.[35] Empathy does not need "correction" by more objective, systematic, or principled moral concerns, or even by care principles generally.[36] If we happen to empathize with those who are more similar to us, this justifies the idea that we are more morally obligated to help or care for those who are more similar to us. Ultimately, differences in empathy explain and justify the different moral obligations that we have to others.

In many ways, Slote's use of empathy to ground care ethics insightfully brings greater attention to the role of empathy in moral action. Nevertheless, his use of Batson's research to undergird his version of care ethics fails to provide genuine support for his view because the type of empathy that Batson researches is not the same type of empathy that Slote discusses. Thus, Batson's empirical conclusions are not particularly relevant to Slote's normative ethics. In addition, Batson's empirical research shows that induced empathy motivates *justice*, not just care or altruism, and so it is misleading to suggest that empathy has a unique support for care ethics over and against other ethical theories. These are not my only objections to Slote's moral theory, and in section 4.4, I explain why our moral obligations ought not be derived from empathy and empathic care.

First, as I showed earlier, Batson's experiments test perspective-taking abilities, but do not gauge emotional response by testing whether the participant is feeling the other's emotion, or merely responding to her own perceived dissatisfaction. This would not be a problem if Slote was particularly interested in perspective-taking empathy, but he does *not* adopt Batson's definition of empathy. Slote defines empathy as "having the feelings of another (involuntarily) aroused in ourselves, as when we see another person in pain."[37] But in Batson's experiments, the feelings of another person were *not* involuntarily aroused, because the experiment involved *inducing* empathy in the participants. Since the subjects did not "voluntarily" take up another's perspective, the feelings of the other person could not have been involuntarily aroused in the observer. Thus, Slote's attempt to provide an empirical basis for care ethics relies on research that is rooted in a different kind of empathy than the one he is interested in. Batson researches the consequences of induced perspective-taking empathy, and Slote is interested in developing a moral theory rooted in the experience of feeling another's emotions.

Second, Batson's experiments show that perspective-taking empathy motivates actions and judgments of *justice*—not just altruism and care—and so it seems plausible that empathy can play a prominent role in other moral theories as well, and I show in the following chapter that it does. To recall, in Batson's experiments, when given the opportunity to change from asymmetrical (unfair advantage) consequences to symmetrical (fair) consequences, 0.38 of the participants in the no-perspective condition changed the distribution from unfair to fair, while 0.83 of those who imagined themselves in the other's position chose the egalitarian distribution. Batson concludes on the basis of this experiment that the imagine-self perspective can stimulate judgments of justice (at least defined as the distributive/egalitarian justice of assigning equal tasks, and not as the procedural justice of coin-flipping), if not altruism. Participants who had no perspective-taking instructions tended to retain their position of advantage, while the participants who imagined themselves in the other person's situation were far more likely to give up their position of advantage in favor of an equal distribution. Batson's study, thus, suggests that induced self-focused perspective-taking empathy can generate judgments of justice, and if this is the case, then empathy's contribution to other types of moral judgment must be examined as well.

Martin Hoffman's psychological theory elaborates how perspective-taking empathy can generate judgments of justice, especially distributive justice. Since perspective-taking empathy can focus attention on others' unjust situations, it can provide a motive to rectify violations of justice to others; the empathic person feels empathic anger and is motivated to rectify the injustice when someone else is treated unjustly.[38] Empathy can also make a substantive contribution to judgments of justice, especially empathy with others in need. Hoffman cites research that shows that bystanders empathize with people who need food and shelter (his Chapters 2–4), and concludes that perspective-taking empathy can motivate people to care about social justice. If someone views food and shelter as basic rights, then a person's empathy for groups of people—such as the disadvantaged—may motivate someone to view such persons as deserving of food and shelter.[39] This empathic response is both a feeling of empathy for the person's distress and also an understanding of the person as a victim of injustice whose rights have been violated.[40]

Finally, Hoffman argues that empathy can motivate a *general* caring principle that transcends particular individuals and lead to an interest in what is right, all things considered.[41] Hoffman argues that empathy does not simply motivate care and increased obligations for *particular* individuals—as Slote claims regarding our obligations to others—but combines with people's other moral convictions to result in care and concern for people *in general*. For example, Hoffman explains how Huck Finn's care and empathetic feeling for (the slave) Jim illustrates the power of empathy not just to befriend Jim and sacrifice his own safety for the sake of Jim's freedom, but also the power of empathy in coming to see that both Jim's situation and the law prohibiting Jim's freedom were unjust.[42] He illustrates how Huck's growing friendship increased care and empathy with a singular person (Jim), and this in turn increased his feeling of obligation to him insofar as it spurred Huck to seek justice for Jim, which is Slote's main idea. But Hoffman suggests that empathy can do more than this: empathy can broaden Huck's realm of concern to include other people *like Jim*, insofar as he regards the laws surrounding slavery as unjust. If empathy with a particular person can increase care, concern, or a desire to do justice for a group of people in general as Hoffman suggests that it does, then Slote's claim that the degree of empathy for someone defines one's moral obligations to others does not match our intuitions about empathy and our moral obligations.[43]

4.4 Empathy and moral obligation

Slote's use of Batson's and Hoffman's research to support his thesis regarding empathy's role in the derivation of moral obligations is problematic because Batson suggests that empathy does *not* enable the development of *genuinely* altruistic concern, as Slote claims, and Hoffman suggests empathy motivates one to act for the sake of justice in addition to care for particular others. However, the real weakness of Slote's position is that it does not take into account the significance of the empirical research that suggests that empathy is biased. This must be taken into account when examining the appropriate role for empathy in articulating standards of correct moral action.[44] In what follows, I first recap Slote's theory and then illustrate why empathy alone cannot be the source of our moral obligations and duties to others. While feeling empathy for another person can be a useful starting point for making a moral judgment, empathy is unsuitable as a criterion of morality because it is an experience, not a normative principle; empathy is neither tantamount to making a moral judgment, nor the sole state from which we ought to derive moral obligations.[45]

To recall, Slote argues that the greater our empathy with another person, the greater our obligations to her; differences in empathy for others correspond to differences in moral obligation. Slote's key illustration of this thesis unfortunately does not provide strong support for this position. He outlines, for example, how a lack of empathy for another reveals that one has less obligation to that other by examining of the morality of abortion. He argues that early fetuses "look more like fish or salamanders or (at least) non-human, lower animals than like human beings, and they lack experience, a brain, and even limbs." This limits our ability to empathize with early fetuses; since "we naturally tend to empathize more with the later stages than with the earlier," "it is morally better, or less bad, to abort an embryo or early-stage fetus than to abort a late-stage fetus."[46] He concludes that the less we empathize with a fetus, as we are less likely to do in an earlier stage of fetal development, the less wrong it is to abort it.

Although this illustration initially seems plausible, people attribute a wide range of emotions, including pain and pleasure, to fetuses, and so Slote's empathy-based argument can lead to the opposite conclusion than the one he suggests. A brief survey of online right-to-life literature suggests that people can easily identify with early-stage fetuses, especially if they are encouraged to see the image of a fetus as very similar to a fully-developed human.[47] Slote's position implies that if a person identifies with a fetus and believes that a fetus in the early stage of pregnancy can feel pain, and empathizes with the fetus's pain, then in that person's view, s/he has a moral obligation to the fetus and it is morally wrong for the fetus to be aborted. If, on the other hand, one does not strongly empathize, then s/he does not have a strong moral obligation to that fetus, normatively speaking. Not only do we not *feel* as if we have a moral obligation to the fetus, we do not actually *have* a strong moral obligation to it.

This example illustrates, rather, that empathically identifying with the other depends on the person's *perception* of another's emotional experience rather than "having the feelings of another (involuntarily) aroused in ourselves, as when we see another person in pain,"[48] (Slote's proposed definition of empathy). Slote's definition of empathy suggests that another's feelings are involuntarily aroused in us when we see them express some emotion, but in the abortion situation, it is not clear what emotion the fetus is expressing. Although one might be able to perceive fetal pain and discomfort at a later stage of pregnancy, the fetus is incapable of expressing emotion in the early stages of pregnancy, certainly not in the same way that a child expresses frustration or an adult expresses pain. Since one must *project* feelings onto the fetus (especially in the earlier phases), this example illustrates that moral obligations at that phase are derived from *projected emotion* rather than genuine empathy. Thus, the example does not well explain how empathy can be the source of our moral obligations to others.

But the more problematic aspect of Slote's example is that it implies that if one cannot identify with something that doesn't look human, then she does not have moral obligations to it. This does not fit well with our everyday intuitions about our obligations to others. For example, most people intuitively believe that we have some sort of obligation to the environment, to protect it so that we will have the natural resources necessary for human survival. But this obligation does *not* seem to be derived from empathy, for we do not empathize with trees, oceans, or wildlife. This disconnect suggests that Slote's claim that our moral obligations correspond to our empathy with others is unsupported by our everyday intuitions, which Slote cites as offering support for his view. Our "natural" empathy with others does not seem to be a good starting point for delineating the scope of moral obligation. Moreover, how similar do two beings need to be in order for one to empathize with another? If one does not empathize with those with Down's syndrome, Slote's position implies that that person does not have moral obligations to them. For example, although one might believe that a girl with Down's syndrome feels physical pain, he might also believe that because she is handicapped, that she cannot experience emotional pain, and will proceed to make fun of her, demean her, and marginalize her. His inability to empathize with her emotions would, on Slote's view, imply that he has no moral obligation to treat her with respect, as he would "normal" people.

While feeling others' pain does seem related to our ideas about right and wrong, the amount or degree of empathy that we feel with others does not usefully define the scope or range of moral obligation to others. Although it is true that we "naturally" empathize with our friends and family members and our obligations to them are stronger, this correspondence does not amount to a normative derivation of obligations. Moral obligations cannot be derived only from empathy or empathic care because empathy is highly variable from one person to the next. Just because we do not understand or feel the emotional responses of those who are different from us does not mean that our moral obligations to them are fewer; likewise, just because we empathize with another's emotion, does not mean that we are obligated to respond altruistically to her—another moral response (such as justice) might be more appropriate. As Hoffman observes, the objects of empathy vary significantly from one person to another, and people have a wide range of empathic abilities; thus, we should be wary of building the edifice of moral obligation on empathic care.

Simply because empathy expresses *prima facie* approval of another's emotion and is in this regard normative, this normative dimension of empathy does not mean that it is tantamount to, or constitutive of, a moral judgment, as Slote suggests. People's empathic abilities are related to their moral beliefs and upbringings, however, empathy is not—and should not be—the basis for moral obligation, since empathy may be biased, can change over time, and is largely influenced by our perceptions about others. Perhaps this is why Hume, who Slote invokes as a forerunner of his view, recognizes the tendency to empathic bias, and thus offers a corrective device, the Common Point of View, for demarcating moral judgment.[49] Hume says that since it would be impossible for people to agree in their sentiments if they made moral judgments from their own individual points of view, they must choose "some common point of view, from which they might survey their object, and which might cause it to appear the same to all of them."[50] The "common point of view" is composed of the perspectives of those individuals who are impacted in the situation and who interact with the person being evaluated. And making a moral judgment from the Common Point of View involves imagining these perspectives, assessing the person's action or character based on the praise or blame assigned by each of these parties, and then expressing approval or disapproval of that person's action or character. In Hume's Common Point of View, empathy is not the *sole* criterion of moral assessment, but it can produce the sentiments that are *characteristic* of moral judgments. This is a much more plausible account of the relationship between empathy and moral judgment than that which Slote proposes.

These criticisms of Slote's theory should not be interpreted as suggesting that empathy cannot play a role care ethics or virtue theory more generally. Nancy Sherman, for example, rightly argues that, insofar as empathy and empathetic imagination can motivate altruism, empathy can contribute to a "conception of altruistic virtues that presupposes empathic imagination."[51] Sherman interprets Batson's program of research as suggesting that "taking the perspective of another person increases empathic arousal, which in turn increases helping on occasions where there are opportunities to help," so that "empathy predisposes us to sympathy."[52] Since empathy often brings about care and sympathy for others, then empathy should be emphasized in a virtue theory that emphasizes care, beneficence, generosity, or compassion, for these virtues "presuppose empathic engagement and [that] a requirement on their cultivation is that we appropriately cultivate that skill."[53] In a virtue theory that emphasizes virtues such as beneficence, compassion, and sympathy, empathy will be important because it is "morally motivating."[54]

However, Sherman points out—like I have—that empathy alone is not enough to bring about moral behavior; there will need to be "normative requirements" to guide the imaginative empathetic experience so that empathy motivates altruistic actions and virtues.[55] She acknowledges that since empathy involves feeling another's emotion, it can result in biased feelings and motives towards others when it is not informed or regulated by moral principles and directives. Additional moral concerns are needed to regulate the workings of empathy, for "to properly predispose empathy toward virtue, we need regulative constraints on our empathy."[56] I agree with Sherman: empathy is alone insufficient to serve as a criterion for moral action, but can play an important instrumental role in motivating the performance of certain virtues.[57] This is why in Chapter 7, I describe in greater detail how empathy should be taught in moral education programs so that it brings about virtuous dispositions and actions.

4.5   Conclusion

This chapter examined several of Batson's empirical studies of empathy and showed that while there is evidence that empathy tends to generate altruism, this thesis should not play a significant role in normative ethics, given that people are biased in favor of those who are similar to themselves, and given that empathy may not motivate *genuine* altruism. This is why I concluded that Slote's method of using the empirical research on empathy to derive a criterion of morality is flawed. Although encouraging people to take up the other's point of view may motivate altruism, it may also motivate concerns for justice. Psychologist Martin Hoffman is correct in suggesting that empathy plays an important and complex role in moral development, in that it can contribute to the development of empathetic virtues and is instrumental to the achievement of a wide range of moral ends.

The claims made in this chapter are central to the book's thesis that empathy alone is not sufficient for moral judgment, deliberation, or action. This chapter thus sets up the argument in the following chapter that perspective-taking empathy can combine with moral commitments and principles to motivate the achievement of a variety of normative ethical ends. As I showed in the previous chapter, perspective-taking empathy is especially important because it can impact our beliefs about others, our judgments about others, and our motivations to perform certain actions or believe certain things. Thus, it needs to work in tandem with moral principles, commitments, and concerns. I turn now to explaining how the epistemic functions of perspective-taking empathy outlined in Chapter 3 can play an instrumental role in moral deliberation.

Part III
Empathy and Ethical Theory

5
Empathy and Moral Deliberation

One of the most important features of empathy is that it brings information to our attention and is one of the few ways that we have to connect with others' emotions and points of view. This enables empathy to have the epistemic functions of information-gathering and understanding others, outlined in Chapter 3. But what can empathy contribute to moral thought and deliberation? Perspective-taking empathy in particular impacts our beliefs about others, our judgments about them, and our motivation to perform certain actions, and so it seems central to moral deliberation. But in order for empathy to contribute to moral deliberation and provide adequate moral guidance, the tendency to empathize with those who are most similar to ourselves, or empathic bias, must somehow be surmounted. This can happen when empathy is used in tandem with moral principles, and informed by moral concerns, so that empathy can motivate the achievement of a variety of ethical ends.

Several philosophers have defended a similar thesis. For example, the theories of moral deliberation offered by R.M. Hare, Diana Tietjens Meyers and Stephen Darwall, among others, recommend utilizing empathy in the moral decision-making process. These theorists believe, as I do, that while empathy brings about awareness of others' reasons, emotions, and concerns, it doesn't *necessarily* offer significant moral guidance. But when someone empathizes, and reflects on her experience using particular moral values, principles, and goals, empathy can play an important role in moral deliberation.

While these philosophers describe empathy's role in particular normative ethical theories, empathy can successfully play a central role in a wide range of ethical theories. Empathy is indispensable to moral theories that recognize that people have differing points of view: empathy can be used to learn what matters to people and, insofar as empathy makes salient others' interests and concerns, can recommend taking those concerns into account in a way that is justifiable to them. To demonstrate how perspective-taking empathy can positively contribute to moral deliberation, this chapter describes empathy's *salience effect*; it then explains how the salience effect generates empathetic deliberation, and then elucidates how empathetic deliberation can transform into different types of *moral deliberation*.

Although it seems intuitive to think that empathy is instrumental to moral deliberation, philosopher Diana Meyers claims that "impartial" ethical theories integrate empathy "without considering the psycho-social obstacles to empathic understanding and thus without appreciating the complexity of moral reflection."[1] I disagree, and show that when perspective-taking empathy is guided by moral principles and values, empathic bias and prejudice can be surmounted, even in impartial moral theories. Moreover, I demonstrate that theories that are *not* impartialist, such as Slote's care ethical theory and Hobbesian ethical theory, may retain empathic bias even though they try to make use of empathy's insights.

To clarify the nature of empathetic deliberation, I end the chapter by distinguishing empathetic deliberation from hypothetical deliberation, which is simulating or imagining the other's psychological state in order to generate provisional choices based on that person's psychology. *Empathetic deliberation* involves feeling another person's perspective and emotions in a way that is sensitive to his situation, so that certain features his perspective becomes salient to the observer and she can evaluate it. Although several utilitarian theorists claim that empathy is useful for deliberating from the objective point of view, they are really endorsing hypothetical deliberation rather than empathetic deliberation. The chapter concludes by showing that given empathy's tendency to bias, a normative ideal of empathy, or a virtuous type of empathy, needs articulation. I call this, following other philosophers, *mature empathy*.

5.1 The salience effect, empathetic deliberation, and moral deliberation

Empathy has what I shall call a *salience effect*. That is, *empathy makes salient another's particular emotions, concerns, reasons, interests, and considerations in such a way that they are relevant and important to the empathizer, so that she is motivated to respond to these concerns.* When, for example, Zack expresses frustration, pain, and anger because he has been bullied due to his sexual orientation, and Amy empathizes, his concerns, situation, and feelings become salient to her. When one becomes aware of the other's point of view, reasons, feelings, desires, and values, then it is possible for her to see his reasons and emotions as *prima facie* valid concerns. (Her particular moral commitments will determine whether she *actually* takes them to be valid concerns.)

To see empathy's salience effect, let us examine the three phases of perspective-taking empathy:

(1) *The matching phase*—when one entertains different beliefs and adopts a different conative relation to the world in order to recreate the other's perspective on the world.
(2) *The simulation phase*—having adopted the other's perspective, one starts thinking about the world from that perspective and entertaining reasons for possible actions and thoughts.
(3) *The attribution phase*—after completing the simulation phase, one ceases to entertain the other's perspective and bases her interpretation of the other's action (or expression) on her knowledge of what happened during the simulation phase.

Empathy's salience effect is present in the second and third phases of empathy. When Amy considers Zack's point of view and comes to feel his emotion and grasp his reasons, the process of empathy makes this information *salient*. The salience effect enables Amy to draw a conclusion in the third phase about what Zack feels in a particular situation and to understand the important reasons, values, and concerns that are associated with his feeling and worldview.

Suppose, for example, that Michael has been making sexual remarks to Emma at work that she finds offensive and inappropriate. Michael presumably does not believe his behavior is offensive, and thinks his remarks are not problematic. But suppose Emma gets angry, and expresses her frustration with Michael, explaining that she dislikes his talking about her sexually at work, saying that it makes her feel simply like a sex object. If Michael has empathy and feels her anger and frustration, then her emotion *makes salient* to him her reasons, values, and concerns. When Michael feels Emma's emotion as she does—not from his own perspective—then her point of view becomes *salient* to him. For Michael to empathize with Emma, Michael must find Emma's emotion intelligible and approve of it as appropriate in the situation.[2]

In situations like these, empathy's salience effect motivates concern for the other's situation. Empathy effects people's beliefs about others and motivations towards them. In Daniel Batson's experiments testing the effects of different kinds of perspective-taking empathy, participants were motivated to perform altruistic actions when the empathetic perspective-taking made certain features of the other person's situation salient to them.[3] This is because perspective-taking empathy's salience effect can help a person access, appreciate, understand, and evaluate other people's reasons, values, and concerns.

When empathy helps a person to feel, think about, imagine, or reflect on another person's feelings, reasons, and responses, it generates *empathetic deliberation. Empathetic deliberation involves keeping in mind the other's relevant feelings, reasons and desires and the way they perceive their lives, and thinking about their situation.* To use the example above, Amy becomes sensitive to Zack's concerns and his reasons for feeling the way he does, and deliberates about the situation using his reasons, feelings, and considerations for wanting such treatment to stop. Empathetic deliberation involves thinking empathetically regarding another person's reasons, feelings, and situation. With empathy, one acquires an appreciation of another's feelings, reasons, beliefs, and point of view.

Empathetic deliberation, though, is not equivalent to *moral deliberation*. Empathetic deliberation becomes moral deliberation when an individual uses moral norms, values, and principles to guide the deliberative process and determine how best to understand that person and the situation. When these features of the person's situation are made salient, one can then use her own personal moral commitments or an impartial decision procedure to decide what to do in a certain situation. This is *moral empathetic deliberation* and it can produce moral deliberation as it is defined by a variety of moral theories. (Since moral deliberation does not necessarily require empathy, moral deliberation is not equivalent to empathetic deliberation.)

5.2   Empathetic moral deliberation in contemporary normative ethics

Two contemporary moral theories that emphasize empathy's role in moral deliberation can be interpreted as offering theories of empathetic moral deliberation that recognize empathy's salience effect. In Diana Meyers' moral theory, which is essentially a theory of empathetic moral deliberation, *empathic thought* is the deliberative ideal. *Empathic thought* involves recognizing oneself as the deliberator *and* recognizing the other in a process of mutual recognition; the two are in a kind of relationship, and the aim of moral deliberation should be to find "a workable continuation of that relationship based on mutual recognition."[4] Empathy should be used to learn about another's reasons, values, and concerns, to answer the question, "How can I *best* respond to you?" The information obtained through empathy should then be considered in light of the individual's own moral commitments and the kind of person she wants to be.[5]

Meyers distinguishes two kinds of empathy that might be relevant to empathic thought: incident-specific empathy and broad empathy. The former involves imaginatively experiencing another's state of mind at a specific time and trying to understand what she is going through in a particular situation. The latter is more expansive insofar as it involves engaging with the other person as a whole, and attempting to understand what it is like to be that person in general.[6] Broad empathy is thus crucial to empathic thought, because it involves imagining the other's state and thinking about who she is as a person. Broad empathy is needed for moral deliberation because "empathic access to the other's perspective discloses the values and disvalues that are at stake for the other."[7] Knowledge of these values and disvalues is needed to deliberate about what is important from a moral point of view. This is because

> A moral interpretation of a situation cannot be confined to the perspective of any one of the participants. Moving back and forth between their empathic understanding of others and their understanding of their own moral identity, people shape and dismiss options according to moral standards and find reasons to settle on one course of action rather than another. Coupled with empathic concern for the other, the guidance of one's moral identity gives this process its moral character.[8]

Meyers says that empathetic moral deliberation involves using empathy and one's personal moral standards to filter information about others, discover the reasons that are relevant to that person, and consider which action to take in light of them. She does not recommend using specifically utilitarian or Kantian criteria in moral deliberation, but indicates that empathic understanding is to be used in tandem with each individual's personal moral principles, ideals, commitments, and virtues, to determine a workable continuation of the relationship.

Myers suggests that empathy's salience effect is present when empathy produces sensitive understanding of the other, oneself, and the relationship. Broad empathy in specific enables one to fully understand and appreciate the other's reasons and values. But moral judgment is a result of the individual's moral identity, which includes commitment to moral principles. Empathy—or empathetic moral deliberation—is "a way of generating proposals" for how to deal with moral issues that "arise in interpersonal relations."[9] Ultimately, though, "impersonal, objective standards" serve as the criteria for right and wrong, and presumably offer guidance in troublesome interpersonal relationships. Given her commitment to these objective moral standards, Myers would likely agree that in relationships of abuse and neglect, broad empathy with the (abusive) other would reveal reasons and values that, when examined through one's moral identity, would recommend that the most workable continuation of the relationship is *severing* it.

Since Myers recognizes empathy's tendency to be biased in favor of those who are most similar to oneself or whose distress is immediate, she emphasizes the importance of respect for persons as "a necessary antidote to the unreliability of empathy."[10] In addition, she argues that empathy should be combined with *dissident speech,* which involves contesting the culturally determined stereotypical images of others and bringing the power of non-conscious prejudices to light by seeing the members of a socially excluded group in a new light. Dissident speech "stymies routine thinking" about the other by refiguring "gender, race, sexual orientation, class, ethnicity, and the like."[11] Although dissident speech aims to correct for empathy's tendency to bias, dissident speech is limited to surmounting the prejudices that we already have and can be made aware of through empathy; to genuinely stymie routine thinking, in my view, empathetic conversations with those are different from ourselves and ethical reflection on what is learned from those perspectives is necessary.

Stephen Darwall's *second-person standpoint* is a theory of moral reflection that accounts for the normativity of our moral obligations. It too appeals to empathy as crucial for moral deliberation. The second-person standpoint is "the perspective you and I take up when we make and acknowledge claims on one another's conduct and will," and is taken up when making demands on how one is to be treated (as a "you").[12] Darwall suggests that empathy plays an epistemic role in bringing about the feelings and beliefs about others and the relationship that are crucial for second-personal deliberation: empathy "works to bring others' views inside our perspective so that they can be part of our own critical reflection and not just recorded as what others think."[13] Second-personal reasons are *agent-relative* insofar as they include a reference to the agent for whom it is a reason[14] and recognizing these reasons requires empathy because it allows the agent to take up the other's perspective and engage in reciprocal recognition of the other.[15]

The second-person standpoint can be interpreted as a deliberative stance that is sensitive to empathy's *salience effect*: by empathizing with others' points of view, a person can appreciate the other's reasons, concerns and values, and not just see them as distant matters. Darwall thus describes second-personal accountability as a form of "social criticism," in that it is a perspective where human beings discuss their concerns and what they can justifiably expect and demand from one another.[16] In this deliberative space, agents can engage in reciprocal recognition of each other as moral agents due to the effects of empathy. Taking up the second-person standpoint enables one to engage in empathetic moral deliberation, which is understood as putting oneself imaginatively into another's standpoint and comparing "the responses that one thinks reasonable from that perspective with the other's actual responses, as one perceives them third-personally."[17] The second-person standpoint is thus guided and constrained by reasonableness, which is norm used to judge another's reasons and responses.[18]

Darwall also recognizes that empathy is limited in that it may be biased against those who are different from oneself, so that the person who empathizes may still be unable to perceive second-personal reasons and their authority. In order for people to "be able to put themselves imaginatively into the other's standpoint and compare the responses that one thinks reasonable from that perspective with the other's actual responses, as one perceives them third-personally," they must not be biased against the other so that they can view the reasons as having a valid source. To guarantee that a person views others' second-personal reasons as valid and authoritative, Darwall adds requirements to the second-person standpoint that will minimize prejudice and bias against others. These include reciprocal recognition, dignity, and respect, which are additional claims, demands, and norms that make sense from a second-person standpoint. These features enable the person who takes up the second-person standpoint to engage in "exchange," which Darwall cites as Adam Smith's term describing the reciprocal acknowledgement of norms that govern parties who are confronting each other as persons: exchange "presupposes that both parties are mutually accountable, having an equal authority to complain, to resist coercion, and so on."[19] Ultimately, to engage in exchange, "one must be capable of the requisite reciprocal recognition, and this requires empathy."[20] Presumably, empathy is the key to dispelling prejudice because, to engage in the second-person standpoint, one must see others as they see themselves and not as the culture has defined them. Empathizing in this way will enable reciprocal recognition of the other.

Meyers' and Darwall's theories of moral reflection expressly emphasize the importance of empathy in deciding a workable solution to one's interpersonal relationships and for feeling the authority of other's reasons in second-person relationships. Both recognize that the information that empathy provides includes insight into the values at stake in a given situation, and insight into the authority of others' demands on the basis of their merits. Both recognize that empathy can perpetuate, as Meyers says, "crude, demeaning, stereotypical thinking about members of target groups," and that empathy's tendency "to be distorted by prejudice must be counteracted."[21] Thus, both theorists require that empathy be used in combination with objective or universal moral principles and requirements that will enable the empathizer to break out of a conventional view of others and see them in a new way. They both agree that empathy alone is insufficient for moral judgment and needs to be combined with other principles in order for it to make a positive contribution to moral judgment.

5.3   Empathetic moral deliberation in Kant's impartialist ethics

Now that we have seen how empathy can contribute to moral deliberation in two contemporary moral theories, I will highlight empathy's positive contribution to a traditional moral theory—Kant's ethics. Surprisingly, Diana Meyers argues that moral theories such as Kant's that require moral judgments to be objective and impartial cannot make significant use of empathy.[22] She claims that moral theories grounded in "impartial reason" are inadequate for addressing prejudice and do not make room for empathy to contribute to one's understanding others.[23] Although such theories may try to use empathy, she says that impartial moral deliberation is incapable of dealing with the problem of cultural prejudice against those who are different or who tend to be stereotyped in society.[24] However, Kantian ethics can make room for empathy to play a role in moral deliberation and the development of virtue in a way that does not preserve stereotypes and bias.

In his discussion of the development of virtue, Kant suggests that empathy and its salience effect are important to recognizing opportunities to follow the moral law and act according to one's duty. Although Kant is well known for arguing that people motivated by sympathy or pity do not act on morally praiseworthy motives, because such passions are heteronomous (or do not spring from reason alone), Kant's writings on the cultivation of feeling in the *Doctrine of Virtue* indicate that empathy plays an important *instrumental* role in moral motivation. Although Kant ostensibly discusses *sympathy*, the phenomena he describes—recounted below—are now called *empathy*. To recall, for Kant, moral requirements are derived from reason by using the different forms of categorical imperative, and an action is morally praiseworthy if it is motivated by reason and a desire to do one's duty for the sake of the moral law. But in his discussion of the duty to cultivate sympathetic feelings towards others, Kant observes that we have natural tendencies to feel others' emotions, and says that that if these feelings can motivate acting according to moral principles, then we have an obligation to cultivate them.

Empathetic feelings include the capacity to share another's emotions, both pleasurable and displeasurable, and Kant says that, "nature has already implanted in human beings receptivity to these feelings."[25] Although sharing others' feelings is a natural inclination, Kant makes it clear that such feelings do not *in themselves* have moral worth. Humans have both (a) the *will to share in others' feelings,* and (b) the natural capacity to acquire the feelings of others *passively*—the *"receptivity,* given by nature itself, to the feeling of joy and sadness in common with others (*humanitas aesthetica*)."[26] The difference between the two types of empathy is that the first is voluntary and the second is involuntary. Since voluntarily feeling empathy involves the deliberate choice to share another's feelings, Kant says that it is free, whereas involuntary empathy is a natural response "like receptivity to warmth or contagious diseases."[27] It is thus unfree. We can only have a moral obligation to do those things that we can voluntarily control and can do "based on practical reason,"[28] thus, we have only an obligation to the first kind of empathy. The second kind of empathy is "contagious" and thus not morally praiseworthy or recommended.[29]

Kant suggests that we have an obligation or duty to feel empathy with others not as an exercise in learning to respond to others' emotions, but because developing one's capacity to be responsive to the feelings of others is an exercise in developing the will. Intentionally feeling the emotions of others will reveal the relevant features and facts about the other person's situation and thus provides an opportunity to act on the moral law. That is, empathy will make relevant features of other's lives and their situations *salient.*

And yet, Kant does not just recommend empathy with one's friends and family. He says we must not avoid going to "sickrooms or debtors' prisons and so forth in order to avoid sharing painful feelings that we may not be able to resist."[30] Kant recommends going to places where we will encounter people in marginalized groups because he implicitly recognizes that people tend to stereotype those in need of aid, and that we tend to feel empathy with those who are like us. He thus recommends that we broaden the range of people with whom we naturally empathize. By encountering actual people in difficult situations, it is more likely that empathy will enable us to connect with another person and not view them as an "other." Spending time with those who are disenfranchised will help us appreciate those people's emotions and experiences, so that we are motivated to help them and defend them against exploitation. Failing to engage with suffering people will cause us to miss out on opportunities to act on the moral law. While the need to act according to the moral law may be *revealed* by reason, empathy helps us to see and feel others' experiences as valid and important. Thus, empathy motivates us to act on duties that "the representation of duty" may not accomplish alone.[31]

Kant's justification of the moral duty to cultivate empathy is that when one's feelings are appropriately subject to reason's commands, they are *ultimately grounded in reason*. This justification is consistent with Kant's rationalistic approach to morality and moral motivation. Since the empathetic feelings and ensuing motivation are merely *instrumental* to moral action, they are not the *source* of the moral action—reason is. This means that actions motivated by empathy can still be considered morally praiseworthy. While it is "not a duty to share the sufferings (as well as the joys) of others, it is a duty to sympathize actively in their fate," and thus it is an "indirect duty to cultivate the compassionate natural (aesthetic) feelings in us" so that we can use them as a "means to sympathy based on moral principles."[32] In other words, by cultivating empathetic responses towards others, the other's situation is made salient in a way that reveals an opportunity to act according to the moral law. Empathy is thus *instrumental* to acting on the moral law because it provides affective feelings that attune one to opportunities to act according to the moral law. This description of how empathy combines with reason to motivate acting according to the moral law could accurately be called Kantian empathetic moral deliberation.

This analysis shows that—contra Diana Myers' claim—empathy can play a central role in an impartial moral theory that construes moral subjects as rational deliberators who are subject to the constraints of consistency.[33] Kant's recommendation to feel empathy with those who are sick or in debtor's prison requires imagining their desires, but also requires thinking about their situation from their point of view in order to know one's moral duty. This kind of empathetic deliberation involves more than just the discovery of others' desires and preferences. Empathy is able to do this because the observer must bring her own sensibility, imagination, and perspective to the empathetic experience, and this motivates her to appreciate the other person's situation and consider her moral duties. The knowledge yielded through empathy is personal, and in this regard, it can be transformative in the sense that one is more sensitive to opportunities to respect others as the moral law commands. Although Kant does not specifically explain how empathy's tendency to bias can be corrected, such as if one were to empathize only with debtors that are similar to oneself, the universality of the moral law requires treating all such debtors, in principle, the same. Insofar as Kant requires reflective judgment on another's feelings, situation, reasons, and desires, and not just discovery of his preferences, he acknowledges empathy's normative dimension as well as its epistemic one.

5.4   Empathetic bias and empathetic deliberation

We have now seen how ethical theories that integrate empathy into moral deliberation must have some way of surmounting the problem of empathic bias. The ethical theories of Darwall, Meyers, and Kant have the resources for doing this. But if a theory employs empathy and doesn't correct for its tendency to bias or prejudice, then integrating empathy will not be useful because empathic bias will be preserved. Although Meyers suggests that this happens primarily with theories of "impartial reason," the tendency to preserve bias can be seen in Michael Slote's care ethical theory as well as Hobbes's egoist moral theory.

Michael Slote's care ethics is an example of a moral theory that not only does *not* correct for bias and prejudice against those who are different from oneself, but uses this fact of empathic bias to justify our moral obligations to others. Slote's version of care ethics maintains that the more we empathize with a person, the greater our moral obligations are to that person; our moral obligations thus derive from empathy. This position implies that if we are prejudiced against a person or group of people, and do not empathize with them, then our moral obligations to them are minimal. If we empathize more with people of our own race or gender, we have greater obligations those of our own race or gender.

Slote justifies this claim on the basis that there is a "strong natural disposition" to empathize more with one's own race, class, gender or religion. This "disposition" is justified, since we cannot know whether it is innate or socially determined.[34] Since Slote defends a Humean, naturalistic account of morality that seeks to justify moral obligation on the basis of natural feelings, empathy's tendency to bias does not need correction.[35] But a moral theory that seeks to outline correct moral action must at least attempt to correct for biases and prejudices. Although Slote states that "there is no reason why an ethics of empathy has to treat this [empathizing with compatriots more than those from other countries] as morally acceptable," he does not explain why, and does not propose a moral principle, such as respect or reciprocal recognition, that would enable an ethics of empathetic caring to surmount the problem of prejudice.[36] Evidently, neglecting the seriousness of empathy's tendency to bias is a problem not just with theories grounded in "impartial reason" but with other moral theories as well.

Thomas Hobbes's attempt to integrate empathy into moral reasoning is also unable to capitalize on empathy's contribution to moral deliberation because it does not offer a way to surmount empathy's tendency to bias. Hobbesian moral theory endorses a "reciprocity principle" as the recommended moral principle, but this principle in combination with empathetic deliberation produces egoistic moral reasoning that does not challenge one's beliefs about others and maintains the status quo.[37]

On the standard interpretation of Hobbes' moral theory (ethical egoism), it is rational to be moral because moral requirements promote peace and stability for people who abide by them. In other words, according to Hobbes, people should be moral for self-interested reasons. This means that making a moral judgment should be about reflecting on what is in one's long-term self-interest. But in Hobbes' defense of the "reality" of the laws of nature, he does not appeal to self-interest, and says that to discover the content of the Laws of Nature, which are given by reason, people should consider the viewpoints of others (using empathetic perspective-taking) and implement a consistency test. That is, one should imagine oneself in another's perspective and compare one's own actions with another's, and doing so will motivate her to see that the laws of nature are reasonable. After listing the Laws of Nature, Hobbes states:

> And though this may seem too subtile a deduction of the Lawes of Nature, to be taken notice of by all men; whereof the most part are too busie in getting food, and the rest too negligent to understand; yet to leave all men unexcusable, they have been contracted into one easie sum, intelligible, even to the meanest capacity; and that is, *Do not that to another, which thou wouldest not have done to thy*

selfe; which sheweth him that he has no more to do in learning the Lawes of Nature, *but when weighing the actions of other men with his own, they seem too heavy, to put them into the other part of the balance, and his own into their place, that his own passions, and self-love, may adde nothing to the weight, there is none of these Lawes of Nature that will not appear unto him very reasonable.*[38]

Hobbes seems to suggest that in order to see that a Law of Nature is reasonable, one should imagine both perspectives on a situation objectively. But another way to interpret Hobbes is to say that one should examine others' actions as if they were one's own, or examine one's own actions through the perspective of others.[39] That is, one could imaginatively switch one's own situation (and emotions, etc.) with another person's, and then use a principle of reciprocity to judge what one ought to do ("Do not do to others what you would have done to yourself"). When a person does this, the demands of morality—which the self-interested person may not want to follow—will now be seen as legitimate reasons (which one can see from the other point of view) and are not just arbitrary.

When moral deliberation involves using a Hobbesian reciprocity principle in combination with empathetic perspective-taking, the judgment yielded will recommend a course of action that is unique to that situation. For example, suppose that Amy owes Zack money, and is considering not paying him back.[40] For Amy to determine whether or not paying Zack back would accord with the moral law, she imagines herself in Zack's place (via projective empathy). Then she asks herself, "Would I want someone who owed me money to not pay me back?" If she wouldn't want Zack to *not* pay her back, she reaches the conclusion that, were she in his position, she would not want someone to fail to repay her. She would want the money back. Amy thus disapproves of failing to pay someone back on the basis of reciprocity: since she wouldn't want others to not repay her money, she is required to repay others when she has borrowed money from them (other things equal).[41] By evaluating the other's relevant preferences, Amy discovers what actions are justified.

Of course, each reciprocity test is unique in Hobbes's theory. Those individuals that imagine themselves in the other's position and don't care if they are repaid will get a different result—namely, that they are not obligated to repay the loan. Hobbes recommends this imaginative exercise because he thinks it will motivate Amy to repay the money: once she is in Zack's position, she will appreciate the reasons for wanting the loan repaid and will see that doing so is reasonable.[42] But the kind of perspective-taking Hobbes recommends is, in the end, self-interested. When Hobbes says to imagine oneself in the other's perspective, he is recommending *self-focused empathy*, where Amy imagines being in Zack's circumstances, but doesn't think about being Zack himself, and imagines *herself* in *his* situation. This kind of empathy not only does not involve the normative dimension of empathy, it doesn't even really gather information about the other person. It recommends gathering information about *oneself* in another person's situation, and this exercise generates the content of the moral judgment. The empathetic portion of the exercise does not require attempting to learn something new about the other person, challenging beliefs about the others, or challenging the status quo. This kind of empathetic reflection does not qualify as genuine empathetic moral deliberation because it does not involve information-gathering about others. The result is that empathy's tendency to bias in favor of those similar to oneself is preserved, and empathy is allowed to function in a non-ideal way.

5.5   Empathetic deliberation is not just hypothetical deliberation

In order to clarify the idea of empathetic deliberation, it is important to distinguish it from hypothetical deliberation, which is taking up another's perspective in order to gather information about her preferences. *Hypothetical deliberation* involves simulating or imagining the other's psychological state in order to generate provisional choices based on that person's psychology. This type of deliberation is often emphasized by utilitarians who recommend learning others' desires or preferences in order to choose the outcome that would maximize greatest overall utility. I show here that while some utilitarian theorists argue that empathy is required to learn others' preferences and thus choose a moral outcome, because these theorists recommend taking up another's perspective without requiring sharing her emotion, empathy's salience effect and its normative dimension are absent or diminished. Thus, these theories of moral deliberation describe hypothetical deliberation rather than empathetic deliberation.

I argued earlier that *empathetic deliberation* involves feeling another person's emotions and perspective in a way that is sensitive to his situation; certain features of his perspective and responses to his situation become salient to the observer so that she then evaluates them. Since empathetic deliberation includes sharing an emotion, and one must have *prima facie* approval of another's emotion to share it, empathetic deliberation thus has a normative dimension. *Hypothetical deliberation* is primarily epistemic rather than normative, in that it involves simulating or imagining the other's psychological state in order to discover another person's desires and preferences. Alvin Goldman defines hypothetical deliberation as when "the practical reasoning system seems to generate provisional choices from imagined goals and beliefs in the same way that it generates real choices from genuine goals and beliefs during ordinary, 'on-line' deliberation."[43]

The difference between empathetic deliberation and hypothetical deliberation needs clarification because some theorists imply that hypothetical deliberation amounts to moral deliberation. For example, Frederique de Vignemont and Uta Frith suggest that Goldman's account of hypothetical deliberation is equivalent to moral deliberation when they say that hypothetical deliberation recommends that, "you simulate what you would like to happen if you were in the situation of another and act accordingly."[44] But this is a misinterpretation of Goldman's view, for he does not recommend hypothetical deliberation as an account of *moral* deliberation. Hypothetical deliberation is best understood as an information-gathering procedure, and given Goldman's claim that simulation can be employed in a variety of moral theories that make inter-personal comparisons, including those of Kant, Rawls, Sidgwick, and Hare, it is doubtful that Goldman believes that using simulation to make a third-person mental ascription also requires doing what that person wants.[45]

To see the difference between these two kinds of deliberation, let us examine hypothetical deliberation at work in a moral theory. The economist John Harsanyi's version of utilitarianism nicely illustrates how hypothetical deliberation is used to make inter-personal comparisons of utility, or comparisons of overall utility between agents with different beliefs, desires, and preference-orderings in utilitarian moral deliberation. In Harsanyi's utilitarian ethics, aggregate utility should be maximized, and utility is measured from the individual's perspective, rather than an external observer's. (This is because the principle of *consumer sovereignty* governs measuring utility levels in economics; an individual is presumed to be the best judge of his or her own welfare.[46]) In order to determine which outcome among several has the greatest aggregate utility, the expected utility each person might receive from particular outcomes must be discovered, and then summed with other people's utility levels to calculate which outcome has the greatest aggregate utility.

Performing this summation requires *comparing* expected aggregate utility levels among individuals, because the strength of people's preferences varies from one to the other. This procedure is known as making an *interpersonal comparison of utility*, and has long been debated among economists and philosophers.[47] Although some philosophers and economists have argued that we cannot know the amount of satisfaction or utility other individuals derive from certain situations,[48] Harsanyi is more optimistic and suggests that while *full* comparability of mental states is never possible, human beings are able to make some interpersonal comparisons of utility. He says that we can use empathy to generate *extended preferences*, (or imaginary preferences), over *extended alternatives* (or imaginary alternatives), and this imaginative exercise will allow the individual to compare the strength of people's preferences.[49]

> Simple reflection will show that the basic intellectual operation in such interpersonal comparisons is *imaginative empathy*. We imagine ourselves to be in the shoes of another person, and ask ourselves the question, "If I were now really in *his* position, and had *his* taste, *his* education, *his* social background, *his* cultural values, *his* psychological make-up, then what would now be my preferences between various alternatives, and how much satisfaction or dissatisfaction would *I* derive from any given alternative?"[50]

Harsanyi says that empathy is needed to appreciate the strength of a person's preferences in light of the causal factors that led her to have those preferences; this will allow her to determine another's amount of preference-satisfaction.[51] For example, the observer Amy imagines herself in Zack's circumstances, with Zack's psychology, desires, background, etc. She then imagines Zack's responses and his preferences over outcomes, and compares the strength of Zack's preferences for certain outcomes. Although Harsanyi describes this process as using empathy, he actually is describing a process more similar to Alvin Goldman's version of simulation, whereby another's beliefs and desires are hypothetical inputs used to generate hypothetical responses. Once Amy simulates Zack's perspective and learns his preferences, she imaginatively orders outcomes on the basis of his preferences, creating his personal utility function.[52]

As Harsanyi describes it, this process certainly requires perspective-taking and imagination to accurately simulate another's desires and discover his preferred course of action. But it does *not* include feeling another's emotion in a way that makes salient that person's reasons, values, and desires (which are independent of his preferences). Thus, Harsanyi does not view empathy as involving a normative dimension and a salience effect. The observer does not reflect, in a deeper way, on the particular moral values and concerns that might be made salient via empathy. This is hypothetical deliberation, rather, because it implements the epistemic dimension of empathy in order to discover another's preferred outcomes. But since this process does not require sharing the other's emotion or evaluating the situation, then it does not include an evaluative or normative dimension and is distinct from what I have described as empathetic deliberation.

The difference between empathetic deliberation and hypothetical deliberation is that empathetic deliberation involves analysis, evaluation, and reflection in a way that expresses normative judgment, while hypothetical deliberation does not. Empathetic deliberation includes feeling the other's emotions and appreciating his situation in a way that enables one to be more sensitive to the moral values and principles that are at stake, while hypothetical deliberation involves merely simulating the other's point of view and learning his preferences. Given this difference, empathetic deliberation can be moral in a way that hypothetical deliberation is not, since it encourages reflection on the other's desires, feelings, and reasons, and does not simply amount to figuring out and doing what the other person wants or desires.

The normative dimension of empathy that is expressed in empathetic deliberation, but not in hypothetical deliberation, is present in the sharing of an emotion, which makes certain features of the other's situation salient to the observer. In order to share Zack's emotion, Amy must approve of it in the sense that she takes it to be appropriate in the situation. (But this is *not* approval in the sense that Amy judges Zack's emotion to be morally correct; rather, it is *prima facie* approval of Zack's emotion, or initial acceptance and endorsement of it given the context and situation.) Empathetic deliberation, then, is more than just imagining the other person's desires and learning his preferences; it involves, in addition, evaluating or judging the other's emotion and reasons for the purposes of assessing what is important in a situation.

Although Harsanyi's account of moral deliberation implements hypothetical deliberation, other utilitarian accounts of moral deliberation, such as R.M. Hare's preference utilitarianism, do make use of empathetic deliberation. According to Hare, an individual makes a moral judgment when she uses empathetic engagement to discern the other's desires or wants, in concert with an impartiality criterion to decide what ought to be done. While this sounds similar to Harsanyi's view, Hare describes moral deliberation as a process in which a person should "disregard the fact that he plays the particular role in the situation which he does," so that he is "prepared to give weight to A's inclinations and interests as if they were his own. This is what turns selfish prudential reasoning into moral reasoning."[53] According to Hare, moral reasoning involves combining four elements: *impartiality* understood as being able to universalize a judgment, *knowledge of the facts* of the situation (what is likely to happen in case of certain events), *knowledge of the inclinations* or interests of the people concerned, learned through empathy, so that he is moved to accept certain principles rather than others, and the *power of imagination* which uses empathy to reveal the other person's interests. Hare implies that other-focused empathy is needed to, one, gather information regarding the others' feelings and preferences, and two, make salient the feelings and concerns that are most relevant to the parties in the situation.

While Hare's version of utilitarianism implements empathetic perspective-taking to gather information, empathy's salience effect is certainly diminished in it. Empathy's salience effect enables an observer to come to see that others' points of view are as important to them as her own view is to her, but once she appreciates this, the utilitarian argues that the only fair way to resolve a dispute between oneself and another is to be *impartial* with regard to the competing interests. This guarantees that whatever outcome is chosen will seem fair to those who are involved. In Hare's preference utilitarianism, then, although empathy is not used to give independent judgment and personalized information, empathy can motivate adherence to a principle of impartiality: by empathizing with, for example, two points of view, and gathering information about two people's values, concerns, desires, and interests, one is motivated to be impartial between these interests, since she "feels" equally for both parties. While it is likely that one would only be motivated to adhere to a principle of impartiality if she were already committed to it ahead of time, my point is that it is *possible* for empathy to support judgments of impartiality through empathetic deliberation of others' perspectives.

Another illustration of empathetic deliberation in impartial judgment that is utilitarian in character is John Rawls' ideal observer theory described in his "Outline of a Decision Procedure for Ethics." In this early piece, Rawls suggests that a competent judge who is trying to be objective should have a "sympathetic knowledge of human interests" because it will decrease personal bias.[54] Rawls suggests that a judge's impartial evaluation requires appreciating the values and interests of various individuals, and by imaginatively empathizing with the parties involved, the judge can come to appreciate their values and their point of view, and understand the interests that are in conflict. The competent judge does not evaluate the validity of an interest by comparing it to "his own de facto preferences." Rather, he should "bestow upon the appraisal of each the same care which he would give to it if that interest were his own."[55] Rawls suggests that empathy can decrease prejudice when someone sees a person's interests and values from that person's internal point of view, so that he can impartially mediate disputes among people with different claims and interests. In this regard, empathy helps one to sort out the values and disvalues that are at stake in a situation, so that one might see others' reasons as valid concerns. This is why the knowledge gained from empathy yields information about others that is *different in kind* from information gained from learning about others externally or theoretically.

Empathy's salience effect thus is important for discerning what is morally important in Rawls' decision procedure, and is not used merely to reveal interests and preferences that simply need balancing. The observer is to reflect on others' interests as they see them, and, through this experience, learn what is most important in the situation. Similarly, Rawls' Veil of Ignorance—which I discuss in the following chapter in greater detail—requires evaluating the feelings and reasons of those who are least advantaged in society (not just discovering their desires and preferences), and learning how best to respond to those concerns using an impartial decision procedure. In both decision procedures, empathy enables the judge to appreciate each party's interest and determine the factors that are most important. She then uses empathetic deliberation to impartially decide how to resolve the conflict of interest.[56] Since Rawls requires reflective judgment on another's feelings, situation, reasons, and desires, and not just discovery of another's preferences, his decision procedure makes use of empathy's normative dimension as well as its epistemic one. This is the key difference between empathetic deliberation and hypothetical deliberation.

5.6   Conclusion

This chapter demonstrated that empathy is important for learning about others' feelings, preferences, and understanding what is morally relevant in a situation. Empathy's salience effect contributes to its effectiveness in moral deliberation because it reveals the importance of the other person's reasons, values, and emotions. Empathy is important in rational, impartial theories of moral deliberation such as Kant's. And yet, if empathy's tendency to bias is not corrected for, then the empathetic deliberation will remain prejudiced and biased. I have argued that empathy's bias can be corrected when the individual is able to view other people as similar to herself, and is able to see how that person's situation and feelings are worthy of moral concern. I now briefly sketch a normative ideal of empathy that could be encouraged by these ethical theories because it is free of bias and can provide adequate moral guidance. Several philosophers have described this ideal as *mature empathy* and so I use this term to describe ideal or virtuous empathy.

Mature empathy is when perspective-taking empathy, or feeling a congruent emotion with another person, in virtue of imagining the other person's perspective, is informed by moral concerns or motivated by moral commitments to produce sensitive understanding of another person. It involves viewing others as having motivating beliefs, feelings, desires, and concerns, and responding to them as if their desires and concerns are justified. Mature empathy involves being perceptive to the other's complex states of mind and social situation, for the purposes of grasping who she is as a person. The mature empathizer has an independent perspective and thinks about the other person as a whole, trying to grasp what it is like to be that person, and comprehend her view of her own situation. In this way, the mature empathizer seeks to understand and appreciate the other's feelings and at the same time tries to learn something new about human experience. The person with mature, well-developed empathy has a better understanding of the other person that can be used to solve moral dilemmas or interpersonal conflicts.

John Deigh argues that in order for perspective-taking empathy to transform into "mature" empathy, one must regard the "other's purposes as worthwhile" and important.[57] He also believes that mature empathy involves taking up another's perspective and being able to recognize "others as autonomous agents and to participate imaginatively in their separate lives."[58] On his view, therefore, the mature empathizer takes the other to have her own independent ends: she consciously or subconsciously believes that the other person is valuable and is not just a means to her own ends. Respecting the other person as human is thus a prerequisite for mature empathy, because one must be able to see and feel how another person's life and perspective are valuable. Mature empathy enables a deeper comprehension of the other's emotions and attitudes, and is needed to connect with others and understand them. Not everyone will develop the capacity for mature empathy, for it requires both intellectual and emotional openness towards others, even those who are radically different from oneself.

Diana Meyers' view of "empathic thought" expresses a kind of mature empathy. Empathic thought involves imagining the other person and her situation to produce sensitive understanding and recognition of the other, oneself, and the relationship, so as to determine the values and goals that are important and relevant in the situation.[59] The individual then uses her own personal moral ideals and commitments to make a moral judgment. Martha Nussbaum states that empathizing with mature empathy makes it "difficult to turn around and deny humanity to the very people with whose experiences one has been encouraged to have empathy."[60] Of course, if a mature empathizer has some other commitment or overriding concern, she could empathize with mature empathy but still go on to perform some action that hurts that person, (such as saving a larger number of people or carrying out orders that she cannot in practice override). Generally, though, experiencing mature empathy makes it difficult to harm or "deny humanity" to the person with whom one empathizes.

The theories of moral deliberation described here can use the broad notion of mature empathy to express the regulative ideal of empathetic deliberation. People can develop mature empathy in different ways, insofar as empathy can combine with moral principles to produce moral motives, as psychologist Martin Hoffman describes.[61] On his view, empathy can go from being a "prosocial motive" to becoming "embedded in" or "bonded with" moral principles to contribute to "prosocial moral reasoning and judgment."[62] This is why empathetic deliberation is more than mere hypothetical deliberation, in that it involves taking into account the consideration of others and other perspectives in a way that is sensitive to the moral claims and values that are at stake in the situation. And while hypothetical deliberation may be needed for some types of moral deliberation, hypothetical deliberation alone is not moral. With this understanding of empathetic deliberation in hand, I turn now to evaluating the way that contractual ethical theories *model* different kinds of empathetic deliberation.

6
Empathy, Contractual Ethics, and Justification

To this point, I have shown that empathy makes a valuable epistemic contribution to producing sensitive understanding of others, and that it can play an important instrumental role in enabling moral deliberation as it is defined in a variety of ethical theories. I now turn to examining empathy's role in *contractual* ethical theories in particular, specifically, those of John Rawls, John Harsanyi and David Gauthier. Contractual ethical theories are distinct from other normative ethical theories because they are based on the idea of rational agreement through a kind of social contract, and seek the public justification of moral principles. Public justification involves showing that an action, principle, or practice is reasonable because a variety of people have reasons in favor of that action, principle, or practice. My aim here is to show that contract theories *model* different types of perspective-taking empathy and empathetic deliberation. This means contract theories express the reasoning of empathetic deliberation, in that they provide a rationale for agreement to moral or political principles that takes into account a variety of perspectives, or points of view that are thought to be irreconcilable. Insofar as contract theories seek to express the reasoning of a variety of perspectives, they seek what could be called both *public justification* and *interpersonal justification*.

This may be a rather surprising thesis, given that contract theories are usually described as a product of *rational choice* and are *rationally justified*; nevertheless, I show that the reasoning modeled in these three social contracts is empathetic, in that the reasoning involves thinking about, imagining, or reflecting on another person's feelings, thoughts, and responses in a certain situation to discover their reasons for supporting particular principles. Ultimately, my analysis will provide a richer understanding of our deliberative processes, and will provide a unique defense of contract ethical theories: they express empathetic deliberation, and the type of empathetic deliberation expressed tells whether the principles are strongly or weakly publicly justified.

I begin by describing how social contract theories model empathetic deliberation, and then show that they model deliberation by constructing a point of view characterized by three features: idealized circumstances for reasoning about the principles, a commitment to rationality as central to agreeing on principles, and value pluralism. These features enable the three theories to model different kinds of empathetic deliberation: other-focused empathy, self-focused empathy, and dual-perspective empathy. I argue that contract theories are understood as seeking public justi-fication, and public justification should be interpreted as a kind of inter-personal justification. Using this interpretation, I show that the kind of empathetic deliberation modeled corresponds to the nature of the interpersonal justification achieved and that it can be strong or weak. I conclude that the empathetic deliberation modeled in Harsanyi's and Gauthier's theories do not achieve strong public justification because they model weaker types of empathetic deliberation.

6.1 Contract theories and public justification

In contemporary moral and political philosophy, there has been a revival in using the idea of the social contract as a way to justify moral or political principles. Justification in moral and political philosophy expresses, roughly, the idea that a moral or political principle is valid if it applies to everyone, or if it is reasonable from each person's point of view. The best known of these theories is John Rawls' theory of justice, but there are several other "contract" theories, including David Gauthier's contractarianism, T.M. Scanlon's contractualism, and John Harsanyi's equiprobability theory of contractual morality.[1] The contractual approach to justification is unique in that it tries to show that certain moral or political principles are justified on the basis that they could be agreed to by the rational (or reasonable) agents governed by them. Essentially, the idea of agreement models what reasons people have to accept or endorse certain principles, policies, etc. That is, the reasons articulated in particular theories capture or model the deliberations of idealized rational agents deliberating in appropriate circumstances. Since the method presumes to capture the reasoning of rational citizens and thus secure rational agreement to principles, it has gained popularity in the last decade as a way of justifying things like capitalism, rights, democracy, and even punishment.[2]

The contractual approach to moral and political philosophy also has its critics. Many philosophers have argued that since contract theories seek hypothetical agreement to moral or political principles, they cannot generate actual obligations to them.[3] But a number of leading contract theorists have argued that hypothetical agreement does not even aspire to show that the legitimacy of our actual political states and institutions follows from hypothetical agreement, and nor do they attempt to derive obligations from our hypothetical consent to those institutions.[4] Rather, hypothetical contractual reasoning has other purposes: hypothetical consent is, as Jerry Gaus says, a "heuristic device for demonstrating that the proposed arrangement is publicly justified: all rational agents would accept it."[5] And Jean Hampton argued that contract theories help us to "work out conceptual answers to moral problems."[6] Samuel Freeman concurs in saying that "the justificatory force of social contract views depends only in part on the idea of agreement; even more essential is the conception of the person and the conception of practical reason that are built into particular views."[7] On these views, the aim of a contract theory is not consent, but justification of the proposed principles or states; the aim is to show that all rational agents have reason to accept certain moral or political principles.

Although Hampton and Freeman defend the contractual approach to moral justification because it is useful for thinking about which moral or political principles are justified, their comments suggest that social contracts merely showcase a particular conception of reason and account of human nature, and then describe the kinds of principles that would be justifiable given these assumptions. But the idea of agreement is central to contract theories because it is reached only when parties can understand and appreciate each other's reasons for wanting certain principles to guide their social interactions. My claim is that contract theories seek to achieve justification rather than articulate assumptions and the principles that follow from them. Justification is achieved when the agreement reached in hypothetical social contracts models *empathetic deliberation*; this deliberation yields reasons for agreement, and these reasons serve as the basis for justification. The *kind* of justification achieved depends on the theory: public justification is the goal in theories that seek to justify moral or political principles that guide citizens, and moral justification is the goal in theories that seek to justify moral principles in interpersonal relationships, such as in Scanlon's contract theory. Since I am interested in how contract theories seek to justify principles to everyone in a society, I focus on the idea of public justification, which is the term most used to refer to the idea of justifying principles in a public way for a group of citizens. For a principle to be publicly justified, it must take into account various perspectives, and show that particular principles would be agreed to from a variety of points of view.

6.2 The elements of social contract theory

The contemporary uses of social contract theory are quite different from the social contracts originally proposed by Hobbes, Locke, and Rousseau. While these theorists claimed that the legitimacy of government is established by the consent of the people, contemporary thinkers such as Rawls, Harsanyi and Gauthier focus not on consent, but on the idea of agreement to moral or political principles based on reasons. Since contemporary social contract theories are hypothetical and thus cannot be binding in the same way that a real contract is, they are thought experiments that express our best reasons for agreeing to principles that commit us to certain moral prescriptions. In recent years, some theorists have argued that the social contract is less about the idea of agreement between individuals regarding the principles that ought to guide society, and more about offering a procedure for *deliberating about* the appropriate moral and political principles in a just society. This is Rawls' view of the social contract method, where the idea is to address the question of justification by working through the problem of deliberation.[8] Political principles are justified by providing a theoretical account of the deliberations that would justify such principles; that is public justification.[9]

And yet, what this deliberation is like is open to interpretation. Many theorists have suggested that the theory of rationality ultimately guides the deliberations of the parties, and game theoretic reasoning provides the solution to each choice situation. But the deliberations of the idealized parties, at least in the justificatory phase of the contract agreement, are guided by empathetic deliberation. Since these parties are interested in the perspectives of others, the reasoning exhibited models perspective-taking empathy. To see this, I begin by showing how the elements of a social contract theory work together in a way that plausibly shows that the reasoning exhibited by the rational agents is open to interpretation.

Although there are a variety of contract theories, I focus on the political contract theories of Rawls, Gauthier, and Harsanyi. David Gauthier's version of contractarianism is a non-tuistic theory (based on preferences that do not necessarily include the well-being of others), John Harsanyi's equiprobability model of moral value judgments is a utilitarian theory, and John Rawls' theory of justice as fairness is a Kantian theory. These theories each provide a hypothetical deliberative model for the public justification of principles. According to this interpretation, the point of a hypothetical contract theory is to justify a moral or political principle to individuals, by showing that it would be chosen by every type of person it would govern. The aim is to reflect on social relations and political institutions from a variety of points of view, in order reveal shared understandings and common beliefs, as well as to identify injustice and unfair social practices. Here I examine the fundamentals of a social contract and show how they set the stage for deliberation.

Rawls' and Gauthier's contract theories are well-known among philosophers, but Harsanyi's is less familiar. In fact, his equiprobability model of social choice is not a social contract *per se*, but is a decision procedure for choosing principles to be used in social choice theory. But the equiprobability model can be considered a kind of hypothetical contract because, like Rawls' theory of justice and Gauthier's contractarianism, it describes a situation in which an ideal deliberator chooses principles to be implemented by social institutions, articulates that deliberator's reasoning in favor of the principles, explains why everyone would agree to them, and justifies the choice of principles with rational choice.[10]

While Gauthier, Harsanyi, and Rawls have similar approaches to deriving and justifying principles of justice and morality, it is well known that these theories are proposed to answer different kinds of questions, and thus, they differ substantially. For example, the question Gauthier is most interested in is, "Can moral constraints be justified on the basis of self-interest, or the idea that everyone has a self-interested reason to be moral?" Rawls asks, "If citizens deliberated behind a veil of ignorance, what principles would they agree are appropriate for guiding social institutions?" And Harsanyi asks, "What principles should be used to decide social welfare, and how can we determine social welfare impartially?" Gauthier uses a bargaining situation to determine the content of his principles, while Rawls uses representative persons in equal positions to *choose* (not bargain about) the content of the principles. Harsanyi proposes the conditions of risk and uncertainty as the appropriate ones for deliberating about social welfare. What unites these theories is the goal of showing that everyone has reason to accept certain principles, and that people from different perspectives can accept them for the practical purpose of social interaction.

To examine the nature of the deliberation in these theories, we must first understand the features of a social contract that make it possible for idealized agents to deliberate on proposals or principles. There are three main features of contract theories, and these features make evaluating the deliberations of the rational agent in these circumstances possible in that they reveal the considerations used to justify the choice of principles:

(1) They each use idealized circumstances and idealized rational agents to reason about principles.
(2) They each use a conception of rationality to justify the choice of particular moral principles or principles of justice.
(3) They each suppose that individuals have different values but are interested in their own welfare.

These features function together to produce deliberations that justify the choice of principles. The circumstances and agents represent a "choice situation" to represent the situation and faculties of people who choose moral or political principles. Many, but not all, contract theories use an *idealized* choice situation to show how rational agents behind a veil of ignorance would choose various principles. Others use a state of nature to illustrate that the principles would be agreed to.[11]

The three theories I discuss use an *idealized* choice situation to articulate the reasoning needed to publicly justify the principles. Gauthier, Harsanyi, and Rawls idealize the persons and circumstances in their "original positions" in three ways:

(a) They use a *veil of ignorance* that prohibits knowledge of one's identity, values, and position in society, so that one is not motivated by strict self-interest.
(b) They use an *informational set* (general or specific, depending on the theory) that describes the preferences, desires, values, and beliefs of the people to be governed by the choice. This is supposed to reflect what we know about actual people who would be governed by the contract.
(c) They situate the contracting parties *equally*. That is, each deliberator supposes that he is equal to his fellows. This supposition has different implications depending on the theory.[12]

Presumably, these features allow contract theories to produce justified principles because they model what we take to be the appropriate perspective for reasoning about moral or political principles.

Second, social contract theories seek rational agreement to the proposed principles, and so each theory must adopt a specific *conception of rationality* to guide a deliberator's choice of moral and political principles. Gauthier endorses "maximizing rationality," the theory according to which it is rational to maximize the satisfaction of one's preferences. The content of one's preferences is not subject to rational evaluation, and reason is neutral with regard to the kinds of preferences one might seek to satisfy. This ultimately explains the choice of contractarian principles in this theory. Harsanyi, on the other hand, endorses a theory of Bayesian rationality, the principles of which describe rational choice under conditions of uncertainty. Using this type of reasoning, people choose outcomes on the basis of certain probabilities, and he says that it supports the choice of a utilitarian principle. Rawls claims that both rationality and "reasonableness" guide the choice of principles of justice.[13] What "reasonable" means is highly debated, but it includes the desire to live according to mutually acceptable principles, so that reasonableness requires taking into account what everyone else would agree to. Having a theory of reason is presumably of central importance in a contract theory because it guides the mutual choice of principles. My goal is to show that while a theory of reason is crucial to bargaining, the degree to which the deliberations are *empathetic* shows how *strongly* the principles are publicly justified.

Third, these contract theories are committed to *value pluralism*, the idea that people hold different desires, interests, and values, and have different conceptions of the good life. Rawls, Harsanyi, and Gauthier suppose that individuals have values and commitments that are not always compatible with the values and commitments of others. This is a crucial tenet of liberalism, which acknowledges the diversity of human interests and the primacy of liberty in fulfilling those interests. But how do people with diverse individual interests come to agree on a common set of rules or principles? Must the governing conception of public reason that guides public justification require shared reasons, or can each citizen have her own reasons to support the justification? Jerry Gaus argues that genuine contract political theories must allow the appeal to different reasons; moreover, "political institutions are justified by appealing to the agent-relative values of each member of the public."[14]

Though I do not defend this position here, the interpretation of contractual reasoning I offer explains how agreement can be reached when citizens deploy agent-relative reasons for agreement. As I explain in section 6.6, the justification of political principles requires empathetic deliberation with those who have different values; this can reveal their reasons for agreement to particular political principles. Public justification is achieved by taking into account the reasoning of a variety of persons, and empathetic deliberation allows a deliberator to gain access to the reasons others use to justify their choice of principles. Empathy enables epistemic access to others' reasons so that the deliberator can deploy these reasons for the purposes of justification, as opposed to simply describing them or stating that they are there. Empathetic deliberation allows one to know and use others' agent-relative reasons. Moral and political theories that seek public justification, then, will rely on empathetic deliberation to consider more points of view, discover others' reasons for preferring certain alternatives into account, and deploy these reasons in the justification of particular moral and political principles.

6.3   The nature of contractual deliberation

It should be evident from what I have said thus far that the nature of contractual deliberation and reasoning is open to interpretation. In order to investigate it further, we must first distinguish between various points of view that are at work in a contract theory. That is, we must first understand the *connection between the hypothetical nature of the contracts and the actual people that they are supposed to speak to—you and me*. The best way to see this is to distinguish the different perspectives of those involved in contractual deliberation. In his essay, "Kantian Constructivism in Moral Theory," Rawls distinguishes three points of view from which to evaluate a social contract: that of the idealized parties in the theory, that of citizens in a well-ordered society, and that of "ourselves—you and me."[15] This clarification allows us to distinguish three points of view from which different evaluations take place: one, those of the idealized agents who are charged with assessing the basic structure of society by considering, two, how things look to the citizens in a well-ordered society, who are the persons affected by it. And three, *we* (the readers) will examine the proposed social contract and decide whether we identify with the representation of persons, reasons, and ideals that are proposed.[16]

To understand the relationship between these three points of view, let us first consider the reasoning of the idealized agents, and how they take into account what is relevant to various people in society. The veil of ignorance requires that the ideal agent must, at least to some degree, choose *as if* she could be any member of society. Of course, even this way of describing the ideal deliberation is open to interpretation. T.M. Scanlon shows that Rawls' social contract has two interpretations. On the one hand, the idea of rational choice under a veil of ignorance suggests that a single individual "accepts a principle because it is one he could not reasonably reject whatever position he turns out to occupy;" on the other hand, rational choice under a veil of ignorance describes a choice that "is supposed to be acceptable to a person in any social position because it would be the rational choice for a single self-interested person behind the veil of ignorance."[17] Scanlon argues that the plausibility of Rawls' theory of justice is enhanced when it is interpreted as an instance of the first form of contractual argument, for it suggests that a principle is justified on the basis that it is reasonable, no matter who she turns out to be in society, and that different reasons and perspectives have been taken into account. Let us take this approach to interpreting the ideal agent's reasoning.

Since the ideal agent is charged with determining whether different individuals would endorse certain principles, she must consider how a principle affects people in different social positions. Essentially, her deliberations must include the relevant considerations of each person, as seen from the agent's own perspective. In Rawls' theory, for example, when principles refer to persons, (such as, for example, whether a person will gain from inequality), "the reference is to representative persons holding the various social positions."[18] Thus, the parties must take up "the position of certain representative individuals" and consider "how the social system looks to them."[19] This is required in other theories as well, and in each choice situation, the rational agent has information (more in Harsanyi's theory, less in Rawls') about the preferences, desires, values, and beliefs of the people to be governed by the choice. It is plausible that the idealized agents could reconstruct a citizen's perspective to make inferences about her range of responses to proposals and whether she will accept or reject certain principles. If this is the case, then the ideal agent will deliberate in a way that models *our* perspective-taking capacities.

What does it mean to say that the thought experiment of rationally choosing behind a veil of ignorance allows the rational agent to deliberate *as if* she were each person (or in each person's perspective) who is impacted by the principle? Gaus and D'Agostino have argued that the best way to understand the relationship between the hypothetical deliberations of idealized agents and the actual agents who the deliberations are supposed to speak to, is to say that the whole hypothetical situation and deliberations *model* the actual justifications that we accept in real life. Their idea is that "the parties' deliberations and the conditions under which they deliberate model our actual convictions about justice and justification."[20] All this means is that social contract theories capture and express how we think about justification, in the sense that they articulate our ideas about how principles must be rationally acceptable to others, which is the essence of justification. My view is that in addition to modeling our actual convictions about justice, the *parties' deliberations* also model *our empathy*, specifically, perspective-taking empathy for the purposes of thinking about others' reasons. The deliberations of the idealized agents are generated *as if* she had simulated the perspectives of those impacted by the principles, in the way that we would do if we were empathizing with others. In this way, her deliberations model our empathic deliberations.

There are three ways to interpret the idea that a contract theory models empathetic deliberation. The strongest thesis regarding contractual deliberation is that the deliberations of an idealized agent *just are* empathetic deliberations. A second, slightly weaker thesis is that empathetic deliberation also happens during an idealized agent's deliberation, but that a substantial portion of the reasoning is *not* empathetic deliberation. A third possibility is to say that part of what social contract theories allow, but don't always include, is empathetic deliberation; hence, agents ought to include empathetic deliberation with the rest of their deliberations as they are engaged in public justification.

Although it initially seems that it would be a mistake to endorse the first thesis and say that contractual deliberation just *is* empathetic deliberation, since much of the deliberation on the part of the idealized agents is non-empathetic, the *justificatory phase* of the reasoning (which includes showing that a set of principles is *publicly justified*) does reflect empathetic deliberation. Although the idealized agents themselves don't take up other points of view, since they are hypothetical deliberators, their deliberations are presented *as if* they had done so. Thus, the way the different points of view are *represented* in a contract theory will correspond with the idealized agent's (more or less) empathetic deliberation. Moreover, empathetic deliberation is appropriate in the justificatory phase of deliberation, and those of us who use social contract methods to consider principles that are publicly justifiable, should engage in empathetic deliberation, as doing so provides a method of grasping the importance and relevance of others' reasons.

Similar theses have been advanced by Jerry Gaus and Susan Moller Okin. Gaus argues that contractual justification requires decentering, where decentering involves moving away from your own perspective in order to take up another person's point of view.[21] Since contract theories seek to justify principles on the basis that they are acceptable to each person, as seen from a personal point of view and not some external point of view, they thus aspire to public justification.[22] Okin's interpretation of Rawls' social contract theory is that the deliberation in the Original Position should be understood as one in which the parties "think from the position of everybody, in the sense of *each in turn*."[23] In addition, she says that the capacity that is essential for being able to think as if in Rawls' original position is the capacity to empathize.[24] My contribution is to show that *other* contract theories that use idealized deliberative situations model empathetic deliberation as well.

While Gaus and Okin indicate that the perspectives of others matter to contractual deliberation, there are *different* ways of conceiving of the perspectives of others, and this can be better understood by examining the nature of empathetic deliberation. Since there are different ways of imagining oneself in the perspective of others, these differences are expressed in contractual reasoning and so different kinds of empathetic deliberation are modeled in different contract theories. The deliberation is *empathetic* insofar as it involves thinking about, imagining, or reflecting on another person's feelings, reasons, and responses in a certain situation, in order to discover her reasons supporting different contracts or principles. Perspective-taking empathy can be used as a rough guide to determining whether a justification could be acceptable, because it involves imagining another's response to a certain principle. Contract theories model empathetic deliberation for the purpose of providing grounds of agreement for points of view that are thought to be irreconcilable.

There are two important implications of this thesis. First, it shows that when hypothetical contracts are used as a heuristic device, they model our actual *psychological* capacities. In this way, contract theories satisfy the meta-ethical constraint of Minimal Psychological Realism.[25] The Principle of Minimal Psychological Realism requires that a moral theory (even if it is a moral ideal), prescribe a decision procedure that is possible for creatures like us. While satisfying this principle does not establish the superiority of contract theories, satisfying it does provide support for the intuitive plausibility of the contractual approach. Even though the deliberations of the rational agents in an idealized situation are abstract, the perspective from which they deliberate and the stipulations of their situation are a model of our way of making empathetic choices. Hypothetical contracts are not, then, as impotent as philosophers have often argued.

Second, viewing hypothetical deliberation as empathetic deliberation will provide a richer understanding of the idea of public justification; contractual justification enables public justification *because* contract theories must consider the points of views of others. To justify a principle to others, the observer must be able to show that it speaks to the concerns of others, and in order to do this, his deliberations must be in some way empathetic. To see how empathetic the deliberation is, the impartial observer's way of reflecting on—or empathizing with—the "others" whose points of view under consideration must be examined. I now examine different *types* of empathetic deliberation, and show that they achieve different degrees of public justification.

6.4   Kinds of empathetic deliberation modeled in social contracts

Since the aim of a political social contract theory is to show that a principle is publicly justified because it is or would be accepted by everyone in society, that theory must have a way of accessing other points of view and finding reasons that support the choice of principles. This is why empathetic deliberation is relevant: it is the method whereby these reasons are accessed, discovered, and brought forward for analysis. To examine the kinds of empathetic deliberation modeled in contract theories, I will use a distinction I have drawn in earlier chapters between other-focused empathy, self-focused empathy, and dual-perspective (combination) empathy to show that the idealized deliberations of three contract theories model different kinds of perspective-taking, for the purposes of accessing the reasons used to justify the choice of principles. My account of empathetic deliberation is relevant to two dimensions of public justification: first, it informs the idealized deliberator's perspective on others' values, interests, preferences, reasons or intentions (explained in section 6.5), and second, it illuminates the degree of public justification achieved in the theory (the topic of section 6.6).

Why do social contract theories model empathetic deliberation rather than mere imaginative simulation of others' perspectives? While simulating and perspective-taking are *necessary* conditions for role-taking and empathetic perspective-taking, they are not *sufficient*, unless they include affectively feeling others' evaluations. The affective part of empathy (the emotion part) is what allows one to really understand another's values, and come to the correct conclusions about what is important to them. Perspective-taking empathy involves imaginatively simulating another person's perspective, responses, and emotions, and seeing things from her point of view, as a way of making her evaluations intelligible. It also involves being sensitive to a person's values in a way that mere belief cannot accomplish. To discover what is important to a person, belief-based theorizing is insufficient—one must attempt to feel what the other person does to genuinely understand what is important to them. "Feeling into" another person's perspective involves simulating the other's evaluations in both an affective and cognitive way, and this enables the observer to grasp the force of the emotion as it is experienced by the other. Thus, the *kind* of information gained through empathy will be more comprehensive and nuanced than that gained from mere simulation.

To see this, let me return to the example of co-workers Anna and Michael discussed in Chapter 3. Michael talks graphically about sex around Anna, comments on her appearance using sexual language, publicly discusses the body parts and appearance of other women in the workplace, and brags about his own sexual prowess. One day, Anna has had enough—she gets angry and yells at Michael. She tells him that she is sick and tired of his sexist comments. She explains why his comments have enraged her, so that Michael can see that from her perspective, his comments are offensive. Now if Michael merely imaginatively simulates Anna's perspective, he may not understand and appreciate Anna's humiliation and frustration. But if, as he listens to her, he feels her anger and frustration, and is able to view his actions from her perspective, then Michael will understand and appreciate Anna's emotions and see why she responded as she did. Even if Michael feels Anna's emotion to only a small degree, he will have different information than if he had merely simulated her perspective: the affective dimension of empathy *makes salient* the information that brings Michael to appreciate and feel Anna's anger. In the same way, the ideal agents in contractual theories must learn what is relevant and important to another person, and this requires one of three types of empathy: other-focused empathy, self-focused empathy, and combination mode.

6.4.1   Rawls' theory of justice

In Rawls' theory, the rational agent behind a veil of ignorance must make a *reasonable* choice of principles of justice. "Reasonableness" requires that the ideal agent in the Original Position take into account the fact that people with different viewpoints, interests, and concerns in life must be willing to accept his choice of principles. Thus, her deliberations must take into account people's similarities, such as their interest in preserving their rights and securing a minimum level of well-being, and their differences, such as their conceptions of the good.

The rational agent behind the veil of ignorance deliberates as if she has taken up each person's perspective and examined her reasons and values. In this way, her deliberations model our—or, as Rawls might say, "yours and my"—*dual-perspective empathy*. In dual-perspective empathetic deliberation, Amy simulates or imagines Zack's beliefs and psychology, sees the differences between those and her own, acquires an emotion that is congruent to Zack's, and works back and forth between her perspective and Zack's; this deliberation recognizes two (or more) perspectives. Because the deliberator must examine what would be reasonable to everyone, her empathetic deliberation must take up others' perspectives to learn about their values, respond to their emotions, and compare them with other perspectives. Empathizing in this way acknowledges the similarities and differences between the individuals in society, and uses what is learned to choose and thus justify the principles chosen from that perspective.

It is important to distinguish this interpretation of the Original Position from one that Rawls rejects: one in which the ideal deliberator takes up the "general point of view," imagines each person's perspective, and uses sympathy to constitute "a common ground for bringing our moral opinions into agreement."[26] This is how Hume describes the appropriate perspective from which make a moral choice, and Rawls aims to distinguish his view from a kind of sentimentalist utilitarianism. (As I explained earlier, we now use the word empathy to describe the phenomena that Hume called sympathy so we should read the above as empathy rather than sympathy). Rawls implies that this interpretation suggests that the deliberator identifies with each person, and responds by approving of some outcome that expresses *the balance of satisfactions* to which he responds in each individual. Rawls rejects this interpretation of the deliberative situation insofar as it expresses the idea that the ideal agent seeks to satisfy desires rather than adjudicate conflicts and assess *reasons* for accepting one set of principles over another. (As I shall show momentarily, this interpretation correctly describes the deliberation in Harsanyi's theory.)

Interpreting the reasoning in Rawls' theory using the idea of empathetic deliberation shows that the ideal agent adjudicates conflicts using dual-perspective empathy. The dual-perspective empathizer can come to appreciate the values and reasons expressed by others, and recognize at the same time that some reasons and values may not be shared by everyone. As I explained in Chapter 3, empathy performs the epistemic function of revealing *reasons* that people in different perspectives have for advancing certain principles, and a dual-perspective empathizer will access reasons empathetically and then adjudicate them by using Rawls' standard of "reasonableness." The idea of reasonableness is captured in the constraints of the Original Position—the motivation of the parties as disinterested, the relationship of the parties as equal, the veil of ignorance, and the sense of justice—and these provide the norms to deliberate about which reasons are justificatory reasons. The other stipulations of the Original Position—the social primary goods, the strains of commitment, the maxi-min principle, the stability requirement, and self-respect—provide the items needed to rank and process claims, and adjudicate conflicts between individuals.

Even though the veil of ignorance effectively eliminates the parties' knowledge of the particular facts about themselves, they do know "general facts about human society," have access to any facts that affect the choice of the principles of justice, and understand political affairs, the principles of economic theory, the nature of social organization, and the laws of human psychology. The ideal agent can use this information thus to learn about the reasons of those who are in her society, since there are no limitations on general information.[27] The deliberating individual could thus be said to empathize insofar as she uses this general knowledge to *reconstruct* the perspective of a representative person. This reconstruction is required in order for her to evaluate a proposal from the perspective of representative individuals, to determine how a proposal affects a person's "life prospects *as viewed from their social station*."[28] When she reconstructs this perspective, she can determine whether the proposal would be justifiable or acceptable to the person, or representative person, impacted by it. This explains how the parties, situated behind a veil of ignorance, being rational and possessing a sense of justice and a desire to find a reasonable basis for agreement on a conception of justice, can evaluate how the proposals impact people in various representative positions. The veil of ignorance is not just a criterion of impartiality that challenges us to "put aside, as best we can, the biases that come from our knowing what principles would suit us personally,"[29] but is a requirement that also requires *appreciating* other people's values and interests.

How genuinely empathetic are the parties? Some have argued that the Original Position does not take into account a variety of perspectives, and the ideal agent is closed to listening to perspectives that would lead to a reevaluation of what is fair or just.[30] But on the interpretation I have offered here, to say that the Original Position reasoning models dual-perspective empathetic deliberation means that it models reasoning that involves discovering reasons that support justice as fairness.

Since this model represents persons as free and equal, and identifies the reasons of justice as those that would be the result of empathetic deliberation, there is no reason to think that the perspective Rawls describes is "monological" or closed to listening to diverse perspectives.[31] If Rawls' theory is understood as a normative description of the reasons that constitute justice as fairness (an issue I consider in section 6.6), then we could conclude, as Christopher McMahon does, that the Original Position can be interpreted as explicating the reasons of fairness that "mutual perspective-taking treats as the focus of moral deliberation."[32] Interpreting the reasoning of the parties in the Original Position as a model of dual-perspective empathetic deliberation captures the sense in which mutual perspective-taking is central to justifying principles of justice.

6.4.2 Gauthier's contractarian ethics

In his contractualist theory presented in *Morals by Agreement*, Gauthier seeks to show that a particular set of principles (the content of which is irrelevant here) is justified or acceptable to everyone in society. In his representation of a deliberative situation, an ideal deliberator's choice of principles shows that certain principles of justice are justified from the individual perspectives of each person. To do this, he proposes the justificatory device of the Archimedean Point, which is roughly equivalent to Rawls' Original Position—it is the perspective appropriate for deliberating about what principles are justified to everyone in society. This perspective is occupied by an ideally rational agent who chooses behind a veil of ignorance "as if he were each of the persons" affected by his choice.[33] A veil of ignorance serves two purposes for Gauthier: first, it guarantees that no one in the proposed society is arbitrarily disadvantaged or advantaged. The choice of principles must not be biased against certain racial, religious, or political groups. And second, the veil simultaneously imposes a requirement of impartiality, prohibiting knowledge of one's identity, values, and position in society in order to allow an impartial consideration of the principles.

Since the ideal agent chooses on behalf of others, her deliberations require some sort of perspective-taking in order to determine what each person would hypothetically choose. The ideal agent in the Archimedean Point conceives of each person as rational, because this conception of persons captures the "utility-maximizing intent of rational actors."[34] The ideal agent thus characterizes each person's preferences, desires, and reasons in a general way, as wanting to maximize individual utility, and this description is true for every individual. Granted, this characterization does not have a very specific content, but that is the aim—to use a general conception of people and their preferences that characterizes "the intent that is common to all."[35] The result is that Gauthier interprets public justification as the project of choosing principles based on reasons that are *common* to everyone rather than identifying different reasons that individuals may have for supporting the principles.[36]

In the Archimedean Point, the ideal agent's deliberations model self-focused empathy because she characterizes each person's psychological phenomena in the same way: by projecting her own psychology onto each individual in society. To recall, in self-focused empathy, Amy acquires Zack's emotion because she simulates being in Zack's circumstances, and responds by feeling an emotion similar to his. This transmission of emotion occurs even though the content of her simulation reflects her own psychology. Since the idealized agent in the Archimedean Point projects her own ideas about others onto them—in this case, that each person wants to maximize his or her interests—she does not "get into" each person's internal perspective and simulate their ideas, reasons, or emotions in order to discover more. In this deliberative setting, the agent seeks to publicly justify principles of constraint by showing that each person has reasons (of self-interest) that support the principles. But this requires her to suppose that each person wants to maximize her own utility. The ideal agent is thus only able to show that the principles chosen in the bargaining situation are justified if people do in fact operate on the basis of self-interest.

The difficulty with this method of deliberation is that it projects a particular conception of persons onto others and uses that to deliberate about what is justifiable from that perspective. The ideal agent supposes that everyone is a rational maximizer, and that each individual in society sees others *as instruments* to their own ends; as a result the only "reasons" they can share are the reasons of prudential self-preservation or self-interest. Of course, if these are the reasons that are given in support of the principles, then the principles are only justified insofar as people "identify with" the idea of themselves as a rational actor; individuals must "identify with" this conception of themselves (that has been given to them in the idealized choice setting), in order for public justification to be achieved. As I explain later, this approach to justification gets the idea of public justification backwards: instead of showing that the contractarian principles are reasonable or rational to people from their own perspectives, they are only justified insofar as people "identify" with the view of themselves as rational actors with the intent to maximize their own utility.

6.4.3   Harsanyi's equiprobability model

John Harsanyi's idealized choice situation differs from Rawls' Original Position and Gauthier's Archimedean Point in several ways. Harsanyi presents his procedure for decision-making on social outcomes as the equiprobability model, which is also a model for deriving social welfare functions via individual decision theory.[37] It involves evaluating people's preferences in an impartial way. Harsanyi's equiprobability model contains an idealized agent deliberating in conditions of risk and uncertainty, so that she does not know who she is, and cannot choose an outcome on the basis of self-interest. In these circumstances, the idealized agent assigns equal chances to being any person in society, so that she has the "same probability of occupying any possible social position."[38] That is, for each person n, she assigns the probability $1/n$ for each position that is assigned a utility level U_1, U_2, U_3, etc.[39] This has the effect of giving each person's utility equal treatment, so that the deliberating agent calculates the *average* utility that could be expected for each outcome.[40] Because the equiprobability model supposes that people should be treated "equally," Harsanyi argues that it is an appropriate model of making moral value judgments and for constructing a social welfare function, since both require treating each person's preferences equally.

Since Harsanyi believes that the equiprobability model can generate judgments that would be identical from one person to the next, it resembles an original-position-style decision procedure that can produce agreement on judgments of desirable social states. (He also claims to have invented the idea of the veil of ignorance before Rawls.) This is why it has been treated as an alternative contractual theory by a number of philosophers. The contractual deliberation in the equiprobability model works in the following way. The idealized deliberating agent assigns equal probabilities to being each person, and then imagines the desires and preferences of each individual in society. Since each person could evaluate expected utility in the same way, and could thus represent social welfare functions identically, each person's impartial assessments of social welfare and orderings of social states could converge with every other's so that "with enough knowledge of other individuals, people could mentally adopt the preferences of others, and the U_i terms in each individual's evaluation of social welfare would converge."[41] Each deliberator then uses "generalized sympathy" (i.e. empathy) to assess preferences and achieve the greatest balance of overall satisfaction in a uniform way. Each person who deliberates using the equiprobability model will get the same results because they will judge preferences in the same way.

Since the equiprobability theory requires imagining each person's preferences, feeling their emotions and being completely engaged in others' preferences, it models *other-focused empathy*. (In other-focused empathy, Amy focuses on Zack's feelings, preferences, desires, or values, and tries to feel what Zack does in his particular circumstances.) In Harsanyi's model, the deliberator considers each person's perspective in order to gather information on each person's preference-orderings. To do this, she takes up a general point of view, imagines each person's preferences and perspective, and then finds a common ground for bringing their moral opinions into agreement. But instead of trying to adjudicate conflicts between parties, the idealized agent tries to treat everyone equally by treating each person's *preferences* equally; since he has an equal chance of being each person, and each person's preferences are equal to every other's, he must figure out which outcome is fair in that it takes into account each person's desires and preferences equally. The equiprobability model thus requires the deliberative agent to be a kind of ideal empathizer, one who feels and appreciates each person's preferences perfectly, and then uses utilitarian principles to determine which outcome would be fair to all.

A worry about Harsanyi's approach is that, rather than conceiving of agreement as a social practice, he emphasizes its role in achieving a uniformity of judgment. Although the deliberations in the equiprobability theory model empathetic thinking, the focus of analysis is an agent's *preferences* rather than her *reasons* for supporting the principles. The result is that the focus is not on public justification to others, for Harsanyi cannot show that utilitarian principles are genuinely publicly justified to others. Although empathetic thinking is modeled in Harsanyi's theory, the Bayesian rationality is what drives the choice, for it recommends opting for principles that have the best prospects under risk, which is average utilitarianism. The result is that the ideal observer will seek to impartially satisfy collective interests rather than use empathy to identify the *reasons* that people have for supporting various principles.

To summarize, let me reiterate that I have not been arguing that the rational agents in these contract theories *actually* empathize with the agents about whom they are deliberating; rather, the idealized situation is set up so that they must consider, at least in a prudential way, what it would be like to be people in different perspectives, and must evaluate principles or proposals from the perspective of each of the individuals who are impacted by them in society. At least in the justificatory phase of the process, they deliberate *as if* they are empathizing with others. Because the veil of ignorance prohibits personal information, but allows general information about individuals and society (again, in a way that varies from one theory to another), it is plausible that the rational agents can reconstruct general perspectives and consider the principles from a variety of perspectives as if they are empathizing. While the three contract theories I have discussed here model empathetic deliberation and seek to justify principles to us, I now turn to explaining why the deliberations modeled in Harsanyi's and Gauthier's theories ultimately do not appeal to others' reasons in a way that is relevant to public justification.

6.5   Empathetic deliberation, public justification and interpersonal justification

Empathetic deliberation, I have argued, is relevant to public justification. If the deliberation in a contract theory models empathetic deliberation, then the justification yielded should be understood as both public *and* interpersonal: this is what it means to appeal to the concept of *justification to others*. Although many theorists have argued that contract theories seek public justification (in that the justification is about justifying things to others on grounds that they can accept), contract theories are also interpersonal, insofar as the perspective from which agreement is sought is based on the idea that such evaluation is conducted according to standards that others can and do accept as being appropriate for the moral point of view. Contract theories thus achieve justification by showing that people have reasons to support certain principles from their own perspectives, and thus, these principles are acceptable to everyone. By showing that the hypothetical deliberations of idealized rational agents model empathetic deliberation, I show that public justification is interpersonal because it involves examining reasons that can be given to others. Engaging in the project of determining which reasons are acceptable to others is interpersonal because it is about the *exchange of reasons*. And this is what empathetic engagement is all about—thinking about how others view things, and how they feel about things. My claim that contract theories model empathetic deliberation leads to a new way of understanding the nature of contractual methods of justification: they seek public justification through interpersonal methods.

Let me say a bit more about public justification and interpersonal justification, since the idea of public justification is a well-known working idea in contemporary political philosophy, and is the focus of study for many scholars in political theory. The basic idea of public justification is that political principles or institutions are justified when they have been shown to be reasonable or acceptable to everyone in the society who will be subject to them. My suggestion is that public justification is a project that seeks to include the points of view of people in different social positions, and thus requires seeing things from different points of view. This means that the way that we conceive of others in public life is constrained by what we believe they would find acceptable as an appropriate way to deliberate about social matters.

The idea of interpersonal justification is less familiar, because the few theorists who have used the idea have replaced it with the idea of public justification.[42] But there are two ways in which public justification can be said to be interpersonal. First, it is interpersonal in the same way that moral justification is said to be interpersonal. Gaus suggests that contract theories are theories of interpersonal justification, insofar as their aim "is to formulate a public conception of justice that provides the foundation for a common moral life among those pursuing diverse values."[43] Essentially, Gaus is saying that justification is interpersonal insofar as it involves justifying moral principles publicly, on the basis that they are acceptable to everyone in society. Additionally, T.M. Scanlon argues that contract theories seek agreement from a variety of perspectives, and in this way they offer a "genuinely interpersonal form of justification."[44] In his version of contractualism, which seeks to contractually justify moral requirements, taking up other people's points of view is required, because on the contractual thought experiment, I, as the deliberator, might actually be that other person.[45] Elizabeth Anderson also states that interpersonal justification involves examining principles and institutions according to standards that others can accept.[46] And David Brink suggests that the contractual method of justifying moral conceptions is interpersonal insofar as it involves attempting to achieve objectivity through taking up a variety of perspectives.[47]

The public justification sought for political principles is *also* modeled on the interpersonal justification of moral theorizing, for social contract theories *model* how we think about moral choice by capturing what we agree is common to moral judgments—that they are *impartial*.[48] And in this case, impartiality is achieved by taking up the moral point of view, or a perspective from which people agree it is appropriate to decide what is morally justified: one that takes into account a variety of perspectives and seeks to balance them or integrate them by using some decision procedure. This idea is modeled by using the "veil of ignorance" aspect that is at work in each of the theories I have discussed, and has the result of requiring that the rational agents in the deliberative setting take into account the reasons and deliberations of others involved in the choice. Since this is the only requirement of the moral perspective, and there are a variety of ways of modeling inter-personal justification, utilitarian, Kantian, and egoist principles can be justified using the contractual method of interpersonal justification. Moreover, the interpretation of contract theories as interpersonal explains why the contractual method must take others' reasons into account: using this device helps to reveal justificatory reasons that are accept-able to all. The aim is to construct an interpersonal justification for points of view that are seemingly irreconcilable, and this can be accomplished when the rational agent behind a veil of ignorance deliberates as if he is empathizing with others. This type of deliberation reveals that the principle is impartial, and at the same time, publicly justified.

Public justification is interpersonal for another reason, and this is that justification is based on pragmatic considerations such as achieving social harmony. That is, public justification is justification to persons with whom we must actually live. In his characterization of public jus-tification, Samuel Freeman suggests that justification is genuinely inter-personal because it is justification to *a person*. He argues that—at least in Rawls' social contract theory—

> "the idea of justification *to* a person is defined by reference to the 'prac-tical task of political philosophy', which in turn consists in its 'social role' or 'public role' in providing a basis for public justification."…"the idea of justification to a person is defined by references to the idea of a well-ordered society. It is because people inevitably have different conceptions of the good and different comprehensive views that contractarians see a need for the idea of 'justification to a person.'"[49]

Freeman's suggestion is that Rawls' concept of public justification is driven by the practical task of needing to find a workable solution to the circumstances of justice: justification to others must be inter-personal insofar as it is addressed to the individuals in society who actually have different conceptions of the good, religious beliefs, and philosophical beliefs. This idea is latent in the other contract theories that seek to achieve justification. In these theories, public justification is interpersonal because it is based on the idea that we confront each other as citizens and persons with whom we must deliberate in order to live our lives together. This is precisely what happens when *we* justify ourselves to others—we show that, looking at the situation from their point of view and taking their feelings into account, they have a reason to support our principle or action.

The advantage of this interpretation of contract theories is that it focuses on the importance of agreement and moves away from the idea that contract theories are primarily about having a theory of rationality and some deliberative constraints in order to justify principles. (Of course, the selection of principles in a social contract may ultimately be driven by certain specified principles of rationality. I am not contesting that here.) While it is imperative to show that certain moral or political principles are rational or reasonable, the contract method reveals the deep connection between justification and acceptability to others in a way that other theories don't. Insofar as hypothetical contract theories try to justify moral and political principles "to everyone," they should be understood as taking all points of view and perspectives as relevant, in some way, to show that moral and political principles are justified *interpersonally* and not just rationally. Since contract theories require justifying principles to others on grounds that they could accept, by determining the reasons and values that others hold and find acceptable, then they seek interpersonal justification and not just rational justification. This is crucial for establishing the idea of impartiality and expressing the way we care about what other rational or reasonable people think about moral requirements. These two features are captured in the criterion of agreement.

The idea that contract theories seek to achieve public justification via interpersonal justification adds to its value as a strategy for justifying principles in modern liberal political philosophy, for it emphasizes the importance of mutual or collective choice. The contract method is proposed as a way to articulate reasons for agreeing to principles that promote social cooperation. Its goal is to reveal similar values and interests, and show how we can choose principles of interaction *together*. By focusing on the idea of agreement, contract theories capture the intuition that our decisions about how to act must somehow take into account the considerations of others by modeling or representing deliberation in the contractual setup.

This is why the interpretation of contract theories as interpersonal provides an important defense of them. If contractual agreement is ultimately explained in terms of the "rationality" of the parties, then the criticism that contract theories of justification are otiose gains traction. For if rationality is sufficient to derive and justify principles, then agreement is unnecessary. There is no reason to distinguish between the contractual approach to the derivation and justification of moral principles and a rational approach, such as a Kantian theory. Contract theories require representing the perspectives of others in order to justify moral and political principles, and this distinguishes them from other kinds of moral or political theories.[50] Hypothetical contract theories emphasize agreement because they are committed to the idea that justification is a joint undertaking. This is why it is so important that we see that such theories model empathetic deliberation: so that we understand that it is through the empathetic consideration of everyone's perspective that we can discover the reasons that are relevant to public justification.

Ultimately, hypothetical contract theories take the *process* by which the parties reach agreement to be significant.[51] Contract theories are sensitive to the fact that a variety of people participate in the choice of principles, and they thus require taking the perspectives of others to be relevant to moral deliberation. The contractual deliberator is thus "influenced by the fact that those for whom she is choosing are different in ways that need to be accommodated, from the start, by the choice she makes."[52] It is intuitive to think that accommodating the considerations of others in contractual deliberation is a way of modeling empathetic deliberation to evaluate others' reasons and values. Since specific people must be accommodated, it is possible for justified principles and practices to not be identical—they may vary according to time, location, culture, and the specific attributes of the parties involved in the deliberation.[53]

Since contract theorists have long argued that contractual agreement is solely a product of rational choice, this view is widely accepted and continues to shape our understanding of how contract theories achieve the justification of moral and political principles. But I have argued that contract theories require interpersonal agreement, in addition to rationality, in order to achieve public justification. This is *not* to say that contract theories are overly rationalistic and individualistic, and that they fail to take account of emotion-based attachments to others and other-regarding commitments, which is what some feminist philosophers, such as Carole Pateman, Annette Baier, and Virginia Held have claimed.[54] We have good reason to believe that contract theories model our ability to reason *and* our ability to empathetically deliberate in an impartial way. But it is a mistake to think that rationality is the *only* reasoning of a contracting agent.[55]

In modifying our understanding of the nature of contract theories to include the idea that they model our empathy, they will become theoretically more appealing. Ultimately, the success of a contract theory that seeks to justify moral and political principles depends on its providing a characterization of persons that is plausible, that we can identify with, and that is an accurate representation of ourselves. The contract approach is a heuristic, and this heuristic is only as powerful as our ability to utilize it. We can use contract theories more if we have a better idea of how a contract theory's ideal deliberators view others in society. If, as I have argued, justification should be achieved interpersonally, empathetic deliberation is crucial to examining the differences in how public justification is achieved.

6.6   Empathy and justificatory reasons

My argument thus far implies that different theories of moral and political principles, such as utilitarian, Kantian, and egoist principles, can be interpersonally justified. But these theories do not achieve public and interpersonal justification equally, and the extent to which a principle is *strongly* justified corresponds to the degree in which public justification or interpersonal justification is achieved. Public justification is achieved by taking into account the reasoning of a *variety* of persons, rather than simply expressing the reasoning of one idealized person, in the way that Ideal Observer theories do.[56] A theory that expresses the reasoning of a variety of persons will thus be more publicly justified because it has considered more points of view and has taken into account more diverse reasons for preferring certain alternatives over others.

While some contract theorists suggest that only the rational point of view matters, perspective-taking empathy allows us to consider perspectives that we otherwise might not, and in this way, others' preferences are made salient to us. This is why we need empathy and to use it in contractual deliberation. For example, empathizing with those who are gay or lesbian will make their reasons for supporting same sex marriage salient—one is likely to view another's reason for wanting to get married as a legitimate reason if he sees that it is the same as his own: the gay or lesbian person loves another and wishes to make that relationship official in the same way that the straight person does. When deliberators are able to take into account a wide range of others' reasons, their view is more strongly justified because it genuinely takes others' views into account and is thus addressed to them. Taking the idea of public justification seriously requires considering the points of view of the actual agents to whom principles will apply, and outlining reasons and concerns that are acceptable to them. If justification to others is viewed as a process of learning the reasons in favor of and against certain political principles, then justification will be seen as a more desirable goal in political theory.

Even though the three contract theories I have discussed here model empathetic deliberation, the deliberations modeled in Harsanyi's and Gauthier's theories ultimately do not appeal to others' reasons in a way that is relevant to the process of interpersonal justification. In Gauthier's theory, the reasons that are required to endorse the principles under consideration are reasons that are related to self-interest; that is, the reasons identified by the Ideal Agent as the reasons that justify the principles are reasons that suggest that it is in my interest to adopt such principles. The Ideal Agent in Gauthier's Archimedean Point uses a specific conception of others to imagine their reasons for action, in the same way that the self-focused empathizer projects how she feels onto others. As a result, she does not really take up the perspective of others in order to determine the reasons that agents would have to support different principles. Rather, the Ideal Agent requires *us* to identify with this view of ourselves in order to see that this is what our reasons are. Instead of empathizing with us, we must ultimately identify with the Ideal Agent, and her ideas about us as rational maximizers. Her empathetic deliberation does not acquire significant information about others' reasons, beliefs, values, and desires, and thus, it cannot achieve interpersonal justification in a significant way. Interpersonal justification involves gaining new information about others, rather than just projecting one's own feelings onto them and identifying reasons that are consistent with that view of them. Gauthier's theory yields principles that are only publicly justified insofar as people (publicly) identify with the conception of themselves as rational maximizers and deploy maximizing rationality to support the principles.

On the other hand, the ideal agent in Harsanyi's hypothetical contract loses the very advantages of having a unique perspective, which is a part of the empathetic experience. Although the empathetic deliberation used in the equiprobability model involves taking up the perspectives of others and seeing things from their point of view, it is performed only for information-gathering. The ideal rational agent only focuses on what others value, prefer, feel, and desire via other-focused empathy, and does not examine the reasons that people have for wanting to support various proposals. But there is a difference between knowing what others prefer (such as Michael's knowing that Anna doesn't like his sex talk at work) and understanding their *reasons* for preferring it (that Anna wants to be respected as a co-worker and not viewed as a sexual object), and Harsanyi's ideal agent only seeks to know others' preferences. Harsanyi's method fails to achieve strong public justification because, by choosing outcomes using average utilitarianism, the reasons for endorsing the principle of equiprobability are based on impartiality rather than inter-personality. Harsanyi's utilitarian principles are not publicly justified because no reasons for public acceptance have been articulated.

Since Rawls' theory models dual-perspective empathy, it acknow-ledges a wide variety of viewpoints and seeks justificatory reasons from a variety of points of view. It thus has the potential for achieving strong public justification. The parties deliberating in the Original Position are interested in the different kinds of reasons expressed by individuals in society, and these reasons are expressed in the original position reasoning. The result is that this theory can examine the *different* reasons that people have for supporting different proposals. Since not all reasons identified will contribute to the process of reaching a determinate solution to the problem of justice, empathetic deliberation may not help in deciding between proposals. But since Rawls' theory models dual-perspective empathy, which takes into account more than one point of view and seeks to understand the similarities and dif-ferences between each view, it can genuinely justify principles *to others* and achieve public and interpersonal justification. Gauthier's and Har-sanyi's theories do not achieve public justification to a similar degree because others' reasons do not contribute significantly to the justificatory process; the justifications are not really addressed *to* others and the variety of perspectives is not taken seriously. In those theories, another principle decides antecedently which "reasons" count as part of the justification.

Let me clarify in greater detail the relationship between public jus-tification and empathy. The idealized parties *model* our empathetic deliberation in order to attain the public justification of principles, and it is *we* that must have empathy and empathetically deliberate when *we* use the contract method. Empathetically imagining the perspectives of others allows us to access and understand the distinctive interests, desires, preferences, reasons, and values of others, especially when we do not share their perspective. When we use empathy in the context of contract theory, it is instrumental to showing that the principles are publicly justified in a way that is ethically objective, in that the principles are mutually chosen. A kind of objectivity can thus be achieved when we empathize with the different view points of others, determine what is valuable, important, and reasonable, and use an impartial criterion to determine which reasons should be used to approve the principles.

This discussion regarding the nature of public justification leads to two questions regarding its nature: First, is a *convergence* of reasons required for public justification, meaning that individuals can deploy different reasons for supporting a principle, or is a *consensus* required, meaning that people must share the same reasons for supporting a certain principle? The view of empathetic deliberation I have defended here is central to the process of discovering the reasons that are constitutive of public justification for both models, whether they are reasons needed for convergence or consensus. Empathetic deliberation will be particularly important for uncovering people's agent-relative reasons, reasons that are usually captured in the convergence model of agreement. In the reason-giving process, reasons and values that people have *in common* that can serve as constraints on agreement are evaluated, and this is why the interpretation of the deliberation as empathetic is crucial to the idea of public justification.[57] Empathetic deliberation can be used to uncover reasons that pass the test of public, interpersonal justification, especially in the justificatory phase of a contract theory.[58]

Evolutionary game theorist Ken Binmore also defends empathy on the basis that it is important for learning about other people's preferences and agent-relative reasons. He argues that the purpose of contract theories is to choose outcomes that are in equilibrium with our other kinds of judgments, and claims that empathy is needed for this kind of reasoning. "In order to use the device of the original position successfully as an equilibrium selection criterion, *we need to be able to empathize with other people*. In particular, we need to recognize that different people have different tastes."[59] Binmore argues that the veil of ignorance provides the conditions needed to model empathetic deliberation, insofar as it requires us to consider the perspectives of others in deliberating about the appropriateness of principles. He suggests that empathetically simulating another's state is useful for gathering information, predicting others' behavior, and ultimately, reasoning about fairness.[60]

In fact, Binmore argues that the best evolutionary explanation for our capacity for empathy is attributed to our need and desire to reason about fairness.

> I suspect that we are able to express empathetic preferences because we need them as inputs when using the device of the original position—and for no other reason. In order to evaluate a social contract behind the veil of ignorance, a person *must* be able to compare being Adam in a particular social contract with being Eve. Since we never need to make such comparisons outside a fairness context, the benefit of being able to use fairness norms in our evolutionary past must have been very high in order to outweigh the cost of carrying

the apparatus for expressing empathetic preferences around in our heads.[61]

Binmore is right to think that empathy is needed to derive fairness norms. Since empathy is how we acquire information about others, and compare it with what we know of ourselves, it is needed to resolve conflicts between people and reach a reflective equilibrium, or agreement on what kinds of reasons are justified in the issue at hand.

The second issue regarding the nature of public justification is, should the reasons that justify a principle be an individual's *actual* reasons, or can the justification appeal to normative reasons that individuals *ought* to have? Empathy can be used to help identify reasons that others presumably ought to hold, given their other commitments. Perhaps this is why T.M. Scanlon argues that social contract deliberation is similar to golden-rule style reasoning: "both thought experiments are devices for considering more accurately the question of what *everyone* could reasonably agree to..."[62] He says that the test of justification in a contract theory is procedurally tantamount to imaginatively "changing places" with others, and involves asking whether one could accept the justification if you were in the other person's position.[63] But empathy can be used to learn people's *actual* reasons as well, and learning these are important when interacting in real-life situations.[64] Since perspective-taking empathy, along with conversations with others, can reveal actual concerns, then it can be used to identify common values and principles that can be used to guide the justificatory process. Empathy can be used to discover and appreciate both actual and ideal reasons, concerns, and values.

6.7   Conclusion

Social contract theories that seek to justify political principles and institutions ultimately seek public justification via interpersonal justification. There are different ways of modeling empathetic deliberation, and these differences correspond to the kind of public justification achieved by the theory. Gauthier's and Harsanyi's contract theories do not achieve strong interpersonal justification, and thus, are not strongly publicly justified. Rawls' Original Position, on the other hand, seeks to respond to the values, reasons, and concerns of people in a variety of circumstances, and since it models dual-perspective empathy, it is more interpersonal, and thus more strongly publicly justified.

It follows from my analysis that contract theories model empathetic deliberation in a way that has important implications for *our* use of them. Hypothetical contract theories have justificatory power in that they show that ideal agents have reason to adopt certain principles; actual agents have reason to adopt them insofar as they, as actual agents, resemble the ideal deliberators. While the ideal deliberators do not empathize, those of *us* who *use* contractual methods will need to imaginatively take up others' perspectives in order to determine if they would endorse certain principles. Contractual thinking requires imagining the responses of others by seeing things from *their* perspectives, and this is what empathy allows us to do—represent the perspectives of others to ourselves in a way that enables us to understand their reasons and values.

If we suppose that contract theories model empathetic deliberation, then we have further evidence that contractual approaches take agreement to respond, in a non-trivial way, to the considerations of actual individuals. Geoff Sayre-McCord notes that this is one of the biggest challenges for contract theories: they must show that moral demands are plausibly a product of what it would be reasonable for people to accept, in a non-trivial way. He suggests that contract theories could do this by showing that what people might agree to is sensitive in some way to (i) the variety of people participating in the choice or (ii) the variety of people being governed by the choice, or (iii) the people who are addressed by the argument.[65]

Showing that contractual deliberations model our empathetic deliberation is evidence that contract theories can (iii) speak to people who are addressed by contract theories, because they model our ability to take into account the feelings, values, and responses of others. Empathy is instrumental to revealing the shared values and reasons needed to reach agreement to principles, and allows us to appreciate and understand the reasons and values of people that are different from ourselves. But since there are different ways to empathetically deliberate, it is important for a theory to genuinely take the reasons and considerations of others into account, so that it has the resources for explaining how they can plausibly be sensitive to the variety of people participating in the choice situation. Otherwise, contract theories are too abstract and idealized to be of use to contemporary political theory, and either neglect the diversity of views, or speak to a version of ourselves that we do not identify with or recognize. If contractual deliberation models empathetic deliberation, then contract theories have a new defense against the charge that they are impractical and irrelevant to moral and political reasoning; rather, they can powerfully contribute to the justification of political principles.

Part IV
Practical Implications

7
Empathy and Moral Education

Empathy is essential to the moral life. The person who empathizes is able to understand others in a sensitive way and gather information about them that can be used to make a moral decision. But can empathy be taught? Recent research in moral education suggests that it can, and the earlier it is taught, the better. Many organizations have developed curricula for teaching empathy, and I will showcase here the variety of methods that are used in these ground-breaking programs. One surprising example is the U.S. Army, which now recommends that leaders in the Army demonstrate empathy to both their peers and subordinates. The 2006 Army Field Manual states that, "Army Leaders [should] show a propensity to share experiences with the members of their organizations. When planning and deciding, try to envision the impact on Soldiers and other subordinates. The ability to see something from another person's point of view, to identify with and enter into another person's feelings and emotions, enables the Army leader to better care."[1]

This chapter will support my overall thesis that empathy alone is insufficient for moral judgment and deliberation, by showing that empathy can contribute significantly to moral development, but that it needs to be taught in tandem with moral principles and values. Empathy can be cultivated to motivate care and sympathy, and to learn more about others who are different from oneself. Philosopher Harvey Siegel argues that the development of empathy as a moral sentiment is important to moral education because "the mature moral agent must be able to put herself in the position of others, and grasp their perspective and feelings, if they are to take seriously into consideration the interests of others."[2] In other words, empathy is an important intellectual habit that should be taught in order to develop moral reasoning skills. Since empathy is an epistemic or intellectual virtue that enables open-mindedness toward others, when it is developed within the context of other moral principles and ideals, it can contribute to the development of moral virtue.[3] The moral education programs reviewed here do this by teaching empathy in a variety of contexts and for a wide range of purposes.

There is little debate among those interested in empathy regarding the merits of teaching empathy: all agree that it should be taught. And yet, those who advocate teaching empathy recommend teaching different *kinds* of empathy and discuss different *purposes* for teaching empathy. I thus survey in this chapter several formal and informal moral education programs and distinguish the philosophical and methodological differences between them, in order to show that empathy must be taught in conjunction with moral values and principles if it is to contribute to moral development. I outline the types of empathy that can be taught, argue in favor of avoiding *passive empathy*, or empathy that involves imagination but is not applied to everyday life or doesn't require students to *do* anything, summarize the different *methods* of teaching empathy, and show how empathy can be taught in a unique social/ moral *context*. Instead of endorsing any one of these methods or contexts against over the others, I emphasize the importance of teaching empathy early on in life and discuss the situational and developmental factors that augment or diminish the capacity for empathy as a person develops.

7.1   Teachable types of empathy

Role-taking and different kinds of perspective-taking empathy (others-focused empathy, self-focused empathy, and dual-perspective empathy) can be taught for diverse purposes, and clarifying these purposes will enable understanding of the likely consequences of teaching a particular kind of empathy.

7.1.1   Others-focused empathy

In others-focused empathy, Amy imagines being Zack, intentionally simulates Zack's situation and/or imagines being Zack, and tries to understand what Zack feels; as a result of this, she feels a similar emotion. Teachers and parents can direct children—and other people, for that matter—to imagine themselves in another's perspective, and insofar as students can successfully do this, then others-focused empathy can be taught or at least induced momentarily. For empathy to become a habit or a natural inclination, students must learn to recognize situations where it is appropriate to imagine the other's perspective and become aware of others emotions, so that they spontaneously take up the other's perspective.

Daniel Batson's experiments on others-focused empathy suggest that this sort of empathy may be taught in order to help motivate care and altruism towards others, and to develop an appreciation for diversity and differences among others. In Batson's experiments on others-focused perspective-taking empathy, participants were asked to focus on the other person and imagine being that person (someone in distress). Researchers found that imagining the *other* person's feelings resulted in increased partiality in favor of the distressed participant and that this directly led to pursuing an altruistic action in relation to that person. Batson and colleagues conclude that, "the imagine-other perspective evoked empathy-induced altruistic motivation directed toward the goal of increasing the other's welfare."[4] Presumably, focusing on another's distressing emotions and situation motivates helping behavior because the details of the other's feelings and situation are vivid in the observer's mind. While Batson's conclusion may be a plausible interpretation of the helping behavior, this sort of partiality and altruism may not always be moral or morally motivated; thus, perspective-taking of this sort is insufficient for moral deliberation and action, and illustrates why empathy must be taught in conjunction with moral principles and values.

Legal scholar Cynthia Ward claims that, in theory, teaching others-focused empathy can also encourage an appreciation of diversity. She argues that focusing on the other's point of view "forces a *de*-emphasis on the empathizer's self in order to freely construct a picture of the other that simultaneously recognizes the fundamental diversity of individuals and their imaginative capacity to understand and connect with each other across the lines of socially created difference."[5] By feeling and appreciating another's emotions and her point of view, a person takes a moment to fully take in the other's position and perspective, and comes to appreciate her point of view, even though it is different from one's own. This is not to say that this kind of empathy can enable people to surmount prejudices and transcend the recognition of difference between oneself and the other, although it may. By role-playing the perspectives of others, individuals can be drawn into the lives of others so that they learn to appreciate the other's differences. The hope is for others-focused empathy to be a vehicle for promoting genuine understanding of others and concern for their welfare. It is possible that by taking up another's perspective or situation, the observer can identify with the other's situation, problems, and concerns and thus reduce racial, gender or socioeconomic prejudice. But since empathy is limited and can be used instead to perpetuate prejudice against others, it will need to be taught in tandem with moral values and principles.

7.1.2   Self-focused empathy

Self-focused empathy, too, can be taught and has pro-social consequences. In contrast to others-focused empathy, self-focused empathy occurs when Amy observes Zack, imagines *herself* in Zack's situation, and comes to feel an emotion that is congruent with Zack's emotion. Whereas others-focused empathy involves imagining how others feel, self-focused empathy involves imagining how *I* would feel in another's situation. Daniel Batson's experiments showed that participants who imagined *themselves* in the other person's position of disadvantage did *not* lead to altruism. Participants who imagined themselves in a disadvantaged other's position were far more likely to respond to the situation by giving up their position of advantage and choosing a situation in which themselves and the others were positioned equally.[6] Batson concluded that self-focused perspective-taking empathy can stimulate judgments of distributive justice (in which a participant chooses egalitarian outcomes) and that it can motivate an interest in fairness and justice. My hypothesis is that imagining the other's perspective causes the person to realize that, were she in the other's position, she would feel frustrated at the unfairness of the present situation, and is thus motivated to rectify it so that it is no longer unfair. This type of perspective-taking empathy motivates judgments of justice because the empathizer comes to understand the other in the same way that she understands her own emotional responses; by imagining herself in another's situation, the "fairness" of a particular distribution of goods becomes more salient to the observer and thus she has a motive to rectify the injustice.

Cynthia Ward also argues that self-focused empathy (what she calls "projective" empathy) can encourage a feeling of equality between persons, in the sense that empathetic interaction enables a person "to see the essential humanity of those whose race, gender, socioeconomic background, or sexual orientation are different from theirs."[7] The idea is that empathy enables one to appreciate and understand the other as an equal and like oneself. The empathizer senses that if she were in the other person's situation, she would behave, believe, and feel the way the other person does, and so she appreciates that other person's self and situation. This is a further ramification of the "understanding others" epistemic function of empathy, in that it can promote a sense of equality between oneself and those with whom one empathizes.

Ward notes that one potentially problematic aspect of self-focused empathy is that, paradoxically, it "draws its power of understanding not from feelings of altruism but from feelings of self-regard."[8] The empathizer responds to the other out of a concern for her own self-interest; that is, the thought process may suggest that if *I* were in your situation, *I* would want to be respected or appreciated in a certain way.[9] Ward also argues that self-focused empathy can also only work to produce a sense of equality and appreciation of another who is different from oneself *if* the empathizer imagines "herself in the events of the other's life with the politically relevant differences—for example, with the other person's race, gender, or socioeconomic class."[10]

While empathy can bring about a sense of equality in the way that Ward describes, self-focused empathy is limited to bringing about a sense of equality only using the categories with which an observer views the other. For example, if Beth projects herself into the perspective of a Black man and focus on his maleness, then she will really only see equality in terms of gender, but not in terms of race (his being a Black male). And in doing this, she may miss out on crucial aspects of his situation and relevant similarities or differences. Coming to see another as an equal requires seeing similarities between oneself and others, and so the ability to see others as equal takes place in the categories that one uses to analyze similarities and differences between oneself and others. This is not necessarily a bad thing, but it illustrates the limits of self-focused empathy for fostering a sense of equality between oneself and others. Self-focused empathy may be more effective at motivating distributive justice than motivating a sense of equality (understood as perceiving the similarity between oneself and others) because self-interest—a motivating factor in self-focused empathy—limits the way a person adopts the other's perspective. There are features of the other's perspective that may lie outside a person's self-interest or self-conception, but which are relevant to viewing others as similar and equal to oneself. Without taking those into consideration, one's appreciation of the other is diminished.

The third mode of empathy, the combination mode, in which Amy goes back and forth between her own perspective and Zack's, is not generally taught, but there is no reason to believe that it cannot be taught in tandem with the other two types. Teaching the combination mode of empathy would emphasize the cognitive dimension of empathy by encouraging imaginative thinking and exploring the many different ways that humans understand and interpret each other. By going back and forth between one's own perspective and others', a person would achieve a deeper understanding of the similarities and differences between herself and others. Fostering this type of understanding of others using perspective-taking is central to building solidarity, reducing prejudice, seeing others as equals, and motivating people to choose just or egalitarian outcomes.

7.1.4   Non-perspective-taking empathy

Can non-perspective-taking empathy (mimicry, classically conditioned empathy, direct association, and mediated association empathy) be taught? Mimicry and classical conditioned empathy cannot be taught formally because they are rooted in spontaneous emotion (moreover, they are not used in moral deliberation and may cause errors in moral judgment). Direct association empathy (in which an individual empathizes because he immediately and non-inferentially associates his own experiences and emotions with another's) and mediated association empathy (in which one empathizes as part of the process of reading or having a verbal conversation) are not usually taught because they require spontaneously connecting another's experiences with one's own. Of course, it is possible that after being taught perspective-taking empathy, a person may get better at mediated association empathy. For example, suppose a fellow student's home burned down. The teacher may *teach* the other students to empathize by saying, "Imagine how Johnny feels" or "Imagine yourself in Johnny's position." This is teaching perspective-taking empathy. Once a person knows how to empathize in this way, he or she may be able to feel sorrow with Johnny on his own without instruction, as Johnny describes his anguish at his home's destruction. Thus, it is possible for mediated association empathy and direct association empathy to be enhanced when students are taught some type of perspective-taking empathy.

7.1.5   Avoiding passive empathy

In sum, several types of perspective-taking empathy can be taught, and these types of empathy can be taught in order to motivate justice, care, altruism, understanding, promote equality, and reduce prejudice against others. However, educational theorist Megan Boler claims that empathy should not be cultivated for the purposes of understanding others if it does not or cannot result in direct action. She and other educational theorists criticize philosophers such as Martha Nussbaum and Cornel West, who praise empathy because of its potential for cultivating democracy or social action, but who support teaching a multicultural curriculum that does not necessarily connect to students' everyday experience or promote reflection on their own actions towards others.[11] This is merely *passive* empathy, which Boler defines as "those instances where our concern is directed to a fairly distant other, whom we cannot directly help."[12] She argues that this is the sort of empathy that is generated by reading novels and texts that aim at producing an appreciation of the other, but does not translate into a contemporary lived context. Boler argues that while empathy can contribute to understanding others through reading novels, for example, by identifying with characters who have suffered or have been marginalized, if empathy is not harnessed to critically reflect on the student's own life and situation, then this activity engenders a kind of passivity. By feeling passive empathy, students do not recognize that they may be part of a system of injustice in their own lives and situations. Specifically, passive empathy "produces no action towards justice but situates the powerful Western eye/I as the judging subject, never called upon to cast her gaze at her own reflection."[13]

Boler's solution to passive empathy is *testimonial reading*, which "requires a self-reflective participation: an awareness first of myself as reader, positioned in a relative position of power by virtue of the safe distance provided by the mediating text" and "an active reading practice that involves challenging my own assumptions and world views."[14] Testimonial reading pushes us to "recognize that a novel or biography reflects not merely a distant other, but analogous social relations in our own environment, in which our economic and social positions are implicated."[15] While reading this sort of literature in a more critical and self-reflective way is better than reading it passively, we will see that for empathy to have an impact in moral education, it must be taught *not just* to include self-reflection on one's place in social relations and power structures but in tandem with specific moral principles, concerns, and values that direct a reader's response. Children should learn not just about the lives of those in distant places, but they should reflect on how they treat their own classmates on the playground; college students should not simply identify systems of power and injustice, but they should ponder their interaction with others and search out ways to respond to the needs of those with whom they empathize through policy changes, non-profit outreach programs, and activism.

7.2   How empathy is taught

It is important to distinguish the *methods* for teaching empathy from the *context* in which empathy is taught. There are at least three *methods* of teaching empathy: induction, rational learning, and modeling. Each of these methods provides essential components for both developing and fostering the constellation of virtues related to empathy.

7.2.1 Induction or inductive discipline

Martin Hoffman's *Empathy and Moral Development* offers a comprehensive theory of how empathy contributes to moral development. He discusses the role of guilt, discipline, moral internalization, culture, and socialization, and shows how they function together to develop empathic abilities over the course of a lifetime. His theory of how empathy is taught to children (especially during the first ten years of life) is called "induction" or "inductive discipline." This is one of three methods he describes of disciplining children.[16] He claims that the type of discipline that cultivates a child's capacity for empathy is induction, "in which parents highlight the other's perspective, point up the other's distress, and make it clear that the child's action caused it."[17] The goal of this type of discipline is for the child to feel empathic distress and guilt, realize the harm her behavior may have caused, and assess the harm in view of her own self-interested desire to perform the action. Essentially, inductive discipline is a way of forcing a child to recognize how her actions affect others, and helping her see how they are perceived by others who are on the receiving end of a harmful action. Inductive discipline brings attention to others' points of view because toddlers and young children are not good at seeing these perspectives on their own. The parents and teachers are there to help children learn how to see things from another's perspective.

Most parents and other moral educators use induction frequently when disciplining children (Hoffman says once every 11 minutes during the second year of life, and once every six to nine minutes in children ages 2–10). An illustration of inductive discipline is as follows: a parent observes young Mary make fun of young Ethan on the playground. The parent approaches Mary and says, "That was very mean of you to make fun of Ethan's shoes (or the way he walks, etc.). Can't you see that that hurts Ethan's feelings and he feels bad when you say those things to him? You would feel bad if Ethan made fun of you. Now tell Ethan you're sorry so he will feel better."

According to Hoffman, there are several things going on in this type of encounter. First, this method calls attention to the other's distress and makes it salient to the child. By showing the child that she too would feel bad if she were in the other's position, the parent arouses the child's empathy and produces empathic distress. Second, this method emphasizes the role the child had in causing the other's distress. This creates the possibility that the child will feel guilty or displeased with herself for wrongfully harming the other. Hoffman emphasizes that drawing attention to the child's causal role is essential because otherwise a child could empathize and cry with the other child without realizing that she was the one that caused his distress.[18] Again, this is part of the "disciplining" part of induction, and it is not necessarily unique to teaching empathy specifically. The point is that children learn empathy through inductive methods when parents and other educators remind them to take into account the other's perspective.

Moreover, this method has an essential epistemic dimension: through inductive discipline, the child recognizes that the other person has reasons and desires of his own (a desire to not be hurt, for example) and that these desires and reasons are legitimate and perhaps even similar to one's own desire to not be hurt. This is empathy's *salience effect*, which I illustrated in Chapter 5. Empathy is the vehicle for bringing one's attention to another's existence and experiences and for becoming aware of her emotions and how they might be similar to one's own. While Hoffman's main point is to show how empathetic training through inductive discipline plays a role in moral development, it is important to show that empathy should be taught not only for moral development but to motivate moral action and decision-making. Although empathy may be useful on its own, the connection between empathy and morality must be drawn so that children are able to use empathy as part of a moral decision-making process as they mature. In short, induction is an informal but ubiquitous method of teaching children to empathize for the purposes of moral action.

7.2.2   Rational, straightforward education

The method of teaching empathy that is frequently employed in schools or other formal organizations involves teaching empathy straightforwardly, in a rational manner using workbooks, art, or group exercises. Tonia Caselman's workbook *Teaching Children Empathy, the Social Emotion* is perhaps the most user-friendly book of its kind, in that it includes lesson plans focused on different aspects of empathy.[19] Lessons include defining empathy, recognizing one's own emotions, developing skills for reading others' emotions, listening to others and empathizing with them, controlling one's own feelings, and putting one's feelings aside in order to focus on another's emotions. There are also moral lessons that connect empathy with various moral values, concerns, and principles such as making friends, resolving conflict, and accepting diversity. Exercises range from traditional worksheets with activities such as word searches, to imaginative writing exercises, group or paired interactive activities that deal with emotions, and personal reflection on one's own empathic skills and abilities. The exercises are appropriate for both elementary and middle school students. As Caselman asserts in her introductory comments, the purpose of the book is to "teach students the value of empathy, assist students in recognizing their own and others' feelings, help students put themselves in 'someone else's shoes' and instruct students how to exhibit understanding and acceptance."[20] While the latter goal is unique to Caselman's programmatic use of empathy, the method of teaching empathy is rational and straightforward, and the acquisition of empathy skills is the primary topic of the lessons.

Two other empathy and moral education programs currently on the market aspire to inculcate empathy through stories. The first, *Through Other Eyes: Developing Empathy and Multicultural Perspectives in the Social Studies* suggests ways to teach understanding of other cultures and critical thinking to elementary and middle school students, and aims to reduce prejudice through empathy using a multicultural curriculum.[21] The authors aim to make historical and social studies relevant by (a) encouraging students to connect their own perspectives and experiences to others' and (b) using thematic analyses (personal and family history, work, migration, and conflict and change).[22] In addition, the authors propose a model of empathetic understanding of others called the *Thinking-Feeling Spiral*, which involves four kinds of learning experiences: "making personal and concrete connections to the topic; inquiring and imagining about someone else's life; investigating content resources to learn more about a group's experience; and 'acting as if' one is actually in another's circumstances, making choices or solving problems."[23] The spiral is intended to represent a symbol of growth, in that going through each phase in the learning experience brings about an ever-deepening understanding as one progresses. The authors claim to build on John Dewey's goals for education in a democratic and inclusive society; their aim is to teach history and social studies so that students can gain an appreciation for other cultures, people, and worldviews and thereby become better-equipped to participate in a democracy.

David Levine's *Teaching Empathy: A Blueprint for Caring, Compassion and Community* is another text that seeks to teach empathy for the purposes of instilling care and compassion rather than for understanding of other cultures.[24] The curriculum includes projects that promote making the school itself feel safe and welcoming to every student who enters; it encourages teachers to model empathy in their interaction with students as the primary method for building trusting relationships; and it includes ways of teaching students specific empathic skills and their "companion behaviors" of listening, compassion, honor, and generosity. The exercises include both individual and group activities such as reading short stories, listening to songs, and evaluating them based on specific criteria related to empathy development. Levine's method is more comprehensive than the other approaches in that it includes reflecting on the teacher's *interaction* with the students. However, it is more abstract; for example, it encourages the teacher to learn how to communicate with children and their parents empathetically with only broad instructions on how to do this. Nevertheless, his approach is another straightforward method of teaching empathy through the school's curriculum and environment.

7.2.3   Modeling empathy

Although the programs canvassed thus far emphasize the need for teachers and parents to model empathy for their students by being empathetic themselves, Mary Gordon's *Roots of Empathy* program has received critical acclaim for the unique way that it promotes a modeling approach to teaching empathy.[25] The *Roots of Empathy* program teaches empathy by introducing a baby into the classroom along with its (female or male) parent. Gordon argues that the program involves the children in "the human dynamic of the parent-baby relationship" by making the relationship between the parent and the child "a template for positive, empathic human relationships."[26] The aim of the program is to take the "learning that occurs with the baby in the classroom and build it into a broader exploration of how humans understand and value themselves and each other."[27]

Students learn empathy through observation of an infant when, as Gordon explains, "through observations of the baby's emotions, children [can] learn about their own emotions and the emotions of others, learn to take the perspective of another, understand the power for resolving conflict that lies in being able to see a situation and the world from another's point of view."[28] Along the way, students gain an experiential insight into parenting that is more powerful than carrying around plastic dolls. Gordon's hypothesis is that good parenting requires the ability to observe the baby, figure out her emotions and what causes them, and respond appropriately to them. These tasks are enhanced with empathy. Since the baby cannot communicate linguistically with the parent, the parent must learn about how babies communicate, and, in some sense, imagine what the world is like from the baby's perspective, so that he can better understand how to respond to the baby.

The students learn the same skills when watching the baby and the parent-baby interaction (as they are being led in the empathetic experience by the *Roots of Empathy* teacher). In one of her examples illustrating how children learn empathy, Gordon describes four-month-old baby Jenna's second visit to the classroom. The class was particularly intrigued with how the baby was struggling to roll over and how she would grasp her feet and pull them up. What impressed Gordon and the teachers was how profoundly the children understood that frustration. One of the children, Daniel, commented, "It must be so scary to not be able to control your own body."[29] Daniel's comment illustrates how the students practiced empathy with baby Jenna—by seeing things from her perspective—in order to better understand what Jenna was experiencing. The children could feel and appreciate Jenna's frustration at being unable to roll over because they used empathy to see the world from her eyes. Children will also learn from observing the parent's empathy with the baby. They will see how the parent accommodates the baby's energy level or mood, tries to figure out what it needs and wants, and discerns how the baby communicates to the parent her need for emotional security.

Gordon's method of teaching empathy is unique because it models emotional engagement and literacy—not simply as a classroom activity, but through interaction with a real live baby with limited verbal communication skills. Children must learn the skills of empathy if they are to enter into the baby's world and comprehend its emotions and desires. Although the baby cannot talk and does not yet harbor prejudice or bias against those who are different from herself, she nonetheless has profound needs for love, security and attachment, and the children must give the baby what she needs and interact with her on her own terms. Gordon reports that even the meanest of bullies connects with the baby at some point over the course of the year. Though Gordon's program is unconventional, it has impressive, statistically-documented results. In contrast to comparable groups, *Roots of Empathy* children demonstrate a/an

- Increase in social and emotional knowledge (increased perspective-taking in 71 per cent of students).
- Increased helping behavior in up to 78 per cent of students, increased peer acceptance in up to 74 per cent of students, increased sharing in up to 69 per cent of students.
- Decrease in social aggression in 39 per cent of students.

- Increase in perceptions of the classroom as a caring environment.
- Increased understanding of infants and parenting.[30]

Gordon attributes the success of the program for increasing empathy-related behaviors to the baby and its ability to connect with students who lack love and affection in their own homes. As I explain later, teaching empathy in this way is a win-win situation in that it is a learning experience for the baby as well: the more a baby is nurtured in its infancy, the greater its empathic abilities and its confidence later on in life.

7.3   The contexts for teaching empathy

This survey of the methods of teaching empathy lays a foundation for understanding how empathy must be taught in a context in conjunction with corresponding virtues, values, and traits in order for it to contribute to moral development. In these formal programs for teaching empathy, as well as in informal inductive discipline, empathy is never taught in isolation, but in conjunction with specific moral directives, values, and principles, for the purposes of reflecting on one's own interactions with others. Although some philosophers have emphasized the importance of the connection between empathy and altruism, the reason for instilling empathy is rarely to produce altruism; rather, the aim is to raise awareness of the other person's emotional state and one's relationship to that person. The goal, beyond that, is to generate moral judgments or actions that have one of three characteristics: care and concern, fairness, or an appreciation of diversity and multiculturalism. The education programs that teach empathy allow it to play this multidimensional role in moral education.

7.3.1   Empathy in the context of care and concern

The *Roots of Empathy* (ROE) program, whose aim is to teach empathy for the purposes of cultivating concern for others' emotions, community, and kindness, nicely illustrates the role that context plays in teaching empathy. ROE teaches care and concern within a rigorous and sophisticated curriculum regarding understanding emotions. The ROE curriculum includes discussion of brain development and the importance of nurturing the baby's brain with love and affection, and emphasizes the ability to recognize another's temperament as well as one's own. Students also learn emotional literacy, or understanding babies' emotions and how they express them. This enables them to understand the critical need for attachment and trust between a child and its parent. By making the classroom a microcosm of democracy and collaboration, students learn the benefits of social inclusion.[31] ROE's agenda goes far beyond indoctrinating empathy, and teaches a constellation of other skills related to emotional understanding and emotional awareness. This comprehensive, inclusive agenda fosters the students' *capability* and *capacity* for empathy, which precedes the experience of empathy, and teaches them the merits of detecting and responding to others' emotions. While the program does not teach specific perspective-taking skills, such as others-focused empathy or self-focused empathy, the program certainly makes it possible for a child to be able to take up another's perspective and take part in perspective-taking empathy.

The uniqueness of the *Roots of Empathy* classroom is that it fosters care and compassion for others through an emotional/affective experience with a baby. Gordon boasts ample evidence that children learn how to understand emotions with a baby because the learning takes place in a non-threatening manner, making the student emotionally open to the baby and its parent. Students learn to spot the signs of affection between the parent and child, to pick up on the non-verbal communication of the baby to the other students, and to feel important as they connect with the baby as they hold, touch, or interact with it. Essentially, the baby can connect with the children in such a powerful way because it can only communicate non-verbally. If children truly want to connect with the baby, they must open themselves up emotionally. This context makes it possible for students to learn empathy along with care and concern for others.

7.3.2   Empathy in the context of the compassionate virtues

David Levine's recommended context for teaching empathy includes the moral values of compassion, care and community. Levine's primary interest in empathy is that it can bring about sympathetic appreciation of another person. In fact, one might argue that given Levine's emphasis on the importance of care, especially on teachers caring for their students, he is actually endorsing empathetic sympathy, which is not equivalent to the imaginative empathy that is being discussed here. Nevertheless, Levine does describe the significance of imagination to empathy,[32] as well as the importance of teachers seeing students' viewpoints and recognizing others' feelings, and these dimensions of his approach can be assessed with regard to the context in which empathy is taught. Levine frequently endorses a number of virtues such as compassion, wisdom, caring, and generosity, as traits that are needed to augment empathy. His curriculum includes exercises that involve taking the perspective of others through stories and songs but then goes significantly beyond this to instill the virtues associated with empathy. While his curriculum at first seems contrived (for example, activities such as singing Levine's own songs), he suggests modifying the activities to suit the needs of the students and the teacher's style. His goal is to introduce the students to a variety of social skills that employ both self-focused and others-focused perspective-taking, in order to develop a community of students and teachers sensitive to each others' needs and compassionately interested in each others' well-being. By teaching perspective-taking empathy in the context of these virtues, the students will develop compassion for others as they practice empathy.

7.3.3 Empathy in the context of diversity and multiculturalism

Tonia Caselman's empathy workbook, on the other hand, teaches empathy in the context of diversity, multiculturalism, and conflict resolution, which she sees as political virtues. Her curriculum primarily attempts to foster others-focused empathy for the purposes of learning more about others and discerning similarities between oneself and others. The motivating principle is that empathy promotes understanding of others in a way that can produce sympathetic actions,[33] aid conflict resolution by enabling one to appreciate the other person's feelings and desires,[34] and promote acceptance of differences among and diversity in others. The activities that motivate accepting others' differences primarily implement self-focused empathy—e.g., one worksheet is entitled "Put Yourself in Someone Else's Shoes"— and presumably, the goal is for a student to see herself in another person or her situation, so that she will see similarities between herself and the other person. For example, in the exercise mentioned above, students are to draw a picture of themselves in another's shoes. Provided that the teacher calls attention to the fact that not only are the other person's shoes different, but that her race, class, gender, or perspective may be different as well, then such activities could promote appreciation for others' differences using self-focused empathy. While some of the activities seem overly simplistic, teachers would likely find much to be of use in this workbook that will help them explain how empathy connects with the particular political virtues Caselman outlines.

7.3.4 Empathy in the context of socialization and behavior modification

These moral education programs implement empathy as a way of teaching a particular ideal social world, one in which children value things like care, compassion, and community. But unlike these programs, teaching empathy within the context of socialization and behavior modification requires appealing to virtues, characteristics and moral principles that are unique to the situation. The goal of inductive discipline is to remedy a child's misbehavior by drawing immediate attention to the problem. First, one must get the child to think about the other's perspective, which involves appealing to a kind of self-focused empathy, and her own role in making the other person feel a particular emotion, so that she will stop the offending behavior–now! While inductive discipline is not comprehensive, it is immediate and specific. Whether or not inductive discipline can genuinely cultivate empathy in children, it is, nonetheless, a method for teaching moral virtue, and especially for pointing out instances of injustice or unfairness.

As we can see, empathy is taught not solely for the purpose of altruism, but rather as a skill needed for making friends, for resolving conflicts, for good parenting, and for becoming a kind and compassionate person. Insofar as empathy is taught as an ability to detect others' emotions, to learn how another person thinks or feels, or to understand others in a deeper way, it is taught as an epistemic skill or ability necessary to acquire sensitive knowledge about others. This is why I emphasized in Chapter 3 that the epistemic functions of information-gathering and understanding others are integral to empathy. Even if empathy is often biased in favor of those who are most similar to oneself, when it is taught, people can learn to expand the range of people and emotions they empathize with, and doing so will enable them to develop other kinds of desirable responses to them. Thus, empathy is essential to moral education.

7.4   Developing the capacity for empathy

Empathy can be taught in both formal and informal ways and it can be taught in different contexts, for different purposes. However, there are additional factors that will also influence an individual's capacity for empathy as she matures. These factors include the early nurturance of empathy and empathetic responding, as well as various social/emotional factors that influence the presence of empathy at any given moment. While empathy can be taught in schools by the teaching staff, there is significant psychological research on social and emotional development in children that suggests that parents play a noteworthy role in developing a capacity for empathy over time.

7.4.1 Factors contributing to empathy development

A number of factors contribute to the development of empathy defined as *feeling a congruent emotion with another person, in virtue of perceiving her emotion with some mental process such as imitation, simulation, projection, or imagination.* This definition has in its extension imitation empathy, classically conditioned empathy, direct association empathy, and mediated empathy. Mark Barnett, a pioneer researcher in the development of empathy, notes that, although this field is still in its nascence, when the evidence is considered, there are several important factors that contribute to the development of a capacity for empathy. These include secure early attachment, parental affection, the availability of a variety of empathic models (both adults and other children), inductive socialization (as described previously by Hoffman), encouragement of the perception of similarity to others, discouragement of excessive interpersonal competition, and encouragement of a positive self-concept.[35] Barnett concludes that the development of empathy and related responses would thrive in an environment that:

(1) satisfies the child's own emotional needs and discourages excessive self-concern, thereby enabling the emotions and needs of others to become more salient;
(2) encourages the child to identify, experience, and express a broad rage of emotions;
(3) provides numerous opportunities for the child to observe and interact with others who, through their words and actions, encourage emotional sensitivity and responsiveness to others.[36]

This research is important for explaining why some people are more receptive to empathy training than others, and why some people have better native empathy skills than others. Essentially, some people have a greater capacity for empathy because they have an emotional head start. Just as the brain develops optimally with secure attachment, the capacity for empathy is correlated to positive emotional experiences; emotional abuse and neglect diminish a child's capacity for empathy.

7.4.2 Caveats to empathy development

Our discussion of various factors contributing to empathy development would be incomplete and perhaps even misleading if it did not include some of the research findings regarding the antecedents that must be in place for empathy to be taught effectively as well as some of the unique circumstances in which empathy failure can be adaptive and thus appropriate. These caveats serve as a reminder that we should not assume that empathy can or should be demonstrated in all circumstances, or with all persons, equally.

For example, psychological studies show that empathetic concern will be engaged on a greater scale if the individual values the welfare of the person in need. Daniel Batson examined whether placing negative or positive value on people and their situations increased perspective-taking empathy. In studies that manipulated the extent to which respondents would value others' welfare, Batson found that individuals report considerably more empathy for a person whose welfare is valued. For example, people were more likely to empathize with a person described as kind versus someone described as self-interested. In essence then, "valuing is an important situational antecedent of empathic concern."[37] His study suggests that empathic concern can be augmented by increasing the empathizer's value of another person's welfare, by using strategies that "reduce prejudice; to improve attitudes toward out-groups [or those who are not socially accepted]; or to produce more positive, cooperative social interactions."[38] Batson's findings do not show that care or concern is necessary for empathy, but only that the more that one values or appreciates that other person, the more the observer empathizes. Since such factors influence the degree to which people actually empathize, it is important for those who teach empathy to help students perceive the value of the other so that they are better able to take up others' perspectives and value their experience.

7.4.3   Failures of empathy

Although a person might have a well-developed capacity for empathy, there are situational cues and factors that affect whether he will empathize at a particular moment. For example, to empathize, one must be emotionally ready or prepared in the sense that he is open to the other's experience. If someone is under tremendous stress, distracted, or having a crisis, he might recognize the other's emotion, but not *feel* the other's emotion because his own present circumstances are not conducive to empathy. In this regard, empathy is like other emotions; it is an evaluative response that is both cognitive and affective, and in some cases, the affect might simply be absent, so that, as Adam Smith says, there is no "correspondence of sentiments."[39] In such cases, there is a failure of empathy because, while one might cognitively judge that it is appropriate to empathize, he may fail to affectively feel the other's emotion.

Another factor that may interfere with empathic responses is actually an adaptive coping mechanism required for certain circumstances. For example, soldiers will likely show a decrease in empathic feelings toward others during wartime (except their comrades), primarily because performing their combat duties would be more difficult if they empathize with their enemies. Similarly, a child's empathic capacities can be diminished if her emotional survival is threatened. For example, if a child is abused or bullied and cannot trust people in her surroundings, she will likely not empathize with others around her. So, although moral education of empathy might take place in elementary and secondary schools, a child's previous social and emotional experiences as a developing infant and toddler may compromise the child's ability to learn empathy even in the most carefully constructed and administered curriculum. This factor underscores the importance of modeling empathy with children when they are young.

7.5   Conclusion

Because there are many ways to teach empathy, the teacher, parent, or practitioner must decide his or her purpose for teaching it, and this in turn will determine the kind of empathy to be taught. Educators should be aware of the types of empathy that can be developed in students and of the different methods for teaching it, as this will maximize the impact on students. Passive empathy, or empathizing with characters in novels without a practical application in the student's life, should be avoided because it does not motivate moral deliberation or action. Most importantly, empathy should always be taught in the context of moral virtues and values so that empathy has direction and purpose.

Moreover, it is important for empathy to be taught early in a child's life and consistently throughout her formal education. Empathy's importance to a child's moral development should even be emphasized in college courses on child development. While many of the developmental psychology texts that mention the need for empathy demonstrate its importance, there is rarely discussion of how to teach it to children.[40] Such information is crucial to future educators. The *Roots of Empathy* curriculum is a well-researched program with promising results that could be implemented rather easily, provided there is institutional support.

Parental involvement in the educational process of teaching empathy must also be emphasized. Parents play a formative role in a child's capacity for empathy, and research on parental behavior in early child-hood has shown it to be strongly correlated with empathic abilities later on in life.[41] Given the many different virtues with which empathy is associated, this parental interaction should not be understated. Parental involvement could be accomplished through parent-teacher school organizations or in newborn training sessions at hospitals. Regardless, given empathy's role in contributing to the development of virtues such tolerance, compassion, understanding, and altruism, and its potential role in moral deliberation and judgment, teaching it should become a priority for parents and educators alike.

8
Conclusion: Implications for Feminist Ethics

This book has covered considerable territory, surveying the nature of empathy, its epistemic functions and how they are important to moral deliberation, why empathy alone is unsuitable as the sole basis of moral judgment, how contractual ethical theories model empathy, and how empathy can be used in moral education. By way of conclusion, I want to make clear the significance of the arguments that have gone before and discuss directions for further research on related topics that I have not treated in detail. There is a great deal of interesting work being done on topics related to empathy—including narrative approaches to empathy, empathy in animals, and empathy in religious ethics (which might see these topics differently from secular ethics)—that I have been unable to examine here.[1] I close by demonstrating the practical application of my argument as it applies to feminist ethics in particular.

8.1 Significance

I began by arguing that philosophers in particular should adopt an account of empathy which allows the phenomena that other disciplines identify as empathy to "count" as empathy; it is undesirable to adopt a narrow concept of empathy—"no, really, *this* is empathy"—because doing so prohibits cross-disciplinary conversation between philosophers and theorists in other fields. Philosophy's most important contribution to the interdisciplinary discussion of empathy is conceptual clarification, not browbeating, and philosophers can be of greatest service to the discussion when they distinguish different types of empathy that others can use to guide their research.

The arguments presented in Chapters 3, 4, and 5 describe perspective-taking empathy's epistemic functions and explain how it can positively contribute to moral deliberation and judgment. While empathy often motivates people to perform certain actions, even altruistic ones, these actions are not necessarily moral. The experience of empathy is often biased in favor of those to whom one is most similar, and what is needed for moral judgment is for someone to empathize and then reflect on the situation using general moral principles. In this way, empathy's tendency to bias is corrected by commitment to moral concerns such as justice, respect, and recognition of the other. Since empathy *can* make important features of a situation *salient*, it can play an important role in moral deliberation and judgment. Thus, it ought to figure more prominently in the articulation of a wide range of ethical theories, which I described in detail in Chapter 5.

Chapter 6 offered a unique interpretation of contract theories: contract theories of ethics exhibit the reasoning of empathetic deliberation. Although contract theories are generally understood as seeking public justification, I showed that public justification is successful only insofar as its reasoning represents interpersonal empathetic deliberation. When contractual theories engage in the project of determining which reasons are acceptable for justifying moral principles, this process is interpersonal because it is about analyzing others' reasons by way of their perspectives and feelings about the situation. Contractual thinking requires imagining the responses of others by seeing things from *their* perspectives, and this is what empathy allows us to do: to represent the perspectives of others to ourselves in a way that enables us to understand their reasons and values. Empathetically imagining the perspectives of others allows us to access and understand the distinctive interests, desires, preferences, reasons, and values of others, especially when we do not share their perspective.

My goal throughout the book has been to show that empathy alone is not necessarily moral, and so I argued in Chapter 7 that empathy must be taught to both children and adults in context, along with moral values and principles. By evaluating the various methods and contexts used to teach empathy, I showed that perspective-taking empathy in particular can be taught for a wide range of purposes, including the development of both moral and epistemic virtue. When empathy is taught at home and in school in tandem with other moral concerns, children develop an understanding of friends, neighbors and fellow classmates that is not based on prejudice or stereotype. In addition, empathy can contribute to the development of virtues such as understanding, acceptance, friendliness, respect, and tolerance.

8.2 Practical implications: Empathy and gender

There are practical implications of my argument for everyday concerns relating to empathy, such as gender roles and expectations. Consider, for example, that a recent USA today article states that women are more charitable than men, in terms of making donations.[2] The director of the Women's Philanthropy Institute, Debra Mesch, is quoted as saying that one explanation for their generosity is that "[w]omen have just been socialized as the care-givers in their families to be more empathetic and altruistic," and "this is being manifested in giving to charity." Her observation suggests that western culture accepts gender stereotypes regarding empathy and does not often challenge these stereotypes to demand more charity of men. While Mesch herself implies that women's empathy is socialized, other theorists imply that women are more naturally suited for giving to charity and being primary care-takers. Thus, they might conclude that men don't need to donate their time and money to others in the way that women do, on the basis that women are more naturally inclined to empathy.

But when we examine whether women are really more empathetic than men—both in their behavior and in their "natural" tendencies—it appears that the women are *not* more empathetic than men, though it depends somewhat on how empathy is measured. In their overview of the research measuring gender differences in empathy, psychologists Randy Lennon and Nancy Eisenberg describe the methods of measuring empathy in subjects and show that on most of these tests, women do not score significantly higher.[3] There are many methods of measuring empathy, including newborn reactive cries, picture/story techniques, self-report of empathy in questionnaires, facial/gestural and vocal measures of empathy, and physiological measures. While women tended to score higher than men on *self-report* tests of empathy and empathic expression (which could be explained by the women conforming to gender expectations and their desire to be socially accepted or admired), "no gender differences were obtained" when the indices measured a response that the participant was unable to consciously control.[4]

Lennon and Eisenberg also suggest that since the type of empathy (emotional contagion, personal distress, or sympathetic responding) being measured in the studies was not clear, it may have been that when the measures were more likely to elicit sympathetic responding, "females appeared to be more emotionally reactive than males."[5] Since the researchers using the indices of empathy did not clarify the type of emotional response elicited in the participants, no reliable conclusions can be drawn regarding the elicitation of empathy, and whether the individual response was indicative of empathy, sympathy, compassion, or care.

Another study measuring the ability to infer the thoughts and feelings of a target person (also called "empathic accuracy") renders data that is consistent with the conclusion drawn by Lennon and Eisenberg. This study tested people's ability to identify others' emotions, and showed that women were better than men at this only when they "were given a task assessing their feelings of *sympathy* toward the target *prior* to performing the empathic accuracy task."[6] In other words, women were better at empathy (identifying the other's emotions) only when they were required to assess their *sympathy* (whether they were positively disposed toward the other and valued his welfare) ahead of time. When in the same experiment women and men were given *payments* in exchange for accurately identifying the other's emotion, *both* men and women's performance improved, and there was no difference in empathic abilities. The researchers conclude that there are motivational differences between men and women, and these differences are based on level of interest, not differences in native ability. In addition, cross-cultural studies of empathy show that gendered empathic responses are culturally shaped, and expressions of empathy vary from one society to another. While there might be differences between the sexes in expression of empathic response, there are a number of other factors related to *socialization*—not native ability—that can explain these differences.[7]

And yet, Michael Slote claims in the *Ethics of Care and Empathy* that women are more empathetic than men. He states that there is "a great deal of (independent) evidence"[8] that this is the case, but the research he cites is not on empathy *per se*. Rather, Slote refers to men's elevated levels of testosterone, research on mirror neuron systems, empirical studies of facial mimicry of others' emotions, and research on the extreme male brain and the female brain that are highly contentious among cognitive scientists. Since these studies are on hormones, the brain and facial expressions, it is not clear how they relate to empathy understood as feeling another's emotion, which is Slote's own definition of empathy.

Nevertheless, the research on the brain and empathy provides insight into the perceived differences in empathy between men and women. Two studies are of particular interest. First, Tania Singer's research shows that neural responses are significantly lower in males than females when they observe a person who has been demonstrated to be "unfair" experience pain. When women observed the "unfair person," they exhibited more brain activity in the frontal lobes than men did. But as Singer and colleagues note, this fact does not render a general conclusion regarding women's native empathy abilities versus men's. They conclude, "in men (at least) empathic responses are shaped by valuation of other people's social behaviour, such that they empathize with fair opponents while favouring the physical punishment of unfair opponents."[9] This difference may of course be due to socialization rather than native abilities, as the study measures brain activity and cannot address whether the brain activity is "natural" or "socialized." Second, in another study, one that Slote cites, people viewed a person in pain, and female participants exhibited stronger motor resonance than male participants and had a stronger physiological response to that person than males did.[10] Slote concludes that since women had more mirroring activity in the frontal lobe and greater physiological responses (such as palmar sweat), women have greater empathy than men when observing others in pain. But just because women had greater activity in the frontal lobe does not mean that they are "naturally" more empathetic than men; this response could be influenced by socialization as well.

The appropriate conclusion to draw from these studies is that women are not necessarily better than men at understanding others' emotions, emotion-matching, identifying others' emotions, or perspective-taking. The research that measures these things suggests that women are *not* better than men at such tasks. However, women do seem to exhibit greater physical responses often *associated* with empathy when they see another person in pain and when the person in pain is "unfair." This suggests that men and women differ in their *physical* "expressions" of empathy, but that they do not differ with respect to the *cognitive* aspects of empathy itself. Given this difference in physical expression versus cognitive tasks, we cannot conclude that women are more *empathetic* than men, unless, of course, we mean that women are better at *expressing* responses correlated with empathy than men. That conclusion does follow from the research.

But this research on brain activity does *not* support the conclusion that there is significant difference in men and women's cognitive ability to empathize. Although some thinkers such as Slote imply that brain activity is tantamount to "natural" ability, a person's brain activity is the merely physical locus of their thoughts, and is not indicative of natural inclination, since thoughts are significantly influenced by socialization. Brain activity is not tantamount to natural ability, nor is it equivalent to feeling a congruent emotion with another person in virtue of perceiving her emotion. Thus, it is important to keep the conclusions of the studies regarding physical expression of empathy independent from those regarding the cognitive aspects of empathy.

8.3   Empathy and feminist ethics

Even if women are not more naturally empathetic than men, there is a tendency to stereotype women as being more empathetic. Should feminist ethicists use this to their advantage, or does a feminist ethic that emphasizes empathy run the risk of being stereotyped as a feminine and for women only? Should feminist ethics make a prominent place for empathy, and if so, why? Empathy should play a fundamental role in feminist ethics, but several caveats are in order. Here I lay out empathy's potential positive contributions to feminist ethics and highlight the dangers of relying on stereotypes of empathy in ethics more generally.

Broadly speaking, feminist ethics seeks to end female subordination and the exploitation of women. But how best to go about doing this is debated among feminist moral theorists.[11] Some feminist theorists have focused on the importance of feminist methodology (as opposed to moral and political agendas) in moral philosophy. For example, Cheshire Calhoun argues that one of the central themes that emerges in women's moral theory is a "resistance to elitism and inegalitarianism in both social life and philosophical work."[12] My methodology here has been feminist in this way, in that it seeks to highlight the similarities between men and women's expressions of empathy and emphasize the likely similarity in native abilities. My account resists elitism (i.e. the suggestion that women are better than men at empathy) and inegalitarianism (i.e. that only women should cultivate empathy towards others). It is constructive and seeks to have practical consequences, which are two characteristics of feminist methodology. In addition, feminist moral evaluation is about learning how to treat each other better by examination of our core commitments; remonstrating with each other for greater respect and appreciation in virtue of our contributions to each other's lives; justifying our reasons, feelings, and desires for certain rights and goods; and attempting to come to a greater understanding of each other in order to modify our existing everyday moral practices. My aim in this book has been to show that empathy can be used to better engage in these projects.

While a practical feminist moral philosophy would also seek to describe women's circumstances and treatment in order to overcome oppression, I have done this to a much lesser extent in this book. Stressing empathy's need to be supplemented with universal or objective moral principles is one way that my account of empathy addresses practical feminist issues such as exploitation, insofar as the exploitation of sentiments such as empathy contributes to female subordination. I argued that relying on empathy alone to make a moral judgment can lead to coercion, manipulation, and exploitation, and this is why it is insufficient for making a moral judgment. Empathizing with another person and then simply doing what the other wants is not moral deliberation—it is moral servitude. Empathy is *instrumental* to the process of moral reflection, insofar as it can reveal another person's desires, reasons and values, but this is not the end of the process. An individual must use her personal moral commitments or an impartial criterion to decide what to do. In addition, empathy *could* be used to raise and to further traditional feminist issues such as co-parenting, equal rights, and equal pay, though I have not done this here.

Although feminist ethics would do well to focus more attention on empathy, simply because a theory implements empathy does not mean it will automatically satisfy the goals of a feminist ethic. For example, Michael Slote's version of care ethics, which is different than accounts of care ethics given by Virginia Held, Sara Ruddick and Nel Noddings, uses empathy to ground care, but his is not a feminist ethic.[13] He argues that empathy can motivate care (understood as a "motivational attitude" involving benevolent feelings for others), and claims that morally correct actions are those that exhibit empathetic caring. While this sounds promising, he also claims that women are more empathetic than men. Since women are more likely to empathize with others and care for them, they are, according to Slote's version of care ethics, morally superior to men.[14]

This initially seems flattering to women, but the implications of this argument run contrary to the main goals of feminist ethics, and, if true, would reinforce female subordination, because caring for others is work. When care is rooted primarily in feelings and attitudes towards others, it runs the risk, as Virginia Held says, of "losing sight of it as work," and thus tends to overlook the question of "who does most of this work."[15] Although Slote's empathic care theory purportedly requires empathic care on everyone's part, it ironically reinforces the stereotypical conception of women as natural caregivers, and thus encourages them to continue doing care work, for men do not possess this natural capacity. The ethic he defends certainly does nothing to reduce the amount of work that women do caring, and it doesn't encourage women to stop performing empathic caring actions that are contrary to their own interests. It also doesn't demand more of men whose apparent natural inclination is to be less empathetic. Slote stops short of saying that care ethics is the ethic of women, but he explicates care ethics as growing out of women's sensibility. His version of care ethics is contrary to the goals of a feminist agenda that seeks to overcome traditional female oppression and, by offering men an excuse for failing to be more empathetic, reinforces traditional distinctions between female and male natures that lead to the systematic subordination of women.

Given that Slote's version of care ethics reinforces gender differences that have led to female subordination, it is evident that the role that empathy plays in an ethical theory is crucial to determining whether a theory is feminist. My own theory of empathetic deliberation is methodologically feminist in that it emphasizes empathy for the purposes of seeing situations from the perspective of others, in order to respond in a morally justified way. When we feel the emotions of others, and see things from their point of view, we learn new interpretations of events and actions that can be used in along with moral principles and commitments to respond to others' concerns in ways that matter to them. Diana Meyers' theory of "empathic thought" is explicitly feminist in that it articulates a normative view of how empathy can be combined with dissident speech—or speech that seeks to dislodge culturally normative prejudice—to overcome the problem of "difference," the systematic unjust social exclusion of minority or powerless social groups, and the exclusion of their points of view.[16]

My view is in the feminist tradition in another way as well, and this regards how I articulate empathy as involving both affect and cognition (or reason). Many debates in ethics are based on the idea that *either* reason or emotion is the basis for moral action. However, the cognitively advanced kinds of empathy that I have emphasized here (such as perspective-taking empathy) involve *both* the rational ability to fit others' beliefs and feelings into our own worldview, and the emotional ability to feel another's emotions in an affective way. Empathy includes elements of both rationality *and* emotion, and if empathy is important to moral deliberation, as I have argued, then emotion and reason are both important to moral deliberation and action. This idea has been a theme in feminist ethics for some time.[17]

8.4　Empathy and virtue

The view of empathy I have outlined here also has practical applications for virtue ethics, especially the development of virtues touted by feminist ethics. The virtues important to feminism can be developed by empathetic perspective-taking, and engaging in different types of perspective-taking empathy can enhance four families of virtues: (1) care, altruism, and compassion; (2) understanding, acceptance, and sense of equality; (3) respect for difference and diversity; and (4) non-violence and peacefulness. Since Nancy Sherman more than adequately analyzes the connection between the psychological studies of empathy and altruistic virtues,[18] and space is limited, I will briefly explain how empathy can be used to teach the virtues described in categories 2–4.

First, *self-focused empathy*, where an observer acquires a target's emotion because she simulates being in her circumstances, and responds by feeling a similar emotion, can be used to teach understanding and acceptance, and to encourage a sense of equality between persons—a core goal of feminist ethics. This is because empathetic interaction enables people, as Cynthia Ward says, "to see the essential humanity of those whose race, gender, socioeconomic background, or sexual orientation are different from theirs."[19] By imagining oneself in another's circumstances, one comes to appreciate and understand that person as similar to oneself and not an alien other. In addition, as Jeanette Kennett argues, emotional contagion and perspective-taking empathy are how "other people's concerns become reasons for us."[20] Perspective-taking empathy enables someone to see that, were she in the other person's situation, she would feel the way the other person does, and so she appreciates that other person's feelings. (Of course, such appreciation is not generated when empathy is biased or when the observer objects to the other person's emotions and actions, so this conclusion does not always follow.)

Second, *others-focused empathy*, where an observer imagines herself not just in the other's circumstances, but imagines being that person, with her beliefs and psychology, so that she acquires an emotion that is congruent with the other's, can be taught to encourage respect for difference and diversity. By taking up another's point of view, one is able to appreciate the ways in which that person's point of view and circumstances are different from one's own, but reasonable and respectable. If, for example, a straight person takes up the perspective of a gay or lesbian person, she can see that from that person's point of view that her inclinations are not harmful to others and make her happy. By role-playing that perspective, one can be drawn into the lives of others so that she learns to appreciate the other's difference from oneself.

Third, perspective-taking empathy can be used to teach non-violence and increase the development of non-violent virtues. Psychologist Martin

Hoffman cites the use of empathy by psychologist John Gibbs in treating juvenile delinquents who tend to be fixated on getting their own needs met and do not consider the future consequences of their actions.[21] His method, called "confronting," primarily involves bringing the person's attention to the harm to others that results from his actions, which elicits and strengthens empathic responses. Confronting also involves compelling the individual to "put himself in another's position and understand the 'chain of injuries' stemming from his harmful actions, including effects on absent and indirect victims."[22] This method of inducing empathy or empathy-like responses is used to reduce the subjects' aggressive behavior and help them examine why the other person is responding the way they are to the situation. Although not explicitly feminist, the virtues of non-violence and reducing aggression are key concerns of women and feminists alike.

In conclusion, feminist ethics is just one of the practical applications of my view of empathy. Empathy can play a very important role in developing virtues that can have a significant impact on social life and political cooperation; and in this regard, my theory of empathy could be applied to realms of inquiry that emphasize the development of social virtues such as understanding, tolerance, and justice. Further work needs to be done articulating empathy's potential for promoting social cooperation and other political virtues, but this connection should not be underappreciated. As Rawls points out,

> The virtues of political cooperation that make a constitutional regime possible are, then, *very great* virtues. I mean, for example, the virtues of tolerance and being ready to meet others halfway, and the virtue of reasonableness and the sense of fairness. When these virtues (together with the modes of thought and sentiments they involve) are widespread in society and sustain its political conception of justice, they constitute a very great public good, part of society's political capital.[23]

Although I have not argued for it here, empathy, and especially *mature empathy*, which I articulated in Chapter 5, is an ability that citizens need in order to have the social virtues that Rawls describes. Rawls' observation regarding social virtues suggests a promising direction for future research on empathy's role in bringing about social unity and contributing to the stability of a society with less crime, hate, poverty, racism, sexism, and homophobia. The arguments I have given here regarding empathy's contribution to moral judgment and deliberation could serve as groundwork for equality movements and political theories that emphasize virtues associated with tolerance, reasonableness, and fairness. Although there is certainly more to say about this and how the theory of empathy I have defended can support Rawlsian political liberalism, I leave these as topics for future research.

Notes

Chapter 1   The Empathy-Morality Connection

1   Maia Slalavitz (2010) "School Bullying Prevention: Teach Empathy at a Young Age," TIME, April 17.
2   Jeremy Rifkin (2009) *The Empathic Civilization: The Race to Global Consciousness in a World in Crisis*, New York: Penguin Group, p. 42.
3   Martin Hoffman (2000) *Empathy and Moral Development*, Cambridge: Cambridge University Press, Chapter 3.
4   Ibid., Chapter 8.
5   Lipps' original interest was the psychology of aesthetics, but Titchener shifted the emphasis to psychology and tried to explain the content of empathy in greater detail than Lipps originally did. According to Lipps, empathy involves inner imitation, and a projection of the self into the objects of perception. See Wispe's discussion, "History of the Concept of Empathy," in Nancy Eisenberg and Janet Strayer (1987) *Empathy and Its Development*, Cambridge: Cambridge University Press, pp. 19–21.
6   In his *Beginner's Psychology*, he explains that the imaginative aspects of empathy distinguish it from sympathy: "We have a natural tendency to feel ourselves into what we perceive or imagine. As we read about the forest, we may, as it were, become the explorer....this tendency to feel oneself into a situation is called EMPATHY—on the analogy of sympathy, which is feeling *together* with another; and empathic ideas are psychologically interesting because they are the converse of perceptions; their core is imaginal and their context is made of up sensations...In memory, their place is taken by the imaginative experiences which repeat over again certain phases of the original situations." Titchener quoted in Ibid., p. 22.
7   This aspect of empathy has been emphasized by Karsten Stueber as relevant to gaining knowledge of other minds, especially in the social sciences, and serves as the foundation for my view that empathy has four epistemic functions, which I describe in Chapter 3. See Karsten Stueber (2006) *Rediscovering Empathy: Agency, Folk Psychology and the Human Sciences*, Cambridge: MIT Press.
8   Psychologists Eisenberg, Miller, Strayer and Batson agree that empathy has products that are not behavioral and that there are ways to measure empathy that do not focus on the resulting behavior. (See Eisenberg and Strayer's concluding chapter in *Empathy and Its Development*, p. 389.) See also Strayer's Chapter 10, Eisenberg and Miller's Chapter 13, and Batson's Chapter 16 of this book for evidence of this idea.
9   Michael Slote (2007) *The Ethics of Care and Empathy*, New York: Routledge, pp. 13, 16.
10   Ibid., p. 16.
11   Holton and Langton argue that empathy cannot be the basis for morality because it will be completely sentimental and subjective, and not objective or systematic. Richard Holton and Rae Langton (1998) "Empathy and Animal

Ethics," in Dale Jamieson, ed. *Singer and his Critics*, Oxford: Blackwell Press, pp. 228–229. I agree that it is not the basis of morality, but believe it should have a prominent role in moral deliberation.

12 *The Ethics of Care and Empathy*, p. 16.

13 Diana Meyers (1994) *Subjection and Subjectivity: Psychoanalytic Feminism and Moral Philosophy*, New York: Routledge, Chapter 6.

14 *Subjection and Subjectivity: Psychoanalytic Feminism and Moral Philosophy*, pp. 34–35. She discusses two kinds of empathy that are relevant to moral judgment: incident-specific empathy and broad empathy. Incident-specific empathy involves feeling another's emotion and imaginatively experiencing another's state of mind at a specific time and trying to understand what she is going through at that moment. The latter is more expansive, and while it is based on an affective experience, involves emotionally connecting and engaging with the other as a whole, trying to understand what it is like to be that person in general, thinking about who she is as a person.

15 Ibid., p. 2.

16 C. Daniel Batson (2009) "These Things Called Empathy: Eight Related but Distinct Phenomena," *The Social Neuroscience of Empathy*, ed. Jean Decety and William Ickes, Cambridge, MA: MIT Press, pp. 4–8.

17 See Rizzolatti, G., Fadiga, L., Gallese, V. and Fogassi, L. (2004) "Premotor Cortex and the Recognition of Motor Actions," *Cognitive Brain Research*, 3 (1996) 131–141; Gallese, V., Keysers, C. and Rizzolatti, G. "A Unifying View of the Basis of Social Cognition," *Trends in Cognitive Sciences*, 8, 396–403.

18 Iacoboni, M. (2009) "Imitation, Empathy, and Mirror Neurons," *Annual Review of Psychology*, 60, 1–19.

19 See Hastings, Paul D., Zahn-Waxler, Carolyn and McShane, Kelly, "We Are, by Nature, Moral Creatures: Biological Bases of Concern for Others," in *Handbook of Moral Development*, edited by Melanie Killen and Judith Smetana, Mahwah, New Jersey: Lawrence Erlbaum Associates, 2006.

20 See especially Ian Ravenscroft (1998) "What is it Like to be Someone Else? Simulation and Empathy," in *Ratio*, XI, 170–185; Robert M. Gordon (1995) "Simulation Without Introspection or Inference from Me to You," in *Mental Simulation*, ed. Martin Davies and Tony Stone, Oxford: Blackwell, and Paul Harris (1992) "From Simulation to Folk Psychology: The Case for Development," in *Mind and Language*, 120: 120–144.

21 See Alvin Goldman (1995) "Simulation and Interpersonal Utility," in *Ethics*, 105: 709–726. See also Robert M. Gordon (1995) "Sympathy, Simulation, and the Impartial Spectator," in *Ethics*, 105: 727–742. See also Alvin Goldman (1993) "Ethics and Cognitive Science," in *Ethics*, 103: 337–360 and Alvin Goldman (1995) "Empathy, Mind, and Morals," in *Mental Simulation*, ed. Martin Davies and Tony Stone, Oxford: Blackwell.

22 Stueber defends empathy and simulation as the primary way we learn about others, versus "theory-theory" versions which claim we learn by applying theoretical information learned externally.

23 These quotes are from his works *Jokes and their Relation to the Unconscious* (1905) and *Group Psychology and the Analysis of the Ego* (1949), respectively.

Quoted in "History of the Concept of Empathy," *Empathy and Its Development*, p. 25.

24 This quote is from his 1959 essay "Introspection, Empathy, and Psychoanalysis," quoted in "History of the Concept of Empathy," pp. 29–30. Kohut captures the sense in which empathizing is a "mode of cognition which is specifically attuned to the perception of complex psychological configurations." (p. 30).

25 Carl Rogers (1959) "The Necessary and Sufficient Conditions of Therapeutic Personality Change," *Journal of Consulting Psychology*, 21(2): 95–103, p. 99.

26 Described in Martin Hoffman (2000) *Empathy and Moral Development: Implications for Caring and Justice*, Cambridge: Cambridge University Press.

27 See Daniel Batson, C., Lishner, D., Carpenter, A., Dulin, L., Harjusola-Webb, S., Stocks, E., Gale, S., Hassan, O. and Sampat, B. (2003) "...As You Would Have Them Do Unto You: Does Imagining Yourself in the Other's Place Stimulate Moral Action?" *Personality and Social Psychology Bulletin*, 29(9): 1190–1201.

28 There is a significant amount of literature on psychopathy and autism, which I do not examine here. The most important discussions include Jeffrie Murphy's (1972) "Moral Death: A Kantian Essay on Psychopathy," *Ethics*, 82: 284–298; John Deigh (1995) "Empathy and Universalizability," *Ethics*, 105: 743–763; R.J.R. Blair (1996) "Theory of Mind in the Psychopath," *Journal of Forensic Psychiatry*, 7: 15–25; Jeanette Kennett (2000) "Autism, Empathy and Moral Agency," *The Philosophical Quarterly*, 52(208): 340–357; Shaun Nichols (2004) *Sentimental Rules*, Oxford: Oxford University Press, Chapter 3; David Shoemaker (2007) "Moral Address, Moral Responsibility, and the Boundaries of Moral Community," *Ethics*, 118: 70–108. See also Alison Denham (2008) "Psychopathy, Empathy, and Moral Motivation," in *Essays on Iris Murdoch*, ed. J. Broakes, Oxford: Oxford University Press.

29 There is extended discussion of this topic in the volume of collected essays by Walter Sinnot-Armstrong (2008) *Moral Psychology: The Neuroscience of Morality: Emotion, Brain Disorders, and Development, Volume 3*, Cambridge: MIT Press. This includes the following essays in this book: Victoria McGeer's "Varieties of Moral Agency: Lessons from Autism (and Psychopathy)," Jeanette Kennett's "Reasons, Reverence, and Value," Heidi Maibom's "The Will to Conform," and Frederique de Vignemont and Uta Frith's "Autism, Morality, and Empathy."

30 *Empathy and Moral Development*, p. 36. See Shoemaker's "Moral Address, Moral Responsibility, and the Boundaries of Moral Community" for discussion of what autistics might do in order to make up for this kind of knowledge.

31 Martin Hoffman was the first to recommend adopting a definition of empathy that embraced the various modes of empathetic responses. Martin Hoffman (1982) "Development of Prosocial Motivation: Empathy and Guilt," in N. Eisenberg, ed. *The Development of Prosocial Behavior*, New York: Academic Press, and Martin Hoffman (1982) "The Measurement of Empathy," in *Emotion in Infants*, ed. C.E. Izard, New York: Cambridge University Press.

32 I use Hoffman's distinction in five modes of empathic arousal (*Empathy and Moral Development*, Chapter 4) to identify the more cognitively-advanced kinds of empathy.

Chapter 2   What is Empathy?

1 Justin D'Arms (2000) "Empathy and Evaluative Inquiry," *Chicago-Kent Law Review*, 74(4): 1478.

2 Peter Goldie (1999) "How We Think of Others' Emotions," *Mind and Language*, 14(4): 394–423, p. 409. *Central imagination* is imagining from the perspective of a specific individual, and in this case, it is specifically from the perspective of the other person.

3 Robert Gordon, "Sympathy, Simulation, and the Impartial Spectator," p. 172.

4 This argument is first given by Mark Barnett, "Empathy and Related Responses in Children," in *Empathy and Its Development* (1987). Goldman follows in "Ethics and Cognitive Science," (1993) and D'Arms in "Empathy and Evaluative Inquiry," (2000). For discussion of the research methods in evaluating emotional match, valence, or blending, see Becky Omdahl (1995) *Cognitive Appraisal, Emotion and Empathy*, Mahwah, NJ: Erlbaum Associates, pp. 16–17.

5 For a helpful overview of the debates in the psychology literature, see Becky Omdahl's *Cognitive Appraisal, Emotion and Empathy*, pp. 14–21.

6 The term "empathy" was introduced into the English language by Edward Titchener in 1909 as a translation of the word *Einfuhlung*.

7 David Hume (1740/2000), ed. Norton and Norton, *Treatise of Human Nature*, Oxford: Oxford University Press, p. 206.

8 Ibid., p. 209. Hume says sympathy is when "we enter into the sentiments" of others, and "partake of their pleasure and uneasiness," p. 234. He also argues that empathy is that part of human personality that impedes self-interest and allows people to cooperate with others. This capacity to relate to the emotions of others is ultimately the basis of our concern for others in society.

9 Although there is no consensus regarding the definition of empathy among philosophers, all philosophers distinguish sympathy from empathy in this way. See, for example, Douglas Chismar (1998) "Empathy and Sympathy: The Important Difference," *Journal of Value Inquiry*, 22: 257–266. See also D'Arms, "Empathy and Evaluative Inquiry," pp. 1477–1479, Stephen Darwall, "Empathy, Sympathy, Care," and Peter Goldie, "How We Think of Others' Emotions." See also Elliot Sober and David Sloan Wilson (1998) *Unto Others: The Evolution and Psychology of Unselfish Behavior*, Cambridge: Harvard University Press, pp. 232–236.

10 Stephen Darwall (1998) "Empathy, Sympathy, Care," *Philosophical Studies*, 89(2–3): 273.

11 Psychologists seem to be more mindful of the difference. See the discussion in Nancy Eisenberg and Janet Strayer, "Critical Issues in the Study of Empathy," in *Empathy and Its Development*, pp. 6–7 and Wispe, "History of the Concept of Empathy," *Empathy and Its Development*, p. 30.

12 Some suggest that empathy and sympathy will not occur independently and that sympathy does require "mind-reading" capacities. This is Shaun Nichols' claim in *Sentimental Rules*, pp. 38–39.

13 *A Treatise of Human Nature*, p. 206.

14 Ibid., p. 208.

15 Hume says this more clearly in his discussion in Section 6, "Of the Influence of the Imagination on the Passions," p. 273.

16 This term is common among both philosophers and psychologists. See Elliott Sober and David Sloan Wilson, *Unto Others*, Peter Goldie, "How We Think of Others' Emotions" and Stephen Darwall, "Empathy, Sympathy, Care."

17 Described by Ross Thompson in "Empathy and Emotional Understanding," in *Empathy and Its Development*, pp. 131–133, and Mark A. Barnett, "Empathy and Related Responses in Children," in *Empathy and Its Development*, pp. 148–153. See, for example, the amusing expressions of an adult and reflected in an infant in Goldman's "Empathy, Mind, and Morals," p. 197.

18 There are a number of studies on this topic and some take motor mimicry to be first depicted by Adam Smith. See Janet Bavelas et al., "Motor Mimicry as Primitive Empathy," in Eisenberg and Strayer, Chapter 14.

19 See Gallese, V., Keysers, C. and Rizzolatti, G. (2004) "A Unifying View of the Basis of Social Cognition," *Trends in Cognitive Sciences*, 8: 396–403; Rizzolatti, G., Fadiga, L., Gallese, V. and Fogassi, L. (1996) "Premotor Cortex and the Recognition of Motor Actions," *Cognitive Brain Research*, 3: 131–141; Marco Iacoboni, M. (2009) "Imitation, Empathy, and Mirror Neurons," *Annual Review of Psychology*, 60: 1–19.

20 Remy Debes (2010) "Which Empathy, Limitations in the Mirrored 'Understanding' of Emotion," *Synthese*, 175(2): 219–239.

21 There are two other states that are similar to, but distinct from, empathy as emotional contagion and sympathy: *emotional sharing* and *emotional identification*. These terms are used by Peter Goldie in "How We Think of Others' Emotions," p. 407, but are also common in the psychology literature. *Emotional sharing* is a state in which two individuals share the same emotion, and know that they share it. An example of this is when a number of people (or just more than one) share a feeling that they receive by the same stimulus, such as the happiness of attending a comedy show or the sadness of experiencing a tragedy. After a fire, flood, or news of death, people may feel the same emotion, and insofar as they take themselves to be responding to the same event in the same way, they experience emotional sharing. This, though, is different from emotional contagion. In emotional sharing, a specific event causes the emotion in two people. In emotional contagion, the presence of the emotion in one person prompts it in the other. Emotional identification sounds similar to empathy, but it is usually thought to be distinct, or at least not a standard case of empathy. In emotional identification, one person identifies with another's emotions, and "one's sense of one's own identity to some extent *merges* with one's sense of the identity of another." Ibid., p. 408. Emotional identification occurs primarily between intimates, people who are close to each other and involved in each others' lives. The intimate nature of the relationship makes it possible for each person to feel the other's emotions and identify with the emotion in the other person in an extremely deep way. For example, if one person in a couple has cancer or a terminal illness, and the partner feels deeply the other's sadness and fear, and identifies with the other person's feeling because he takes the other to be part of himself, then this is emotional identification. In another case, a parent might identify with a child's feeling in a way she feels the child's excitement as the child does. Emotional identification involves a mutual bond between individuals that is absent

in emotional sharing. It may plausibly be considered a kind of intense empathy, since it occurs in intimate relations, but is not what we generally refer to as empathy.

22 Adam Smith (1759/2002) *The Theory of Moral Sentiments*, Cambridge: Cambridge University Press, p. 12.

23 I discuss this more in the following chapter (Section 3.3.1).

24 It is also useful to distinguish perspectival from aperspectival imagination. Peter Goldie uses the terms "central" and "acentral" imagination to describe this difference. Acentral imagination involves taking up an imaginative stance by "imagining from no point of view." This imagination is not performed from a particular person's perspective, but from an external or objective perspective. "How We Think of Others' Emotions," p. 410. This is acentral imagination, which is imagining things, say, as one would a scene from a movie. For example, as I walk from my apartment to a restaurant downtown, I may imagine that I am being approached by a stalker, but instead of imagining it from his perspective or mine, I imagine the situation from an external viewpoint, in a way that the stalker is unseen by me. Thus, what I imagine is a scenario where a woman (myself) is walking downtown with a stalker following behind, but from no particular person's vantage point.

25 This term corresponds to Hoffman's "self-focused role-taking" (and the second to his "other-focused role-taking") in *Empathy and Moral Development*, p. 54.

26 Cited in Holton, Richard and Langton, Rae (1998) "Empathy and Animal Ethics," *Singer and his Critics*, Oxford: Blackwell Press, p. 412. See Kahneman and Tversky (1982) "The Simulation Heuristic," in Slovic, Kahneman and Tversky, eds. *Judgment Under Uncertainty: Heuristics and Biases*, Cambridge: Cambridge University Press.

27 Goldie's discussion of empathy is different from my own, primarily because he takes empathy to be about imagining how someone else feels from their narrative perspective, and not about shared emotions, which I take to be crucial to the definition of empathy.

28 For discussion on a variety of problems of empathic accuracy, see William Ickes, ed. (1997) *Empathic Accuracy*, New York: Guilford Press.

29 Consider Robert Gordon's example of the actor Ray McAnally playing a Prime Minister. He realized when he was filming a scene at 10 Downing Street, surrounded by pictures of other Prime Ministers, himself in the middle of the Prime Minister's world, "It's not that I'm *pretending* to be the Prime Minister...I *am* the Prime Minister." The idea is that while he was pretending to be the Prime Minister, he was so other-focused in the Prime Minister's psychology, he *forgot* that he was doing so. See Robert M. Gordon, "Simulation Without Introspection," p. 65.

30 Not many theorists who study empathy identify this mode. Psychologist Martin Hoffman calls it "combination" empathy, where observers can shift back and forth between other-focused and self-focused role-taking and "experience them as co-occurring parallel processes" (*Empathy and Moral Development*, p. 58).

31 John Deigh, "Empathy and Universalizability," p. 759.

32 Sometimes, theorists mistakenly treat empathy and role-taking as equivalent, but empathizing is affective in a way that imaginative role-taking is not.

33   Piaget cited in "History of the Concept of Empathy," p. 24.
34   Goldman says that paradigmatic cases of empathy are those that "consist first of taking the perspective of another person, that is, imaginatively assuming one or more of the other person's mental states" which "are then operated upon (automatically) by psychological processes, which generate further states that (in favorable cases) are similar to, or homologous to, the target person's states." "Ethics and Cognitive Science," p. 351.
35   "Empathy, Sympathy, Care," p. 261.
36   "Empathy, Sympathy, Care," pp. 267–268.
37   The psychologist Kohut emphasized that empathy involves thinking oneself into another's perspective in a way that involves a "vicarious introspection" where we feel another's experience "as if it were our own and thus revive our inner experiences" of something similar. This way of empathizing is more projective, but could still be considered empathizing. (H. Kohut (1959) "Introspection, Empathy, and Psychoanalysis," *Journal of the American Psychoanalytic Association*, 7: 459–483, p. 461. I discuss empirical studies on these types of empathy in Chapter 4.)
38   For further discussion on this topic, see the essays in William Ickes, ed. (1997) *Empathic Accuracy*, New York: The Guilford Press.
39   Even Martin Hoffman's theory of empathy includes this aspect, even though he focuses on empathic distress. See *Empathy and Moral Development*, p. 30.
40   See especially Peter Goldie, "How We Think of Others' Emotions."
41   "Empathy and Universalizability," p. 761, my emphasis.
42   Martha Nussbaum (2001) *Upheavals of Thought*, Cambridge: Cambridge University Press, p. 329.
43   The literature in *Empathy and Its Development* confirms this. See also philosopher Nancy Sherman, who adheres to the traditional understanding of empathy as requiring similar feelings: empathy is the "emotional and cognitive capacity to enter another's world sufficiently to identify with that person...through an act of imagination and simulation we appreciate, however fleetingly, something of what another experiences, sees, fears, and desires." Nancy Sherman (1998) "Empathy, Respect, and Humanitarian Intervention," *Ethics and International Affairs*, Vol. 12, p. 115. See also Justin D'Arms, "Empathy and Evaluative Inquiry," p. 1481.
44   On the view that emotions are cognitive, an emotion essentially involves making a judgment or an evaluation. Michael Stocker, who endorses this view, says that emotions in general are central to moral evaluation, because "emotions are grounds of evaluations of people, actions, and practices, and [that] emotions figure in making moral evaluations." Michael Stocker and Elizabeth Hegemon (1996) *Valuing Emotions*, Cambridge: Cambridge University Press, p. 138. The view that emotions are non-cognitive supposes that emotions are pure feelings, and that they lack meaning, intentionality, and representation (in that they do not represent anything about the world). Hume's view of emotions is an example, for he states that emotions are primarily impressions (or copies of) another's idea and that they do not involve any sort of linguistic representation.
45   This is a version of Gerald Gaus's theory of emotion in Gerald Gaus (1990) *Value and Justification*, Cambridge: Cambridge University Press, Chapter 2.
46   In a cognitive theory of emotion, it is possible for emotions and beliefs to conflict, because the emotion is hooked up to some cognitive state with

stronger affective feeling; it is also possible to have an emotional response without *significant* propositional content. For other concerns with a cognitive account of emotions, see Cheshire Calhoun, "Cognitive Emotions?" in Robert C. Solomon, ed. (2003) *What is an Emotion? Classic and Contemporary Readings*, Oxford: Oxford University Press.

47 The account I endorse here suggests that (many) emotions such as empathy contain moral judgments, rather than the view that moral judgments contain emotions. The latter view is defended by Jesse Prinz as *emotionalism*, or the view that moral judgments are grounded in (non-cognitive) emotional responses. See Jesse Prinz (2007) *The Emotional Construction of Morals*, Oxford: Oxford University Press, Chapters 1–2.

48 On Gaus's view, an emotion can have as its content a variety of psychological states, and is similar to beliefs and intentions. For example, X(Fear) [Tigers], X(Fear)[Tigers are running after me] and (fear) [I believe tigers are running after me] are different emotions. Since my aim here is to explain the affective and cognitive dimensions of empathy, my discussion here is cursory. For a detailed discussion see *Value and Justification*, p. 53ff.

49 Using this method, it seems to follow that a sadist could empathize with a masochist, since he understands and appreciates that the other finds "pleasure in his pain." They both take pleasure in the masochist's pain and feel a similar emotion—pleasure.

50 Compare, for example, Jesse Prinz, who argues that moral judgments contain emotions such as empathy, and that they are inextricably linked; moral concepts are essentially related to emotions. My view is that emotions have an epistemic role or component, and while our emotions influence moral judgment, they are not sufficient or constitutive of our moral judgments. See *The Emotional Construction of Morals*, Chapter 3.

51 See Chapter 2 of *Empathy and Moral Development*. One study reports children as young as nine performing spontaneous role-taking empathy, so it is safe to say that perspective-taking empathy develops later in life, as it requires greater cognitive development.

52 His explanation of how cognitive development is directly related to the development of empathy is in *Empathy and Moral Development*, Chapter 3.

53 He says a mechanism of empathy is one which tends "to influence the emotional reactions of one person—'the observer'—so as to produce a match (roughly, some sort of congruence) between these emotions and those of another person—the 'model.'" "Empathy and Evaluative Inquiry," p. 1480ff.

54 Martin Hoffman, "Development of Prosocial Motivation: Empathy and Guilt," in N. Eisenberg, ed. (1982) *The Development of Prosocial Behavior*, New York: Academic Press and "The Measurement of Empathy," in C.E. Izard, ed. (1982) *Emotion in Infants*, New York: Cambridge University Press.

55 Comprehensive views have been adopted by other psychologists, for example, Mark H. Davis (1994) *Empathy: A Social Psychological Approach*, Madison, WI: Brown and Benchmark, and Becky Omdahl (1995) *Cognitive Appraisal, Emotion, and Empathy*, Mahwah, NJ: Erlbaum Associates.

56 This figure is a modified version of the "Organizational Model" of empathy presented in Mark H. Davis, *Empathy: A Social Psychological Approach*, p. 13. It is slightly changed to better show the causal relations between the four states. It is worth noting that Michael Morrell also adapts this approach to empathy. See Michael Morrell (2010) *Empathy and Democracy: Feeling,*

Thinking, and Deliberation, University Park: Penn State Press. Morrell refers to this as the "process model of empathy," p. 62.

57   See also primate and evolutionary scientist Frans B.M. de Waal's "Russian doll" model of empathy that includes various levels of emotional contagion and perspective-taking, for the purposes of investigating empathic behavior in certain primates. See Frans B.M. de Waal (2008) "Putting the Altruism Back into Altruism: The Evolution of Empathy," *The Annual Review of Psychology*, 59: 279–300, pp. 287–288.

58   *Unto Others*, p. 234. Sober and Wilson say that O's actually feeling E is required in order to be *accurate* empathy. Otherwise, it would be a misfire of empathy based on a false belief.

59   For Hume and the psychologists, there is no the need for a person to *believe* that someone has an emotion in order for it to be transmitted. She must have an "idea" that converts to a lively impression. This account at least provides an explanation of how the transmission takes place. For an interesting discussion on this topic, see Shaun Nichols (2004) "Imagining and Believing: The Promise of a Single Code," *Journal of Aesthetics and Art Criticism*, 62(6): 129–139.

60   See *Rediscovering Empathy*, pp. 2–3. Stueber defends empathy as the epistemically central method for understanding other agents within folk psychology, and states that even if theoretical knowledge is used to obtain knowledge of other minds, empathy (as a kind of simulation) plays a distinct and central role apart from this in coming to know other minds. (See his Chapter 3, which addresses this topic.)

61   See especially the work of Alvin Goldman, Robert Gordon, and Karsten Stueber, who defend the idea that empathy as a kind of mental simulation can yield knowledge of other minds.

62   Justin D'Arms also argues that empathy can play a crucial role in acquiring justified beliefs, and says that some experiences of empathy provide us with information that can "expand our sensibilities [our dispositions to experience particular kinds of emotional reactions in response to particular sorts of cues] and convictions so as to make room for new sources of value and interest." Ibid., p. 1494, inserted definition of "sensibility" on p. 1490.

63   Martin Hoffman shows that cognition plays an important role in the *development* of empathic abilities. (*Empathy and Moral Development*, Chapter 4.)

64   Lorraine Code, "I Know Just How You Feel: Empathy and the Problem of Epistemic Authority," p. 92.

Chapter 3   The Epistemic Functions of Empathy

1   *Rediscovering Empathy; Agency, Folk Psychology, and the Human Sciences*, pp. 5, 19, 26. The question he addresses is, do we get knowledge of other minds by knowing others by using external knowledge or theories about others and apply them to them, so that "empathy as a form of mental simulation or imitation is epistemically superfluous"? Or is simulating another's mind our primary way of knowing them? My view is that empathy one of the very important ways that we get knowledge about other minds, but I will not seek to defend empathy against the "theory-theory" view of other minds. Nancy

Sherman (1998) and Justin D'Arms (2000) also suggest that empathy has epistemic functions. See also Derek Matravers (2011) "Empathy as a Route to Knowledge," in *Empathy: Philosophical and Psychological Perspectives*, ed. Amy Coplan and Peter Goldie, Oxford: Oxford University Press.

2 Stueber offers a theory of understanding others (in the human sciences) that places empathy as simulation prominently in the process of learning about others and ourselves. In his second chapter ("Folk Psychology and Rational Agency"), Stueber argues that having access to our own reasons for action from a first person perspective is central to our understanding of ourselves, and defends this as part of the plausibility of the folk psychology conception of the mind. The argument I make here builds on his defense of empathy.

3 Stephen Darwall, "Empathy, Sympathy, Care," p. 270.

4 Remy Debes, "Which Empathy? Limitations in the Mirrored 'Understanding' of Emotion," p. 4.

5 Jodi Halpern (2001) *From Detached Concern to Empathy: Humanizing Medical Practice*, Oxford: Oxford University Press, p. 87.

6 Ibid., p. 88.

7 Justin D'Arms, Nancy Sherman and Remy Debes discuss intelligibility of emotions: D'Arms says that "when we have an affective response to a situation, we look for, and are sensitized to, features of the situation that render that response at least intelligible, and at best appropriate." ("Empathy and Evaluative Inquiry," p. 1496) Sherman says that "empathy is a form of understanding" and "informs our appreciation of others." (Nancy Sherman (1998) "Empathy and Imagination," in *Midwest Studies in Philosophy, Volume XXII: The Philosophy of Emotions*, ed. Peter A. French and Howard K. Wettstein, Notre Dame: University of Notre Dame Press, p. 110). Remy Debes argues that empathy involves finding another's emotion intelligible in "Which Empathy? Limitations in the Mirrored 'Understanding' of Emotion," p. 4ff.

8 Hoffman's *Empathy and Moral Development* focuses specifically on empathic distress. While the majority of his conclusions and arguments address empathic distress (which involves empathy focused on a victim), these modes of arousal do not apply only to distress and can include happy emotions.

9 *Empathy and Moral Development*, pp. 37–38.

10 Ibid., p. 46.

11 *Empathy and Moral Development*, p. 49.

12 See also Nancy Eisenberg et al. (1997) "The Development of Empathic Accuracy," in William Ickes' *Empathic Accuracy*, New York: Guilford Press, p. 77 for a summary of the different ways one might role-take. John Flavell's role-taking model of empathy is essentially an information-processing model of how we know others' perspectives. It is discussed in Goldstein and Michaels (1985) *Empathy: Development, Training, and Consequences*, Hillsdale, NJ: Erlbaum Associates, p. 21.

13 *Empathy and Moral Development*, pp. 58–59.

14 This is Remy Debes' term. He argues that "mirrored" empathy (a kind of contagious empathy) involves trivial understanding and that this is not the same as genuine understanding required for empathy to be a kind of normative judgment in "Which Empathy? Limitations in the Mirrored 'Understanding' of Emotion."

15 *Rediscovering Empathy*, p. 20.

16   Ibid., p. 21.

17   See the essays in Eisenberg's *Altruistic Emotion, Cognition, and Behavior* and Ervin Staub's commentary in *Empathy and its Development* where he states: participatory empathy (a kind of cognitive empathy) "is directly involved in gathering information and accurately knowing another person" (p. 106) and Janet Strayer, "Affective and Cognitive Perspectives on Empathy," in *Empathy and its Development*, p. 223.

18   Psychologists Eisenberg, Miller, Strayer, and Kohut agree that empathy has products that are not behavioral and that there are ways to measure empathy that do not focus on the resulting behavior. (See Nancy Eisenberg and Janet Strayer (1987) *Empathy and Its Development*, Cambridge: Cambridge University Press, p. 389.) See their concluding chapter, "Empathy Viewed in Context," Strayer's Chapter 10, Eisenberg and Miller's Chapter 13, and Batson's Chapter 16 of this book for evidence of this idea.

19   Simulation theorist Alvin Goldman's term is *mindreading*, and he argues that by representing another's mental state to oneself, one can make inferences about that person's feelings, values, responses, or preferences. Alvin Goldman (2006) *Simulating Minds: The Philosophy, Psychology and Neuroscience of Mindreading*, Oxford: Oxford University Press, Chapter 1.

20   *Rediscovering Empathy*, p. 124. Alvin Goldman's "simulation" theory of understanding also consists in three distinct phases, but with different inputs.

21   Stueber's model of empathic process (like Goldman's) is essentially an information-processing model. Goldman argues that empathy can be used to gather information about others by simulating that person's emotions and facts about them via a hypothetical deliberation system, which then generates further knowledge about that person. "Every normal agent has a set of mental mechanisms for generating new mental states from initial ones, for example, a decision-making system that takes desires and beliefs as inputs and churns out decisions as outputs. Such mechanisms or systems might be employed in a derivative fashion to simulate and ascribe mental states to oneself and others." Alvin Goldman (1995) "Simulation and Interpersonal Utility," *Ethics*, 105, p. 718.

22   In a statement attacking an Israeli plan to demolish Palestinian homes in Gaza, Lapid cited seeing a suffering Palestinian woman on TV who reminded him of his grandmother: "I did think, when I saw a picture on the TV of an old woman on all fours in the ruins of her home looking under some floor tiles for her medicines—I did think, 'What would I say if it were my grandmother?'" Lapid engaged in perspective-taking empathy even though the woman was an enemy, and viewed Israel's actions through the eyes of its enemies. "Israeli Official Offers Empathy but Hits a Nerve" by James Bennet, *New York Times*, May 24, 2004.

23   See Nancy Eisenberg et al., "The Development of Empathic Accuracy" in William Ickes (1997) *Empathic Accuracy*, New York: Guilford Press, for a discussion of the role of perspective-taking in empathizing.

24   "Simulation and Interpersonal Utility," p. 723. Empathizing with one's countrymen, friends, family or social group yields more accurate information because there is more content-based similarity; the two have more in common in terms of the content of their beliefs, values, etc.

25   *From Detached Concern to Empathy: Humanizing Medical Practice*, p. 87.

26 Ibid., p. 91.
27 Ibid., p. 91.
28 Ibid., p. 92.
29 This definition of a reason follows T.M. Scanlon (1998) *What We Owe to Each Other*, Cambridge: Harvard University Press, Chapter 1.
30 Korsgaard, Christine (1996) *The Sources of Normativity*, Cambridge: Cambridge University Press, p. 143. Korsgaard's central argument regarding normativity is that obligations come about when someone requests that others view him as he views himself, as a person with "demandingness," which he has in virtue of being a human. That is, he makes himself a law to others by requiring them to acknowledge his humanity; from this arises the obligation to respect him.
31 Darwall agrees: if we cannot see another's reasons for an emotion, then we cannot participate with others in the first-person emotion or attitude ("Sympathy, Empathy, Care," p. 270).
32 Since empathy involves making another's emotion intelligible in light of her situation and psychology, empathy is a faculty well-suited for identifying *agent-relative* reasons, or reasons that one particular agent has, but others do not. Empathizers are able to recognize that others have reasons of their own because they suppose the other has ends and goals that are distinct from one's own. Empathy affectively engages one's interest in another, and makes it possible for her to appreciate the other's reasons and see them as plausible.
33 For more on this, see Lorraine Code (1994) "'I Know Just How You Feel': Empathy and the Problem of Epistemic Authority," in Ellen Singer More and Maureen A. Milligan, eds. *The Empathic Practitioner: Empathy, Gender, and Medicine*, New Brunswick: Rutgers University Press, p. 92.
34 Rogers defines empathy as "to perceive the internal frame of reference of another with accuracy and with the emotional components and meanings which pertain thereto as if one were the person, but without ever losing the 'as if' condition." Rogers, C.R. (1959) "A Theory of Therapy, Personality and Interpersonal Relationships, as Developed in the Client-centered Framework," in S. Koch (ed.), *Psychology: A Study of Science*, Vol. 3, pp. 210–211; 184–256). New York: McGraw Hill. For him, understanding is crucial to empathy because it requires grasping the other's perspective on life "as if" you were the other person.
35 Clinicians such as Sigmund Freud, Carl Rogers and Heinz Kohut emphasized that empathy is an affective response on the part of the observer (namely, feeling the other's emotion) as well as a cognitive response of seeing the other's emotion as intelligible, and that the cognitive and affective responses go hand in hand. See "History of the Concept of Empathy," by Lauren Wispe in *Empathy and Its Development*, pp. 25, 29–30.
36 This idea is also expressed by Adam Smith. If we hear someone expressing "general lamentations," it prompts a "disposition to sympathize" but creates "rather a curiosity to inquire into his situation..." *Theory of Moral Sentiments*, p. 14.
37 "Empathy and Evaluative Inquiry," p. 1495.
38 In direct association, someone associates the other's emotion with her own experience, takes the other's emotion to be appropriate in the situation,

and responds by feeling the same emotion that the other does. Mediated association empathy and role-taking empathy are cognitively advanced types of empathy that require the observer to mentally process the other's situation and her emotion; if she responds by feeling the other's emotion, then it must be because she takes it to be an appropriate response given the situation.

39 *Upheavals of Thought*, p. 329.
40 Thanks to Jonny Anomaly for pressing me on this issue. We have emotions that we are ashamed of or disapprove of, such as inappropriate anger, misdirected jealousy, and the instinct to retaliate for insignificant harms. We can "empathize" with (or sympathetically understand) those who have such emotions, when we recognize that although we disapprove of the other's feeling that emotion, we also disapprove of it in ourselves and are thus sensitive to that person's situation.
41 Adam Smith, *Theory of Moral Sentiments*, p. 20.
42 This is precisely Debes' point. The higher-order empathy requires understanding and approval of an emotion in a way that is normative, and is distinct from empathy that would result via direct representation or "mirroring" another's actions, somatic sensations and emotions (the thesis advanced by social neuroscientists).
43 Donald Davidson (1986) "Judging Interpersonal Interests," *Foundations of Social Choice Theory*, edited by Jon Elster and Aanund Hylland, Cambridge: Cambridge University Press, p. 205.
44 Olga Tsoudis (2002) "The Influence of Empathy in Mock Jury Criminal Cases: Adding to the Affect Control Model," *Western Criminology Review*, 4(1): 55–67.
45 Ibid., p. 64.
46 Douglas O. Linder (1996) "Juror Empathy and Race," *Tennessee Law Review*, 63: 887–916. Linder cites lawyers' writings since 1929 that bolster support for this thesis.
47 Ibid., p. 907.
48 Ibid., p. 900.
49 In fact, according to psychologists, the empathy of facial mimicry, motor mimicry, and emotional contagion do change people's feelings and dispositions, especially in those of children. See Ross A. Thompson, "Empathy and Emotional Understanding: The Early Development of Empathy," *Empathy and Its Development*, pp. 119–145.
50 "Juror Empathy and Race," p. 916.
51 "Empathy and Imagination," p. 111.
52 Justin D'Arms argues that empathy is for "learning about what matters and why." ("Empathy and Evaluative Inquiry," p. 1470) He says that some experiences of empathy provide us with information that can "expand our sensibilities [disposition to experience particular kinds of emotional reactions in response to particular sorts of cues] and convictions so as to make room for new sources of value and interest." ("Empathy and Evaluative Inquiry," p. 1494, definition of "sensibility" inserted from p. 1490.
53 Both quotes in "Empathy and Evaluative Enquiry," p. 1499.
54 See Richmond Campbell, who argues that there are transition phases between our emotions and our beliefs, and that sometimes they are

incongruous until the belief state dominates the habitual emotional reaction. (Campbell (2007) "What is a Moral Judgment," *Journal of Philosophy*, Vol. 104(7).)

55 Jurors who observe, for example, a quadriplegic victim of a criminal assault usually have a more intense empathetic reaction than appellate judges who know of the victim's quadriplegia only through a written record. The hypothesis is that observing another's distress, rather than merely imagining it, play an important role in provoking the conditioning, association, and mimicry that are part of strong empathetic reactions (Linder, "Juror Empathy and Race," p. 897).

56 *Rediscovering Empathy*, p. 3.

57 This is the first of his "Eleven Lessons" from *The Fog of War: Eleven Lessons from the Life of Robert S. McNamara*: Directed by Errol Morris, Sony Pictures Classics, 2003. McNamara was U.S. Secretary of Defense from 1961–1968.

58 Two classes of individuals, psychopathic and autistic people, have been said to lack the ability to recognize another's emotion or the ability to appreciate the significance of another's emotions, and presumably lack the epistemic abilities that I outline here.

59 Temple Grandin (2008) *The Way I See It: A Personal Look at Autism and Asperger's*, Arlington TX: Future Horizons, pp. 136–137.

60 Ibid., p. 138.

Chapter 4   Empathy, Altruism and Normative Ethics

1 Michael Slote (2007) *The Ethics of Care and Empathy*, New York: Routledge, p. 13.

2 Ibid., p. 16.

3 The non-cognitive mode of *imitation* has been shown to have prosocial consequences and affects the way people perceive and interact with their social environment. Jean Decety and colleagues discovered that in studies where one subject was imitated (by mimicking his or her non-verbal behavior) and one subject was not, the imitated subject was more likely to help the experimenter when she tripped; another study tested the effects of mimicking language, and showed that when waitresses verbally mimicked their customers when taking their orders (as opposed to merely paraphrasing the order), they received better tips—the difference was more than 50 per cent between the amount of tips received from mimicry versus nonmimicry. Decety et al. conclude that mimicry "affects us in a way that goes beyond building a special bond with the mimicker. It makes us generally more prosocial as people." (Rick B. van Baaren, Jean Decety, Ap Dijksterhuis, Adries van der Leij and Matthijs L. van Leeuwen (2009) "Being Imitated: Consequences of Nonconsciously Showing Empathy," *The Social Neuroscience of Empathy*, edited by Jean Decety and William Ickes, Cambridge, MA: MIT Press, pp. 31–42.)

4 There are many more empirical studies on empathy and pro-social behavior in *Empathy and Its Development* and *Altruistic Emotion, Cognition and Behavior*.

5 His research started in the late 1970s but is collected in Batson (1991) *The Altruism Question: Toward a Social-Psychological Answer*, Hillsdale, NJ: Erlbaum Publishers.

6 Ibid., Chapter 8.

7 Ibid., p. 127.

8 Batson does not test what I called in Chapter 2 "dual-perspective empathy" (what Hoffman calls combination empathy) where one switches back and forth between another's perspective and one's own. It may of course be the case that some people *do* think in this way, but that Batson does not test for it in the experiment.

9 Daniel Batson, C., Lishner, D., Carpenter, A., Dulin, L., Harjusola-Webb, S., Stocks, E., Gale, S., Hassan, O. and Sampat, B. (2003) "'...As You Would Have Them Do Unto You': Does Imagining Yourself in the Other's Place Stimulate Moral Action?" *Personality and Social Psychology Bulletin*, 29(9): 1190–1201. The studies discussed here are from this article. For similar studies, see also Batson, C.D., Early, S. and Salvarani, G. (1997) "Perspective-taking: Imagining How Another Feels Versus Imagining How You Would Feel," *Personality and Social Psychology Bulletin*, 20: 751–758.

10 Batson's research is supported anecdotally by Adam Smith, who suggested that the capacity to "change places in fancy" with others is a principle that can "interest him in the fortune of others, and render [others'] happiness necessary to him, though he derives nothing from it, except the pleasure of seeing it." Adam Smith, *The Theory of Moral Sentiments*, pp. 11, 12.

11 "'...As You Would Have Them Do Unto You': Does Imagining Yourself in the Other's Place Stimulate Moral Action?" p. 1195.

12 Of the participants who had no perspective-taking instructions, 13 (of 24) flipped the coin, and of those who took up an imagine-self perspective, 15 (of 24) flipped the coin. This is a statistically insignificant difference, and shows that an imagine-self-perspective does not motivate choosing a just or fair action, at least defined in terms of the procedural justice of coin-flipping. In fact, when asked later what the most moral thing would have been to do, 0.71 of the participants in the no-perspective condition and 0.63 of those in the imagine-self condition thought that flipping the coin was the most moral, while only 0.33 of the imagine-other thought that coin-flipping was the most moral. Taking up the imagine-self perspective had virtually no effect in influencing the belief that flipping a coin would have been the most moral action to take in a situation where procedural justice could be achieved (coin-flipping) and distributive justice (assigning equal tasks) could not.

13 The researchers did not include an imagine-other condition, because they had clear evidence that this form of perspective-taking would induce not only distributive justice, but altruism.

14 Only 0.15 participants total flipped, and only 0.10 thought flipping the coin was the most moral thing to do.

15 *The Altruism Question*, p. 113.

16 *Empathy and Moral Development*, pp. 206–208.

17 *Empathy and Moral Development*, p. 62.

18 For example, Eva Kittay describes the inability of people to connect with her intellectually disabled daughter as follows: "her limitations in communication

make much of what goes on in her mind opaque to those around her" and what others "project onto her and what is really her own experience cannot but remain conjectures." See Eva Kittay (2005) "Equality, Dignity, and Disability," in Mary Ann Lyons and Fionnuala Waldron, eds. *Perspectives on Equality: The Second Seamus Heaney Lectures*, Dublin: The Liffey Press, p. 97.

19 Adam Smith argued that rational people will not empathize with those with a "loss of reason" because they feel "anguish...at the sight of such an object" and think that happiness "cannot be the reflection of any sentiment" of such a miserable person. *The Theory of Moral Sentiments*, p. 15. Smith's sentiment towards those with intellectual disabilities is unfortunate, but it may reflect what many "normal" adults feel when interacting with someone who is intellectually disabled. Consider your observations of persons with Down's syndrome, who typically have overt expressions of emotion, but that are often inappropriate. For example, they might laugh after spilling some milk. Since people with intellectual disabilities have odd emotional responses to some situations, we have difficulty identifying with them in virtue of the fact that the response is not rational.

20 *Empathy and Moral Development*, p. 62.

21 Hume made the same observation: "We sympathize more with persons contiguous to us, than with persons remote from us: With our acquaintances than with strangers: With our countrymen, than with foreigners." (*Treatise of Human Nature* (section 3.3.1), p. 371. He also notes that since we give the "same approbation to the same moral qualities" in one country and another, though, that sympathy may vary, but our esteem (or judgment of right and wrong) does not vary. Thus, he says, esteem does not proceed from sympathy.

22 *Empathy and Moral Development*, p. 213.

23 Ibid., p. 214.

24 Ibid., p. 216.

25 Hoffman states specifically that "*empathic morality, at least empathic morality alone, may not be enough*" to live up to moral philosophy's criterion of impartiality. (*Empathy and Moral Development*), p. 16.

26 Philosophers Karsten Stueber and Shaun Nichols dispute the empathy-altruism hypothesis. See Steuber's discussion of empathy and altruism in the Stanford Encyclopedia of Philosophy (http://plato.stanford.edu/entries/empathy/index.html) and Shaun Nichols, *Sentimental Rules*, Chapter 2. Nichols argues that studies in developmental theory indicate that "altruistic motivation is independent of sophisticated mindreading abilities like perspective-taking." *Sentimental Rules*, p. 48. Philosopher Elliot Sober and biologist David Sloan Wilson argue that Batson's psychological evidence for altruism is inconclusive and that there are better—evolutionary—explanations for altruism: altruistic people (and other animals) are more reproductively fit and evolutionarily stable than those who are not altruists. See Elliot Sober and David Sloan Wilson (1998) *Unto Others: The Evolution and Psychology of Unselfish Behavior*, Cambridge, MA: Harvard University Press.

27 See *Altruistic Emotion, Cognition, and Behavior*, p. 106.

28 Batson, *The Altruism Question*, p. 50.

29 Michael Slote, *The Ethics of Care and Empathy*, p. 15.

30 Ibid., p. 13.

31 Ibid., p. 16.
32 Ibid., p. 33.
33 Ibid., p. 31.
34 Ibid., p. 16.
35 This view is described in Chapter 2 of *The Ethics of Care and Empathy*.
36 Holton and Langton argue that empathy cannot be the basis for morality because it will be completely sentimental and subjective, and not objective or systematic. Richard Holton and Rae Langton, "Empathy and Animal Ethics," in *Singer and his Critics*, pp. 228–229.
37 *The Ethics of Care and Empathy*, p. 13.
38 *Empathy and Moral Development*, p. 228.
39 Hoffman even goes on to argue that empathy can motivate support for Rawls' difference principle, but I will not examine that argument here.
40 *Empathy and Moral Development*, p. 229.
41 Ibid., pp. 225–226.
42 Ibid., p. 226.
43 Slote says that our intuitions about empathy and obligations are that the more we empathize, the greater we believe our obligations to be, etc.
44 Martin Hoffman agrees: "in view of empathy's vulnerability to over-arousal and familiarity and here-and-now bias, I would not want to follow Hume and rely on collective empathic responses to validate moral judgments." *Empathy and Moral Development*, p. 246.
45 Although there are many interpretations of Hume's moral theory, I do not intend to survey them here. No matter if Hume is interpreted as a subjectivist, sentimentalist, emotivist, ideal observer theorist, general point of view theorist, or an expressivist about moral judgment, empathy is still an initial starting point for making moral judgments and is not constitutive of a moral judgment.
46 All quotes *The Ethics of Care and Empathy*, p. 18.
47 See, for example, the fetal images at http://www.priestsforlife.org/images/index.aspx; http://www.nrlc.org/abortion/facts/fetaldevelopment.html. Accessed February 27, 2011.
48 *The Ethics of Care and Empathy*, p. 13.
49 Hume suggested that when we share the affective responses of those with whom we have no connection, and feel pleasure because they are pleased, or pain because they are not, that emotion is caused by empathy and it is this sharing (or approving) of others' responses or sentiments that is the basis of making a moral judgment. David Hume, *Treatise of Human Nature*, pp. 234–235, and 369–378, Sections 2.2.5 and 3.3.1.
50 *Treatise of Human Nature*, Section 3.3.1 par. 30, p. 377.
51 Nancy Sherman, "Empathy and Imagination," pp. 111–112. Nussbaum similarly argues that empathy is not required for compassion, but may lead to it, in her *Upheavals of Thought*, pp. 329–334.
52 "Empathy and Imagination," pp. 111–112.
53 Ibid., p. 109.
54 Ibid., pp. 112–113.
55 Ibid., pp. 109–110.

56 Ibid., p. 113. In the following chapter, I explain what those regulative constraints might be and explain how they turn empathetic thinking into moral thinking and deliberation. My point here is that to avoid becoming simply freewheeling emotion, empathy should be guided by what I would describe as normative principles or eudaimonistic values in a theory of virtues that encourage emotional engagement and sensitivity to others.

57 Sherman argues in another paper that empathy is, in this way, relevant to making certain kinds of policy decisions, such as in motivating a commitment to humanitarian intervention. She implies that it is not enough to have knowledge of people in other societies; rather, insofar as empathy is central appreciating others' situation, empathetic capacities are important to "buttressing a theory of political humanitarianism" because empathy "predisposes us to active forms of respect and to a responsiveness to violations of respect." (Nancy Sherman (1998) "Empathy, Respect, and Humanitarian Intervention," *Ethics and International Affairs*, Volume 12, p. 115.)

Chapter 5   Empathy and Moral Deliberation

1 *Subjection and Subjectivity*, p. 42.

2 For a more detailed analysis of the requirement of intelligibility and the way that empathy expresses approval, see my Chapter 3.

3 "'…As You Would Have Them Do Unto You': Does Imagining Yourself in the Other's Place Stimulate Moral Action?" pp. 1190–1201.

4 *Subjection and Subjectivity: Psychoanalytic Feminism and Moral Philosophy*, p. 134.

5 Ibid., p. 134.

6 Ibid., p. 35.

7 Ibid., p. 134.

8 Ibid., p. 135.

9 Ibid., p. 135.

10 Ibid., p. 137.

11 Ibid., p. 60.

12 Stephen Darwall (2006) *The Second Person Standpoint: Morality, Respect, and Accountability*, Cambridge: Harvard University Press, p. 3.

13 Ibid., p. 170.

14 Ibid., p. 6.

15 Ibid., p. 48.

16 Ibid., p. 170.

17 Ibid., p. 48.

18 In addition, empathy can bring about feelings and attitudes that can motivate one to accept certain moral norms as governing her behavior. Empathy can be motivating because it "can interact with normative psychology in the exchange of reactive attitudes and the engendering of conscientious feelings and even normative acceptance." *The Second Person Standpoint*, p. 170.

19 *The Second Person Standpoint*, p. 48.

20 Ibid., p. 48.

21 Both quotes p. 43.

22 Representative theories include Kantian ethics, utilitarianism, and Rawls' theory of justice. Meyers argues that these theories cannot address prejudice, for they view it as an intellectual moral vice, rather than a problem that is rooted in feelings and cultural norms. Such theories lead to unjust social exclusion, the institutionalization of exclusion, and purposeful disregard of the viewpoint of the excluded. *Subjection and Subjectivity*, pp. 2–3.

23 Meyers' primary target is Kant's categorical imperative. She considers various ways empathy could be integrated into a universalizable maxim, but shows that they all fail. In my view, her characterization of Kant's ethics is oversimplified, for the categorical imperative is more than just universalizability. Moreover, Meyers does not take into account other elements of Kantian moral theory that are amenable to empathy. While she may be successful in showing that it is difficult to integrate empathy into a sole universalizable, consistent maxim, no moral theory, not even Kant's moral theory, would suggest that this is possible or desirable.

24 Although Meyers mentions a few "impartial reason" theories that *have* emphasized the importance of empathy (Tom Hill's integration of empathy into a Kantian theory of autonomy and Susan Okin's view of empathy as part of the Rawlsian veil of ignorance), she does not examine them in detail.

25 Immanuel Kant (1797/1996) Mary Gregor, ed. *The Metaphysics of Morals*, Cambridge: Cambridge University Press, Cambridge, p. 204 [6:456].

26 Ibid., p. 204. The distinction Kant makes roughly corresponds to my distinction between empathy as simulative imagination and empathy as emotional contagion.

27 Ibid., p. 205.

28 Ibid., p. 205.

29 See my Chapter 2 for further elaboration of contagious empathy. Modern examples include mimicry or imitation empathy and classically conditioned empathy.

30 *The Metaphysics of Morals*, p. 205.

31 Ibid., p. 205.

32 Ibid., p. 205.

33 This is her characterization of impartial moral theories in *Subjection and Subjectivity*, p. 2. Meyers also characterizes these beings as averse to affect, emotion, and feeling.

34 *The Ethics of Care and Empathy*, pp. 35–36.

35 From *The Ethics of Care and Empathy*: "I don't think we can know at this point whether social prejudices or stereotypes are responsible for (certain) mature adults' tendencies" to empathize with some more than others (pp. 35–36). Also, "The ethics of empathy may here be hostage to future biological and psychological research, but I don't think that takes away from its *promise* as a way of understanding and justifying (a certain view of) morality." (p. 36)

36 Ibid., p. 36.

37 Meyers' criticism of "impartial reason" is thus best interpreted as a criticism against Hobbesian reasoning. In her description of how "impartial reason" theories might make use of empathy, Meyers suggests that impartial would reason would ask questions like "Would I want to be treated like that if I were you?" (p. 39) or "How do my principles apply to you, given your

circumstances and subjectivity?" (p. 40). Such questions sound surprisingly similar to Thomas Hobbes' defense of the "reality" of the laws of nature.

38 Thomas Hobbes (1651/1996) Richard Tuck, ed. *Leviathan*, Cambridge: Cambridge University Press, Chapter 15, section 79, pp. 109–110, emphasis added.

39 In another passage, Hobbes more overtly suggests that empathetic perspective-taking is instrumental to determining whether an action is morally acceptable: "There is an easy rule to know upon a sudden, whether the action I be to do, be against the law of nature or not...*that a man imagine himself in the place of the party with whom he hath to do, and reciprocally him in his*. Which is no more but a changing, as it were, of the scales." S.A. Lloyd (2009) *Morality in the Philosophy of Thomas Hobbes: Cases in the Law of Nature*, Cambridge: Cambridge University Press, p. 17.

40 This illustration explains in another way Kavka's well-known argument that Hobbes' moral theory uses the Copper Rule. (See Gregory Kavka (1996) *Hobbesian Moral and Political Theory*, Princeton, NJ: Princeton University Press.)

41 Since the content of the moral law is based on *individual* desires and interests in Hobbes' view, there is no guarantee that the content of the moral law will be agreed upon by everyone who performs the test. That is, there is no guaranteed congruence between people's individual moral judgments.

42 Hobbes's recommendation to imagine the other's perspective thus does not compromise the rationalist character of his theory: the requirement to seek peace—by following moral constraints—is utility-maximizing and thus rational. Hobbes' recommendation for perspective-taking can even be given an egoist rationale: moral reasoning is in service to the Right of Nature.

43 "Simulation and Interpersonal Utility," p. 719.

44 Frederique de Vignemont and Uta Frith (2008) "Autism, Morality and Empathy," in Walter Sinnott-Armstrong, ed. *Moral Psychology Volume 3*, Cambridge: MIT Press, p. 273.

45 "Simulation and Interpersonal Utility," p. 721.

46 There are a number of different ways to measure utility in economics: ordinal utility (which measures preference rankings), cardinal utility (which measures the strength of preferences in their rankings), and expected utility (which measures preferences for certain lotteries or probabilities), etc. I will examine how empathy is used to calculate cardinal utility and not expected utility. Contemporary theorists who rely on interpersonal comparisons of utility to render judgments regarding social states now focus on comparing *strength of preference* across individuals. In social choice theory, for example, this is used to decide how to allocate resources by determining who is in the greatest need of resources, or who would enjoy or appreciate the use of scarce resources the most.

47 T.M. Scanlon argues that making an interpersonal comparison of utility can best be understood as asking, "Would it be better to be individual *j* in state *x*, or individual *i* in state *y*?" and then determining which outcome maximizes overall utility. He distinguishes three interpretations of the question: (1) as a value judgment, (2) as an *intrapersonal* comparison, or (3) as a question about the *strength* of people's preferences. Thomas Scanlon (1991) "The Moral Basis of Interpersonal Comparisons," in Jon Elster and John Roemer, eds. *Interpersonal Comparisons of Well-being*, Cambridge: Cambridge University Press, pp. 31–32.

48 Lionel Robbins is perhaps the most well-known economist who argued that mental states, including utilities, could not be measured. Lionel Robbins (1938) "Interpersonal Comparisons of Utility: A Comment," *The Economic Journal*, 48(192): 635–641.

49 John Harsanyi (1977) *Rational Behavior and Bargaining Equilibrium in Games and Social Situations*, Cambridge: Cambridge University Press, p. 53.

50 John Harsanyi (1982) "Morality and the Theory of Rational Behavior," in Amartya Sen and Bernard Williams, eds. *Utilitarianism and Beyond*, Cambridge: Cambridge University Press, p. 50, emphasis mine.

51 Thus, Harsanyi's idea of utility is best interpreted as "preference-satisfaction" and not expected utility, which is simply a representation of preferences. John Weymark argues that Harsanyi's discussion of psychological reactions and satisfaction as part of an interpersonal comparison reflects his belief that well-being is more than just preferences. John Weymark (1991) "A Reconsideration of the Harsanyi-Sen Debate on Utilitarianism," in Jon Elster and John Roemer, eds. *Interpersonal Comparisons of Well-being*, Cambridge: Cambridge University Press, p. 308.

52 Goldman even goes so far as to say that the information gathered from simulation can be considered empirically legitimate knowledge ascriptions in "Simulation and Interpersonal Utility," p. 721ff.

53 R.M. Hare (1963) *Freedom and Reason*, Oxford: Clarendon Press, p. 94.

54 John Rawls (1951) "Outline of a Decision Procedure for Ethics," in Samuel Freeman, ed. The *Collected Papers of John Rawls*, Cambridge: Harvard University Press, 1999, p. 3.

55 Ibid., p. 3.

56 John Deigh's description of moral evaluation seems similar to Rawls's ideal observer theory. He suggests that making a moral decision involves using empathy to figure out what is important to another person, and then using a "criterion by which to arbitrate" interpersonal conflicts. ("Empathy and Universalizability," p. 762.)

57 Deigh uses this distinction to describe the difference between "mature" empathy and "immature" empathy. ("Empathy and Universalizability," pp. 759–761.)

58 "Empathy and Universalizability," p. 760.

59 Diana Meyers, *Subjection and Subjectivity: Psychoanalytic Feminism and Moral Philosophy*, pp. 34–35. She discusses two kinds of empathy that are relevant to moral judgment: incident-specific empathy and broad empathy. Incident-specific empathy involves feeling another's emotion and imaginatively experiencing another's state of mind at a specific time and trying to understand what she is going through at that moment. The latter is more expansive, and while it is based on an affective experience, involves emotionally connecting and engage with the other as a whole, trying to understand what it is like to be that person in general, thinking about who she is as a person. I discuss her theory in greater detail in the following chapter.

60 *Upheavals of Thought*, p. 334. Nussbaum argues that a villain can empathize with her victim, but on my view, it is a mistake to see a villain's imaginative perspective-taking as empathy because he does not experience a similar emotion.

61 See Chapters 9, 10, and 11 of Hoffman's *Empathy and Moral Development*.

62 *Empathy and Moral Development*, p. 244.

Chapter 6   Empathy, Contractual Ethics, and Justification

1   See John Rawls (1999) *A Theory of Justice, Revised Edition*, Cambridge: Harvard University Press; David Gauthier (1986) *Morals By Agreement*, Oxford: Clarendon Press; John Harsanyi (1977) *Rational Behavior and Bargaining Equilibrium in Games and Social Situations*, Cambridge: Cambridge University Press; and T.M. Scanlon (1998) *What We Owe to Each Other*, Cambridge: Harvard University Press.

2   See Gerald F. Gaus (1989) "A Contractual Justification of Redistributive Capitalism," in John W. Chapman and J. Roland Pennock, eds. *Nomos XXXI: Markets and Justice*, New York: New York University Press; Jules L. Coleman (1992) *Risks and Wrongs*, Cambridge: Cambridge University Press; Christopher Morris (1991) "Moral Standing and Rational-Choice Contractarianism," in P. Vallentyne, ed. *Contractarianism and Rational Choice*, Cambridge University Press; James M. Buchanan (2005) "Contractarian Presuppositions and Democratic Governance," in Geoffrey Brennan and Loren Lomasky, eds. *Politics and Process: New Essays in Democratic Thought*, Cambridge: Cambridge University Press; and Matt Matravers (2000) *Justice and Punishment: The Rationale for Coercion*, Oxford: Oxford University Press.

3   The list here is long, but Ronald Dworkin's argument that "hypothetical contract is not simply a pale form of an actual contract; it is no contract at all," is perhaps best known. Ronald Dworkin (1978) *Taking Rights Seriously*, Cambridge: Cambridge University Press, p. 151.

4   This is clearer in Rawls' and Harsanyi's theories than it is in Gauthier's. Some suggest that Gauthier wants hypothetical agreement on principles to show that we need to revise our current set of moral principles and take a revisionary approach to them.

5   Gerald Gaus, "A Contractual Justification of Redistributive Capitalism," p. 93.

6   See Jean Hampton (1993) "Feminist Contractarianism," in Louise Antony and Charlotte Witt, eds. *A Mind of One's Own*, Boulder: Westview Press, p. 235. She says a Hobbesian contract theory like Gauthier's is interested in hypothetical contracts in order to reveal that "the agreed-upon outcome is rational for all of us" in the sense that it requires thinking about political principles that would be mutually advantageous. On the other hand, a Kantian social contract like Rawls' tries to show that moral principles and conceptions are provable theorems derived from a kind of "moral proof procedure" that is expressed in the contractarian reasoning process (p. 235).

7   Samuel Freeman (1990) "Reason and Agreement in Social Contract Views," *Philosophy and Public Affairs*, 19(2): 122–123.

8   *A Theory of Justice, Revised Edition*, p. 16.

9   Jerry Gaus has been perhaps the foremost proponent of the idea of public justification. See Gerald F. Gaus (1996) *Justificatory Liberalism: An Essay on Epistemology and Political Theory*, New York: Oxford University Press. See also Gerald F. Gaus (2005) "The Place of Autonomy in Liberalism," in John Christman and Joel Anderson, eds. *Autonomy and the Challenges to Liberalism*, Cambridge: Cambridge University Press, pp. 272–306, and (2003) *Contemporary Theories of Liberalism*, London: Sage Press. See also

Samuel Freeman (2007) "The Burdens of Public Justification: Constructivism, Contractualism, and Publicity," *Politics, Philosophy & Economics*, 6(1): 5–43.

10 Both Rawls and Gauthier believe Harsanyi's decision-procedure to be a competitor to the decision-procedures they advance in their explicitly contractual theories.

11 Gaus's theory is an example of a contract theory that does not use idealized circumstances and ideally rational agents to show that the justified principles are rational. He instead uses a state of nature argument to provide a benchmark of what a reasonable agreement or bargain would include, and provides a theory of rationality to explain why it is rational. (Gerald F. Gaus (1990) *Value and Justification*, Cambridge: Cambridge University Press, Chapter 8.)

12 Although Gauthier allows for unequal bargaining positions in the bargaining phase of the choice of principles, in the justificatory phase of the project, he supposes that the parties are equally situated and have equal value. (See Chapter 8 of *Morals By Agreement*.)

13 This made clear in his later work. See John Rawls (1993) *Political Liberalism*, New York: Columbia University Press, especially pp. 49–61. For a detailed treatment, see James W. Boettcher (2004) "What is Reasonableness?" *Philosophy and Social Criticism*, Vol. 30 (5–6): 597–621.

14 Gerald F. Gaus, "A Contractual Justification of Redistributive Capitalism," p. 91.

15 "Kantian Constructivism," pp. 320–321. See also *Political Liberalism*.

16 Gaus has emphasized the importance of this distinction for understanding the hypothetical nature of contract theories. See his "Contemporary Uses of the Social Contract," in the *Stanford Encyclopedia of Philosophy*. http://plato.stanford.edu/entries/contractarianism-contemporary/. Accessed July 14, 2010.

17 T.M. Scanlon, "Contractualism and Utilitarianism," in Amartya Sen and Bernard Williams, eds. (1982) *Utilitarianism and Beyond*, Cambridge: Cambridge University Press, p. 282.

18 *A Theory of Justice, Revised Edition*, p. 56.

19 Ibid., p. 81.

20 "Contemporary Approaches to the Social Contract," in Stanford Encyclopedia of Philosophy by Gerald Gaus and Fred D'Agostino: http://plato.stanford.edu/entries/contractarianism-contemporary/ section 1.3.

21 Gerald F. Gaus, *Justificatory Liberalism*, pp. 118–119.

22 Several philosophers have been engaged in this project of defending the contractual account of justification. See especially Gerald F. Gaus, *Justificatory Liberalism*; Cynthia Stark (2000) "Hypothetical Consent and Justification," *Journal of Philosophy*, 97(6): 313–332; Christopher Morris (1996) "A Contractarian Account of Moral Justification," in Walter Sinnot-Armstrong and Mark Timmons, eds. *Moral Knowledge? New Readings in Moral Epistemology*, New York: Oxford Press, p. 216.

23 Susan Moller Okin (1989) "Reason and Feeling in Thinking about Justice," *Ethics*, 99, p. 288. She argues that Rawls' theory of justice cannot be a product of rational choice, and is "a theory that requires empathy even on the part of those artificial moral agents who inhabit the original position…" On her view, Rawls does not "acknowledge any role for empathy or benevolence in the formation of his principles of justice" because he is more interested in depicting the Kantian and rationalistic heritage of his theory. (Both quotes

p. 275.) I disagree with Okin that Rawls' theory cannot be a product of rational choice; on my view, the choice of the principles is rationally justified, but this is a separate question from whether it is publicly justified.

24 Susan Okin (1989) *Justice, Gender, and the Family*, USA: Basic Books, p. 98.

25 See Owen Flanagan (1991) *The Varieties of Moral Personality*, Cambridge: Harvard University Press, p. 32.

26 *Theory of Justice, Revised Edition*, pp. 162–163.

27 Ibid., p. 119.

28 Ibid., p. 56, my emphasis.

29 Brian Barry (1989) *Theories of Justice: A Treatise on Social Justice, Volume 1*, Berkeley: University of California Press, p. 332.

30 Christopher McMahon (2002) "Why There is No Issue Between Habermas and Rawls," *The Journal of Philosophy*, 99(3): 128.

31 Amartya Sen gives a similar argument. He says that the impartiality expressed in the Original Position is "closed" and that impartial assessment is confined to a fixed group that he calls a focal group. He argues that under Rawls' veil of ignorance "there is no insistence at all that perspectives from outside the focal group be invoked," so that his procedure "is not geared to addressing the need to overcome group prejudices." Amartya Sen (2002) "Open and Closed Impartiality," *The Journal of Philosophy*, 99(9): 446. The Rawlsian veil of ignorance can only address interpersonal differences between individuals; it does not address shared prejudices or biases, and can exclude the voice of people who are not included in the focal group, but whose lives are affected by the focal group (pp. 447–449). Though Sen does say that Rawls' way of evaluating society with a public framework of thought implies that various perspectives are taken into account, he is wrong to think that this framework is biased. The constraints that shape the Original Position are ones that we agree on because they are constitutive of the moral perspective, and these beliefs about what is moral determines what is considered a bias. We should thus not worry about bias in the Original Position. Thanks to Jerry Gaus for clarification on this point.

32 Christopher McMahon, "Why There is No Issue," p. 128. Habermas argues that the moral point of view involves a "joint process of Ideal role-taking" in which everyone is required to take the perspective of everyone else." And in the "interlocking of perspectives" an "ideally extended we-perspective" is generated and this is the perspective from which everyone can test whether they wish to make "a controversial norm the basis of their shared practice" (p. 111). But it is important to note that role-taking and identifying with others is not constitutive of moral impartiality for Habermas. Rather, "moral impartiality is constituted by reasons governing the resolution of conflicts of interest, reasons relative to what would be in everyone interests" (p. 116).

33 *Morals By Agreement*, p. 255.

34 Ibid., p. 256.

35 Ibid., p. 257.

36 Ibid., p. 257.

37 To remind the reader, a social welfare function is a representation of the welfare of society (or, the representation of overall preference satisfaction).

38 John Harsanyi "Morality and the Theory of Rational Behavior," in Amartya Sen and Bernard Williams, eds. (1982) *Utilitarianism and Beyond*, Cambridge: Cambridge University Press, p. 45. More specifically, it states that someone

has an *"equal probability* of being *put in the place* of any one among the *n* individual members of society, from the first individual (say, the one in the *best* social position) to the *n*th individual (say, the one in the *worst* social position)" (p. 50).

39 Ibid., p. 45.

40 It is important to note here that the specified utilities should probably be understood as representing a person's *preferences over social states*, so that her utility curve represents her preferences for particular outcomes of social states. Thus, there is no problem of using principles of individual rationality to evaluate social choices, a point made by Dennis Mueller. Dennis Mueller (2003) *Public Choice III*, Cambridge: Cambridge University Press, p. 570.

41 *Public Choice III*, p. 571.

42 In *Value and Justification*, Gaus says that the aim of moral theory is to achieve interpersonal justification of public moral principles. He now uses the term "public justification" of moral principles instead of "interpersonal justification."

43 Gerald Gaus, *Value and Justification*, p. 21.

44 "Contractualism and Utilitarianism," p. 117.

45 Scanlon, *What We Owe to Each Other*, p. 191.

46 See Elizabeth Anderson (1999) "What is the Point of Equality?" *Ethics*, 109(2): 287–337.

47 David Brink (2001) "Realism, Naturalism, and Moral Semantics," *Social Philosophy and Policy*, 18(02): 154–176.

48 Gaus offers a similar thesis when he says that objectivity requires "decentering" and realizing that others have a perspective on things that is different from others, and that their reasons are not ones we may necessarily share. (*Justificatory Liberalism*, pp. 46 and 118.) My claim is that we do this with empathy.

49 Samuel Freeman (2007) "The Burdens of Public Justification," *Politics, Philosophy, and Economics*, 6(1): 27.

50 See also Gerald F. Gaus, *Value and Justification*, p. 329. Gaus argues that in contract theories, the deliberations of the parties are *not* identical, and so the contract method is not otiose.

51 This is also emphasized by Freeman in his "Moral Contractarianism as a Foundation for Interpersonal Morality," in James Dreier (2006) *Contemporary Debates in Moral Theory*, Oxford: Blackwell Publishers.

52 Geoff Sayre-McCord, "Contemporary Contractarian Moral Theory," in Hugh LaFollette (1999) *The Blackwell Guide to Ethical Theory*, Oxford: Blackwell Publishers, p. 258.

53 It is also likely that there will be fundamental similarities to the choice of justified principles, due to similarities in human values and commitments. But the *specific* content of the principles may vary from one contract situation to the next and still be justified.

54 Carole Pateman's critique of the social contract is perhaps the best known. She argues that the individual who enters a social contract depends on a prior, sexual contract that subjects women to the law of male sex-right. (Carol Pateman (1988) *The Sexual Contract*, Stanford, CA: Stanford University Press.) Annette Baier argues that there is a male "fixation" on contract theories that

take morality to be about "cool, distanced relations between more or less free and equal adult strangers..." Annette Baier (1986) "Trust and Anti-Trust," *Ethics*, 96(2): 248. And Virginia Held argues that contract theories that use rational, economic man as representative of humanity use assumptions and conceptions that "seem highly questionable," "hold out an impoverished view of human aspiration," and "overlook or discount in very fundamental ways the experience of women." See Virginia Held (1993) "Non-contractual Society: A Feminist View," *Canadian Journal of Philosophy*, Supplementary Volume 13: 113.

55 As game theorist Ken Binmore argues, even *"Homo economicus* must be empathetic to some degree." Ken Binmore (1996) *Game Theory and the Social Contract Volume 1: Playing Fair*, Cambridge: MIT Press, p. 28.

56 This is essentially Jean Hampton's point in "Feminist Contractarianism," when she claims that there is no reason to posit more than one party in Rawls' original position. Gauthier and Harsanyi also suggest that their contract theories express the reasoning of one person.

57 Gaus argues that contractual justification based on common values is both teleological and deontological. (*Value and Justification*, Chapter 7.) Deontological arguments articulate the shared moral presuppositions that are fundamental to the contractors' value systems and teleological arguments show that a principle is part of a code that describes the idea of the common good (p. 364).

58 See Samuel Freeman's "Reason and Agreement in Social Contract Views," pp. 144–147 for elaboration of this point.

59 *Game Theory and the Social Contract, Volume 1*, p. 290, my emphasis. Binmore proposes a contract theory that implements a veil of ignorance, and calls the preferences derived from it *empathetic preferences*, because they are derived from imaginative identification with others.

60 Ibid., p. 28.

61 Ken Binmore (1998) *Game Theory and the Social Contract, Volume 2: Just Playing*, Cambridge: MIT Press, p. 13.

62 "Contractualism and Utilitarianism," p. 280.

63 "Contractualism and Utilitarianism," p. 276.

64 Alison Jaggar argues that a problem with reversibility tests is that they are "designed as philosophical idealizations, abstracting those features of real-life situations that distort actual moral thinking." Alison Jaggar "Taking Consent Seriously: Feminist Practical Ethics and Actual Moral Dialogue," in Earl R. Winkler and Jerrold R. Coombs, eds. (1993) *Applied Ethics: A Reader*, Oxford: Blackwell Publishers, p. 73. She thinks that while idealized situations can isolate the relevant features of a moral decision, they are too idealized to apply to real people and real situations. "...The real-life people with whom we are instructed to identify may not themselves be fully informed, rational, and uncoerced." Ibid., p. 73. But if social contracts reflected only the actual concerns of actual agents, they would not be able to derive *justified* principles—they would merely represent a bargain. Thus, it is good for social contracts to address both actual and ideal reasons and values in order to achieve interpersonal justification.

65 "Contemporary Contractarian Moral Theory," pp. 257–258.

Chapter 7   Empathy and Moral Education

1   U.S. Army Field Manual (FM) 6-22, *Army Leadership* (Washington, D.C.: U.S. Government Printing Office [GPO] October 2006), pp. 4–9, cited in Harry Garner (2009) "Empathy: A True Leader Skill," *Military Review*, pp. 84–92.
2   Harvey Siegel (1990) *Educating Reason*, New York: Routledge, p. 43.
3   For a discussion on whether empathy is a virtue, see Heather D. Battaly, "Is Empathy a Virtue?" in Amy Coplan and Peter Goldie, eds. (2011) *Empathy: Philosophical and Psychological Perspectives*, Oxford: Oxford University Press.
4   Batson et al., "'...As You Would Have Them Do Unto You': Does Imagining Yourself in the Other's Place Stimulate Moral Action?" p. 1195.
5   Cynthia V. Ward (1994) "A Kinder, Gentler Liberalism? Visions of Empathy in Feminist and Communitarian Literature," *The University of Chicago Law Review*, 61(3): 947.
6   By contrast, those who did not engage in any perspective-taking did *not* choose this approach. See Batson et al., "'...As You Would Have Them Do Unto You': Does Imagining Yourself in the Other's Place Stimulate Moral Action?" p. 199.
7   Cynthia Ward, "A Kinder, Gentler Liberalism? Visions of Empathy in Feminist and Communitarian Literature," p. 935.
8   Ibid., p. 938.
9   This is similar to the rationale of an agent behind Rawls' Veil of Ignorance, though that reasoning is closer to the combination mode of empathy (using self-focused and others-focused empathy). For a complete analysis of empathy and Rawls' Veil of Ignorance, see my Chapter 6.
10   Cynthia Ward, "A Kinder, Gentler Liberalism? Visions of Empathy in Feminist and Communitarian Literature," p. 940.
11   Megan Boler (1999) *Feeling Power: Emotions and Education*, New York: Routledge Press, pp. 158–160.
12   Ibid., p. 159.
13   Ibid., p. 161.
14   Ibid., p. 166.
15   Ibid., p. 170.
16   The others are "power assertion" and "love withdrawal." For discussion of these, see *Empathy and Moral Development*, Chapter 6.
17   *Empathy and Moral Development*, p. 143.
18   Ibid., p. 151.
19   Tonia Caselman (2007) *Teaching Children Empathy, the Social Emotion: Lessons, Activities and Reproducible Worksheets (K-6) That Teach How to "Step Into Others' Shoes"*, Chapin, SC: Youth Light Books.
20   Ibid., p. 6.
21   Joan Skolnick, Nancy Dulberg and Thea Maestre (2004) *Through Other Eyes: Developing Empathy and Multicultural Perspectives in the Social Studies*, Don Mills, Ontario: Pippin Publishing Corporation.
22   A chapter is devoted to developing empathy through each of these themes. See Chapters 4–7 for each of these topics.
23   Ibid., p. 4.
24   David Levine (2005) *Teaching Empathy: A Blueprint for Caring, Compassion and Community*, Bloomington, IN: Solution Tree.

25 Mary Gordon (2005) *Roots of Empathy: Changing the World Child By Child*, New York, New York: Experiment Publishing. Programs are currently in place in public elementary schools in Canada, New Zealand, and some countries in Europe. Programs have just started in Seattle, WA, and are being considered in the New York City public school system.

26 Ibid., p. 6.

27 Ibid., p. 21.

28 Ibid., p. 21.

29 Ibid., p. 45.

30 Statistics accessed: http://www.rootsofempathy.org/documents/ROE%20Research%20Report%2009.pdf October 2, 2010.

31 Mary Gordon, *Roots of Empathy: Changing the World Child by Child*, pp. 60–63.

32 Levine, *Teaching Empathy*, p. 36.

33 Caselman, *Teaching Children Empathy*, p. 68.

34 Ibid., p. 84.

35 Mark A. Barnett, "Empathy and Related Responses in Children," in Nancy Eisenberg and Janet Strayer, eds. (1987) *Empathy and Its Development*, Cambridge: Cambridge University Press, pp. 150–156.

36 Ibid., p. 157.

37 C. Daniel Batson (2007) "An Additional Antecedent of Empathic Concern: Valuing the Welfare of the Person in Need," *Journal of Personality and Social Psychology*, 93(1): 72.

38 Ibid, p. 73.

39 This is Smith's way of explaining successful empathy in his *Theory of Moral Sentiments*, p. 21. His example is about telling a joke; though you may judge a joke to be funny, or at least recognize that the joke is appropriate to cause laughter, if you are in a bad mood, or are preoccupied, you simply may not laugh.

40 See for example, Kathleen Stassen Berger (2005) *The Developing Person: Through the Lifespan, 6th Edition*, New York: Worth Publishers.

41 Koestner, R., Franz, C. and Weinberger, J. (1990) "The Family Origins of Empathic Concern: A 26-year Longitudinal Study," *Journal of Personality and Social Psychology*, 58(4): 709–717. Adult levels of empathic concern were most strongly related to: paternal involvement in child care, maternal tolerance of dependent behavior, maternal inhibition of child's aggression, and maternal satisfaction with the role of mother.

Chapter 8   Conclusion: Implications for Feminist Ethics

1 Examples include: Suzanne Keen (2007) *Empathy and the Novel*, New York: Oxford University Press; Marc Bekoff (2008) *The Emotional Lives of Animals: A Leading Scientist Explores Animal Joy, Sorrow, and Empathy—and Why They Matter*, Novato, CA: New World Library; Frans de Waal (2010) *The Age of Empathy: Nature's Lessons for a Kinder Society*, New York: Three Rivers Press; Edward Farley (1996) *Divine Empathy: A Theology of God*, Minneapolis: Augsburg Fortress.

2 Jessica Durando (2010) "Women More Generous, More Likely to Donate, Study Says," *USA Today*, October 21. http://www.usatoday.com/yourlife/mind-soul/doing-good/2010-10-21-1Acharity21_ST_N.htm. Accessed January 29, 2011.

3   Randy Lennon and Nancy Eisenberg (1987) "Gender and Age Differences in Empathy and Sympathy," in *Empathy and Its Development*, Chapter 9.

4   Ibid., p. 203.

5   Ibid., p. 203.

6   Klein K. and Hodges S. (2001) "Gender Differences, Motivation, and Empathic Accuracy: When it Pays to Understand," *Personality and Social Psychology Bulletin*, 27(6): 720–730. (Emphasis mine.)

7   See Claudia Strauss (2004) "Is Empathy Gendered and, If So, Why? An Approach from Feminist Psychological Anthropology," *Ethos*, 32(4): 432–457.

8   *The Ethics of Care and Empathy*, p. 71.

9   Singer, T., Seymour, B., O'Doherty, J.P., Stephan, K.E., Dolan, R.J. and Frith, C.D. (2006) "Empathic Neural Responses are Modulated by the Perceived Fairness of Others," *Nature*, 439: 466–469.

10 Yang, C.Y., Decety, J., Lee, S., Chen, G. and Cheng, Y. (2009) "Gender Differences in the Mu Rhythm During Empathy for Pain: An Electroencephalographic Study," *Brain Research*, 1251: 176–184.

11 For example, Alison Jaggar outlines four criteria of a feminist ethical theory, or a theory that serves women's interests equally to men's. These include (a) the assumption that women and men do not share precisely the same situation in life, (b) the theory recommends actions "that will tend to subvert rather than reinforce the present systematic subordination of women," (c) it provides strategies for dealing with issues that arise in private or domestic life, and (d) it takes "the moral experience of all women seriously, though not, of course, uncritically," Allison Jaggar, "Feminist Ethics" in L. Becker and C. Becker, eds. (1992) *Encyclopedia of Ethics*, New York: Garland Press, p. 364. See also Annette Baier (1985) "What Do Women Want in a Moral Theory?" *Nous*, 19: 53–63 for a similar argument.

12 Cheshire Calhoun, "Introduction," in Cheshire Calhoun, ed. (2004) *Setting the Moral Compass: Essays by Women Philosophers*, Oxford: Oxford University Press, p. 13.

13 See Virginia Held (2006) *The Ethics of Care: Personal, Political, Global*, Oxford: Oxford University Press; Sara Ruddick (1995) *Maternal Thinking: Towards a Politics of Peace*, Boston: Beacon Press, and "Care as Labor and Relationship," in Joram G. Haber and Mark S. Halfon, eds. (1998) *Norms and Values: Essays on the Work of Virginia Held*, Lanham, Md.: Rowman and Littlefield; Nel Noddings (1986) *Caring: A Feminine Approach to Ethics and Moral Education*, Berkeley: University of California Press.

14 Slote states, "An advocate of care ethics (along the lines of the present book) would then, presumably, have to agree/admit that, in the sphere of morality, women are basically superior to men...," *Ethics of Care and Empathy*, p. 72.

15 Virginia Held, "Taking Care: Care as Practice and Value," in *Setting the Moral Compass: Essays by Women Philosophers*, p. 63.

16 See my Chapter 5 for a complete analysis of Myers' view, articulated in *Subjection and Subjectivity: Psychoanalytic Feminism and Moral Philosophy*.

17 See for example: Martha C. Nussbaum (2001) *Upheavals of Thought: The Intelligence of Emotions*, Cambridge, England: Cambridge University Press; Nussbaum, Martha (1990) *Love's Knowledge*, Oxford: Oxford University Press; Greenspan, Patricia (1988) *Emotions and Reasons: An Inquiry into Emotional Justification*, New York: Routledge, Chapman and Hall; Patricia Greenspan

(1995) *Practical Guilt: Moral Dilemmas, Emotions and Social Norms*, New York: Oxford University Press; Lugones, Maria (1987) "Playfulness, 'World'-traveling, and Loving Perception," *Hypatia*, 2: 3–19.

18 Nancy Sherman (1998) "Empathy and Imagination," *Midwest Studies in Philosophy XXII*: 82–119.

19 Cynthia Ward, "A Kinder, Gentler Liberalism? Visions of Empathy in Feminist and Communitarian Literature," p. 935.

20 Jeannette Kennett (2002) "Autism, Empathy and Moral Agency," *The Philosophical Quarterly*, 52(208): 345. She argues that the developmental literature also suggests that empathy gives "insight into other selves which is so epistemically useful in our daily lives" and contributes to "the development of one's own sense of self" (p. 356).

21 *Empathy and Moral Development*, pp. 290–293.

22 *Empathy and Moral Development*, p. 292.

23 John Rawls "The Idea of an Overlapping Consensus," *The Collected Papers of John Rawls*, p. 439.

Bibliography

Anderson, Elizabeth. 1999. "What is the Point of Equality?," *Ethics*, 109(2): 287–337.

Antony, Louise and Witt, Charlotte, eds. 1999. *A Mind of One's Own*, ed. Boulder: Westview Press.

Arrow, Kenneth. 1951. *Social Choice and Individual Values*. New York: John Wiley and Sons.

Baier, Annette. 1985. "What Do Women Want in a Moral Theory?," *Nous*, 19: 53–63.

———. 1986. "Trust and Anti-Trust," *Ethics*, 96(2): 231–260.

———. 1987. "The Need for More than Justice," *Canadian Journal of Philosophy*, Supplementary Volume 13: 41–56.

Barnett, Mark. 1987. "Empathy and Related Reponses in Children," *Empathy and Its Development*, ed. Nancy Eisenberg and Janet Strayer. Cambridge: Cambridge University Press.

Barry, Brian. 1989. *Theories of Justice: A Treatise on Social Justice, Volume 1*. Berkeley: University of California Press.

Batson, C.D. 1991. *The Altruism Question: Toward a Social-Psychological Answer*. Hillsdale, NJ: Erlbaum Press.

———. 2007. "An Additional Antecedent of Empathic Concern: Valuing the Welfare of the Person in Need," *Journal of Personality and Social Psychology*, 93(1): 65–74.

———. 2009. "These Things Called Empathy: Eight Related but Distinct Phenomena," in *The Social Neuroscience of Empathy*, edited by Jean Decety and William Ickes. Cambridge, MA: MIT Press.

Batson, C.D., Early, S. and Salvarani, G. 1997. "Perspective-taking: Imagining How Another Feels Versus Imagining How You Would Feel," *Personality and Social Psychology Bulletin*, 20: 751–758.

Batson, C.D., Lishner, D., Carpenter, A., Dulin, L., Harjusola-Webb, S., Stocks, E., Gale, S., Hassan, O. and Sampat, B. 2003. "'...As You Would Have Them Do Unto You': Does Imagining Yourself in the Other's Place Stimulate Moral Action?," *Personality and Social Psychology Bulletin*, 29(9): 1190–1201.

Bekoff, Marc. 2008. *The Emotional Lives of Animals: A Leading Scientist Explores Animal Joy, Sorrow, and Empathy – and Why They Matter*. Novato, CA: New World Library.

Berger, Kathleen Stassen. 2005. *The Developing Person: Through the Lifespan, 6th Edition*. New York: Worth Publishers.

Benhabib, Seyla. 1987. "The Generalized and the Concrete Other: The Kohlberg-Gilligan Controversy and Feminist Theory," in *Feminism as Critique: On the Politics of Gender*, ed. Seyla Benhabib and Drucilla Cornell. Minneapolis: University of Minnesota Press.

Bennett, James. 2004. "Israeli Official Offers Empathy but Hits a Nerve," *New York Times*, May 24.

Binmore, Ken. 1996. *Game Theory and the Social Contract, Volume 1: Playing Fair*. Cambridge: MIT Press.

——. 1998. *Game Theory and the Social Contract, Volume 2: Just Playing.* Cambridge: MIT Press.

Blair, R.J.R. 1996. "Theory of Mind in the Psychopath," *Journal of Forensic Psychiatry*, 7: 15–25.

Blum, Lawrence. 1980. *Friendship, Altruism and Morality.* London: Routledge and Kegan Paul.

——. 1988. "Gilligan and Kohlberg: Implications for Moral Theory," *Ethics*, 98: 472–491.

Boettcher, James W. 2004. "What is Reasonableness?," *Philosophy and Social Criticism*, 30(5–6): 597–621.

Boler, Megan. 1999. *Feeling Power: Emotions and Education.* New York: Routledge Press.

Boucher, David and Kelly, Paul, eds. 1994. *The Social Contract from Hobbes to Rawls.* New York: Routledge.

Brennan, Samantha. 1999. "Recent Work in Feminist Ethics," *Ethics*, 109: 858–893.

Brink, David. 2001. "Realism, Naturalism, and Moral Semantics," *Social Philosophy and Policy*, 18(02): 154–176.

Buchanan, James M. 2005. "Contractarian Presuppositions and Democratic Governance," in *Politics and Process: New Essays in Democratic Thought*, ed. Geoffrey Brennan and Loren Lomasky. Cambridge: Cambridge University Press.

Calhoun, Cheshire. 2003. "Cognitive Emotions?," in *What is an Emotion? Classic and Contemporary Readings*, ed. Robert C. Solomon. Oxford: Oxford University Press.

Calhoun, Cheshire, ed. 2004. *Setting the Moral Compass: Essays by Women Philosophers.* Oxford: Oxford University Press.

Campbell, Richmond. 2007. "What is a Moral Judgment?," *Journal of Philosophy*, 104: 321–349.

Caselman, Tonia. 2007. *Teaching Children Empathy, the Social Emotion: Lessons, Activities and Reproducible Worksheets (K–6) That Teach How to "Step Into Others' Shoes".* Chapin, SC: YouthLight Books.

Chismar, Douglas. 1988. "Empathy and Sympathy: The Important Difference," *Journal of Value Inquiry*, 22(4): 257–266.

Code, Lorraine. 1994. "'I Know Just How You Feel': Empathy and the Problem of Epistemic Authority," in Ellen Singer More and Maureen A. Milligan, eds. *The Empathic Practitioner: Empathy, Gender, and Medicine.* New Brunswick: Rutgers University Press.

Coleman, Jules L. 1992. *Risks and Wrongs.* Cambridge: Cambridge University Press.

Coplan, Amy and Goldie, Peter. 2011. *Empathy: Philosophical and Psychological Perspectives*, ed. Oxford: Oxford University Press.

Copp, David. 1991. "Contractarianism and Moral Skepticism," in *Contractarianism and Rational Choice*, Peter Vallentyne, ed. Cambridge: Cambridge University Press.

D'Arms, Justin. 2000. "Empathy and Evaluative Inquiry," *Chicago-Kent Law Review*, 74(4): 1467–1500.

Darwall, Stephen. 1998. "Empathy, Sympathy, Care," *Philosophical Studies*, 89(2–3): 261–282.

——. 2006. *The Second Person Standpoint: Morality, Respect, and Accountability.* Cambridge: Harvard University Press.

Davidson, Donald. 1986. "Judging Interpersonal Interests," in *Foundations of Social Choice Theory*. Edited by Jon Elster and Aanund Hylland. Cambridge: Cambridge University Press.

Davis, Mark H. 1994. *Empathy: A Social Psychological Approach*. Madison, WI: Brown and Benchmark.

Debes, Remy. 2010. "Which Empathy? Limitations in the Mirrored Understanding of Emotion," *Synthese*, 175(2): 219–239.

Decety, Jean and Ickes, William. 2009. *The Social Neuroscience of Empathy*. Cambridge: MIT Press.

Deigh, John. 1995. "Empathy and Universalizability," *Ethics*, 105(4): 743–763.

Denham, Alison. 2008. "Psychopathy, Empathy, and Moral Motivation," in *Essays on Iris Murdoch*, ed. J. Broakes. Oxford: Oxford University Press.

de Waal, Frans B.M. 2008. "Putting the Altruism Back into Altruism: The Evolution of Empathy," *The Annual Review of Psychology*, 59: 279–300.

de Waal, Frans B.M. 2010. *The Age of Empathy: Nature's Lessons for a Kinder Society*. New York: Three Rivers Press.

Dreier, James. 2004. "Decision Theory and Morality," in *The Oxford Handbook of Rationality*, ed. Alfred Mele and Piers Rawling. Oxford: Oxford University Press.

Durando, Jessica. 2010. "Women More Generous, More Likely to Donate, Study Says," *USA Today*, October 21.

Dworkin, Ronald. 1978. *Taking Rights Seriously*. Cambridge: Cambridge University Press.

Eisenberg, Nancy. 1986. *Altruistic Emotion, Cognition, and Behavior*. Hillsdale, NJ: Erlbaum Press.

Eisenberg, Nancy, ed. 1982. *The Development of Prosocial Behavior*. NY: Academic Press.

——. ed. 1989. *Empathy and Related Emotional Responses*. San Francisco: Jossey-Bass Inc., Publishers.

Eisenberg, Nancy, and Strayer, Janet, eds. 1987. *Empathy and Its Development*. Cambridge: Cambridge University Press.

Elster, Jon and Hylland, Aanund, eds. 1986. *Foundations of Social Choice Theory*. Cambridge: Cambridge University Press.

Farley, Edward. 1996. *Divine Empathy: A Theology of God*. Minneapolis: Augsburg Fortress.

Flanagan, Owen. 1991. *The Varieties of Moral Personality*. Cambridge: Harvard University Press.

Flanagan, Owen and Jackson, Kathryn. 1990. "Justice, Care and Gender: The Kohlberg-Gilligan Debate Revisited," in *Feminism and Political Theory*, ed. Cass Sunstein. Chicago: University of Chicago Press.

Freeman, Samuel, ed. 2003. *The Cambridge Companion to Rawls*. Cambridge: Cambridge University Press.

Freeman, Samuel. 1990. "Reason and Agreement in Social Contract Views," *Philosophy and Public Affairs*, 19(2): 122–157.

——. 2006a. "Moral Contractarianism as a Foundation for Interpersonal Morality," in James Dreier, ed. *Contemporary Debates in Moral Theory*. Oxford: Blackwell Publishing.

——. 2006b. *Justice and the Social Contract: Essays on Rawlsian Political Philosophy*. Oxford: Oxford University Press.

——. 2007. "The Burdens of Public Justification: Constructivism, Contractualism, and Publicity," *Politics, Philosophy & Economics*, 6(1): 5–43.

Garner, Harry. 2009. "Empathy: A True Leader Skill," *Military Review*, 84–92.

Gallese, V., Keysers, C. and Rizzolatti, G. 2004. "A Unifying View of the Basis of Social Cognition," *Trends in Cognitive Sciences*, 8: 396–403.

Gaus, Gerald F. 1989. "A Contractual Justification of Redistributive Capitalism," *NOMOS XXXI: Markets and Justice*, ed. John W. Chapman and J. Roland Pennock. New York: NYU Press.

——. 1990. *Value and Justification*. Cambridge: Cambridge University Press.

——. 1996. *Justificatory Liberalism*. Oxford: Oxford University Press.

——. 2003. *Contemporary Theories of Liberalism*. London: Sage Press.

——. 2005. "The Place of Autonomy in Liberalism," in John Christman and Joel Anderson, eds. *Autonomy and the Challenges to Liberalism*. Cambridge: Cambridge University Press.

Gaus, Gerald F. and D'Agostino. 2008. "Approaches to the Social Contract," in *Stanford Encyclopedia of Philosophy*. http://plato.stanford.edu/entries/contractarianism-contemporary.

Gauthier, David. 1986. *Morals By Agreement*. Oxford: Clarendon Press.

——. 1988. "Morality, Rational Choice, and Semantic Representation: A Reply to My Critics," *Social Philosophy and Policy*, 5(2): 173–221.

——. 1991. "Why Contractarianism?," in *Contractarianism and Rational Choice*, ed. Peter Vallentyne. Cambridge: Cambridge University Press.

——. 1993. "Between Hobbes and Rawls," in *Rationality, Justice, and the Social Contract*.

Gauthier, David and Sugden, Robert, eds. 1993. *Rationality, Justice, and the Social Contract*. Ann Arbor: University of Michigan Press.

Gilligan, Carol. 1982. *In a Different Voice: Psychological Theory and Women's Development*. Cambridge: Harvard University Press.

Goldie, Peter. 1999. "How We Think of Others' Emotions," *Mind and Language*, 14(4): 394–423.

Goldman, Alvin. 1993. "Ethics and Cognitive Science," *Ethics*, 103: 337–360.

——. 1995a. "Empathy, Mind, and Morals," in *Mental Simulation*, Martin Davies and Tony Stone, eds. Oxford: Blackwell.

——. 1995b. "Simulation and Interpersonal Utility," *Ethics*, 105: 709–726.

——. 2006. *Simulating Minds: The Philosophy, Psychology and Neuroscience of Mindreading*, Oxford: Oxford University Press.

Goldstein, Arnold and Michaels, Gerald, eds. 1985. *Empathy: Development, Training, and Consequences*. Hillsdale, NJ: Erlbaum Associates.

Gordon, Mary. 2005. *Roots of Empathy: Changing the World Child By Child*. New York, New York: Experiment Publishing.

Gordon, Robert. 1995. "Sympathy, Simulation, and the Impartial Spectator," *Ethics*, 105(4): 727–742.

——. 1995. "Simulation Without Introspection or Inference from Me to You," in *Mental Simulation*, Martin Davies and Tony Stone, eds. Oxford: Blackwell.

Grandin, Temple. 2008. *The Way I See It: A Personal Look at Autism and Asperger's*. Arlington TX: Future Horizons.

Greenspan, Patricia. 1988. *Emotions and Reasons: An Inquiry into Emotional Justification*. New York: Routledge.

——. 1995. *Practical Guilt: Moral Dilemmas, Emotions and Social Norms*. New York: Oxford University Press.

Halpern, Jodi. 2001. *From Detached Concern to Empathy: Humanizing Medical Practice*. Oxford: Oxford University Press.

Hampton, Jean. 1980. "Contracts and Choices: Does Rawls have a Social Contract Theory?," *Journal of Philosophy*, 77: 315–338.

——. 1991. "Two Faces of Contractarian Thought," in *Contractarianism and Rational Choice*, Peter Vallentyne, ed. Cambridge: Cambridge University Press.

——. 1993. "Feminist Contractarianism," in *A Mind of One's Own*, Louise Antony and Charlotte Witt, eds. Boulder: Westview Press.

——. 1994. "The Failure of Expected-Utility Theory as a Theory of Reason," *Economics and Philosophy*, 10: 195–242.

——. 2006. *The Intrinsic Worth of Persons: Contractarianism in Moral and Political Philosophy*. Cambridge: Cambridge University Press.

Hare, R.M. 1963. *Freedom and Reason*. Oxford: Oxford University Press.

——. 1981. *Moral Thinking*. Oxford: Clarendon Press.

Harsanyi, John. 1977. *Rational Behavior and Bargaining Equilibrium in Games and Social Situations*. Cambridge: Cambridge University Press.

——. 1980. *Essays on Ethics, Social Behavior, and Scientific Explanation*. Dordrecht: D. Reidel Publishing Co.

——. 1982. "Morality and the Theory of Rational Behavior," *Utilitarianism and Beyond*, Amartya Sen and Bernard Williams, eds. Cambridge: Cambridge University Press.

Hastings, Paul D., Zahn-Waxler, Carolyn and McShane, Kelly. 2006. "We are, by Nature, Moral Creatures: Biological Bases of Concern for Others," *Handbook of Moral Development*, edited by Melanie Killen and Judith Smetana. Mahwah, NJ: Lawrence Erlbaum Associates.

Hausman, Daniel. 1995. "The Impossibility of Interpersonal Comparisons," *Mind*, 104: 473–490.

Held, Virginia. 1987. "Non-Contractual Society: A Feminist View," *The Canadian Journal of Philosophy*, Supplementary Volume 13: 121–137.

——. 2006. *The Ethics of Care: Personal, Political, Global*. Oxford: Oxford University Press.

Hill, Jr. Thomas. 1989. "Kantian Constructivism in Ethics," *Ethics*, 99: 752–770.

Hobbes, Thomas. 1651/1996. *Leviathan*, Richard Tuck, ed. Cambridge: Cambridge University Press.

Hoffman, Martin L. 1982. "Development of Prosocial Motivation: Empathy and Guilt," in N. Eisenberg, ed. *The Development of Prosocial Behavior*. New York: Academic Press.

——. 1982. "The Measurement of Empathy," in *Emotion in Infants*, ed. C.E. Izard. New York: Cambridge University Press.

——. 2000. *Empathy and Moral Development: Implications for Caring and Justice*. Cambridge: Cambridge University Press.

Holton, Richard and Langton, Rae. 1999. "Empathy and Animal Ethics," *Singer and his Critics*. Oxford: Blackwell Press.

Hume, David. 1740/2000. ed. Norton and Norton, *Treatise of Human Nature*. Oxford: Oxford University Press.

Iacoboni, Marco. 2009. "Imitation, Empathy, and Mirror Neurons," *Annual Review of Psychology*, 60: 1–19.

Ickes, William, ed. 1997. *Empathic Accuracy*. New York: Guilford Press.

Izard, Carol E., ed. 1982. *Emotion in Infants*. Cambridge: Cambridge University Press.

Jaggar, Alison. 1992. "Feminist Ethics," in *Encyclopedia of Ethics*, L. Becker and C. Becker, eds. New York: Garland Press.

———. 1993. "Taking Consent Seriously: Feminist Practical Ethics and Actual Moral Dialogue," in *Applied Ethics: A Reader*, ed. Earl R. Winkler and Jerrold R. Coombs. Oxford: Blackwell Publishers.

Kahneman, Daniel and Tversky, Amos. 1982. "The Simulation Heuristic," in *Judgment Under Uncertainty: Heuristics and Biases*, edited by Kahneman, Slovic and Tversky. Cambridge: Cambridge University Press.

Kahneman, Slovic and Tversky, eds. 1982. *Judgment Under Uncertainty: Heuristics and Biases*. Cambridge: Cambridge University Press.

Kant, Immanuel. 1797/1996. *The Metaphysics of Morals*, Mary Gregor, ed. Cambridge: Cambridge University Press.

Katz, Robert L. 1963. *Empathy: Its Nature and Uses*. New York: Macmillan Company.

Kavka, Gregory. 1986. *Hobbesian Moral and Political Theory*. Princeton: Princeton University Press.

Keen, Suzanne. 2007. *Empathy and the Novel*. New York: Oxford University Press.

Kennett, Jeanette. 2000. "Autism, Empathy and Moral Agency," *The Philosophical Quarterly*, 52: 340–357.

———. 2008. "Reasons, Reverence, and Value," in *Moral Psychology Volume 3: The Neuroscience of Morality: Emotion, Disease, and Development*, ed. Walter Sinnott-Armstrong. Cambridge: MIT Press.

Kittay, Eva. 2005. "Equality, Dignity, and Disability," in *Perspectives on Equality: The Second Seamus Heaney Lectures*, Lyons, Ann and Waldron, Fionnuala, eds. Dublin: The Liffey Press.

Klein, K. and Hodges, S. 2001. "Gender Differences, Motivation, and Empathic Accuracy: When it Pays to Understand," *Personality and Social Psychology Bulletin*, 27(6): 720–730.

Koestner, R., Franz, C. and Weinberger, J. 1990. "The Family Origins of Empathic Concern: A 26-year Longitudinal Study," *Journal of Personality and Social Psychology*, 58(4): 709–717.

Kohlberg, Lawrence. 1981. *The Philosophy of Moral Development: Moral Stages and the Idea of Justice*. San Francisco: Harper and Row.

Kohut, H. 1959. "Introspection, Empathy, and Psychoanalysis," *Journal of the American Psychoanalytic Association*, 7: 459–483.

Korsgaard, Christine. 1996. *The Sources of Normativity*. Cambridge: Cambridge University Press.

Krisjannsen, Kristan. 2004. "Empathy, Sympathy, Justice and the Child," *Journal of Moral Education*, 33(3): 291–305.

Kukathas, Chandran and Pettit, Philip. 1990. *Rawls' A Theory of Justice and Its Critics*. Stanford, Calif.: Stanford University Press.

LaFollette, Hugh, ed. 1999. *The Blackwell Guide to Ethical Theory*. Oxford: Blackwell Publishers.

Lennon, Randy and Eisenberg, Nancy. 1987. "Gender and Age Differences in Empathy and Sympathy," in *Empathy and Its Development*, ed. Eisenberg and Strayer.

Levine, David. 2005. *Teaching Empathy: A Blueprint for Caring, Compassion and Community*. Bloomington, IN: Solution Tree.

Linder, Douglas O. 1996. "Juror Empathy and Race," *Tennessee Law Review*, 63: 887–916.

Lloyd, S.A. 2009. *The Philosophy of Thomas Hobbes: Cases in the Law of Nature.* Cambridge: Cambridge University Press.

Lugones, Maria. 1987. "Playfulness, 'World'-traveling, and Loving Perception," *Hypatia*, 2: 3–19.

Mandle, Jon. 1999. "The Reasonable in Justice as Fairness", *Canadian Journal of Philosophy*, 29(1): 75–107.

Matravers, Matt. 2000. *Justice and Punishment: The Rationale for Coercion.* Oxford: Oxford University Press.

McMahon, Christopher. 2002. "Why There is No Issue Between Habermas and Rawls," *The Journal of Philosophy*, 99(3): 111–129.

Mele, Alfred and Rawling, Piers, eds. 2004. *The Oxford Handbook of Rationality.* Oxford: Oxford University Press.

Mendus, Susan. 2002. *Impartiality in Moral and Political Philosophy.* Oxford: Oxford University Press.

Meyers, Diana Tietjens. 1994. *Subjection and Subjectivity.* New York: Routledge Press.

More, Ellen Singer and Milligan, Maureen, eds. 1994. *The Empathic Practitioner: Empathy, Gender, and Medicine.* USA: Rutgers University Press.

Morris, Christopher. 1996. "A Contractarian Account of Moral Justification," in *Moral Knowledge? New Readings in Moral Epistemology*, Walter Sinnott-Armstrong and Mark Timmons, eds. New York: Oxford Press.

Morris, Errol. 2003. *The Fog of War: Eleven Lessons from the Life of Robert S. McNamara.* Sony Pictures Classics.

Murphy, Jeffrie. 1972. "Moral Death: A Kantian Essay on Psychopathy," *Ethics*, 82: 284–298.

Mueller, Dennis. 2003. *Social Choice III.* Cambridge: Cambridge University Press.

Nagel, Thomas. 1970. *The Possibility of Altruism.* Princeton: Princeton University Press.

Nichols, Shaun. 2004. *Sentimental Rules.* Oxford: Oxford University Press.

Nichols, Shaun. 2004. "Imagining and Believing: The Promise of a Single Code," *Journal of Aesthetics and Art Criticism*, 62(6): 129–139.

Noddings, Nel. 1986. *Caring: A Feminine Approach to Ethics and Moral Education.* Berkeley: University of California Press.

Nussbaum, Martha. 1990. *Love's Knowledge.* Oxford: Oxford University Press.

——. 2002. "Rawls and Feminism," in *The Cambridge Companion to Rawls*, ed. Samuel Freeman. Cambridge: Cambridge University Press.

——. 2003. *Upheavals of Thought: The Intelligence of Emotions.* Cambridge: Cambridge University Press.

Okin, Susan Moller. 1989. "Reason and Feeling in Thinking about Justice," *Ethics*, 99: 273–293.

——. 1990. "Feminism, the Individual, and Contract Theory," *Ethics*, 100: 658–669.

——. 1991. *Justice, Gender and the Family.* USA: Basic Books.

Omdahl, Becky. 1995. *Cognitive Appraisal, Emotion, and Empathy.* Mahwah, NJ: Erlbaum Associates.

O'Neill, Onora. 1993. "Justice, Gender, and International Boundaries," in *The Quality of Life*, ed. Martha Nussbaum and Amartya Sen. Oxford: Clarendon Press.

Pateman, Carole. 1988. *The Sexual Contract*. Stanford: Stanford University Press.

Piaget, Jean. 1932/1965. *The Psychology of Moral Development*. New York: Free Press.

——. 1968. *The Moral Judgment of the Child*. London: Routledge and K. Paul.

Piper, Adrian M.S. 1991. "Impartiality, Compassion, and Modal Imagination," *Ethics*, 101(4): 726–757.

Prichard, H.A. 1912. "Does Moral Philosophy Rest on a Mistake?," *Mind*, 21: 21–37.

Prinz, Jesse. 2007. *The Emotional Construction of Morals*. Oxford: Oxford University Press.

Rawls, John. 1993. *Political Liberalism*. New York: Columbia University Press.

——. 1999. *A Theory of Justice, Revised Edition*. Cambridge: Harvard University Press.

——. 1999. *Collected Papers of John Rawls*, ed. Samuel Freeman. Cambridge: Harvard University Press.

Ravenscroft, Ian. 1998. "What is it Like to be Someone Else? Simulation and Empathy," *Ratio*, 11: 170–185.

Rifkin, Jeremy, 2009. *The Empathic Civilization: The Race to Global Consciousness in a World in Crisis*. New York: Penguin Group.

Rizzolatti, G., Fadiga, L., Gallese, V. and Fogassi, L. 1996. "Premotor Cortex and the Recognition of Motor Actions," *Cognitive Brain Research*, 3: 131–141.

Robbins, Lionel. 1938. "Interpersonal Comparisons of Utility: A Comment," *The Economic Journal*, 48(192): 635–641.

Roemer, John. 1996. *Theories of Distributive Justice*. Cambridge: Harvard University Press.

Ruddick, Sara. 1995. *Maternal Thinking: Towards a Politics of Peace*. Boston: Beacon Press.

——. 1998. "Care as Labor and Relationship," in Joram G. Haber and Mark S. Halfon, eds. *Norms and Values: Essays on the Work of Virginia Held*. Lanham, Md.: Rowman and Littlefield.

Sample, Ruth. 2002. "Why Feminist Contractarianism?," *Journal of Social Philosophy*, 33(2): 257–281.

Sayre-McCord, Geoff. 1994. "On Why Hume's 'General Point of View' Isn't Ideal – and Shouldn't Be," *Social Philosophy and Policy*, 11: 202–228.

——. 1999. "Contemporary Contractarian Moral Theory," in *The Blackwell Guide to Ethical Theory*, ed. Hugh LaFollette. Oxford: Blackwell Publishers.

Scanlon, Thomas. 1991. "The Moral Basis of Interpersonal Comparisons," in *Interpersonal Comparisons of Well-being*, ed. Jon Elster and John Roemer. Cambridge: Cambridge University Press.

——. 1997. "Contractualism and Utilitarianism," in *Moral Discourse and Practice*, ed. Stephen Darwall, Allan Gibbard and Peter Railton. Oxford: Oxford University Press.

——. 1998. *What We Owe to Each Other*. Cambridge: Harvard University Press.

Scheffler, Samuel. 1992. "Responsibility, Reactive Attitudes, and Liberalism," *Philosophy and Public Affairs*, 21(4): 299–323.

Siegel, Harvey. 1990. *Educating Reason*. New York: Routledge.

Sen, Amartya and Williams, Bernard, eds. 1982. *Utilitarianism and Beyond*. Cambridge: Cambridge University Press.

Sen, Amartya. 2002. "Open and Closed Impartiality," *The Journal of Philosophy*, 99(9): 445–469.

Sherman, Nancy. 1998a. "Empathy, Respect, and Humanitarian Intervention," *Ethics and International Affairs*, 12: 103–119.

——. 1998b. "Empathy and Imagination," *Midwest Studies in Philosophy, Volume XXII: The Philosophy of Emotions*, ed. Peter A. French and Howard K. Wettstein. Notre Dame: University of Notre Dame Press.

Shoemaker, David. 2007. "Moral Address, Moral Responsibility, and the Boundaries of Moral Community," *Ethics*, 118: 70–108.

Singer, T., Seymour, B., O'Doherty, J.P. Stephan, K.E., Dolan, R.J. and Frith, C.D. 2006. "Empathic Neural Responses are Modulated by the Perceived Fairness of Others," *Nature*, 439: 466–469.

Sinnot-Armstrong, Walter, ed. 2008. *Moral Psychology: The Neuroscience of Morality: Emotion, Brain Disorders, and Development, Volume 3*. Cambridge: MIT Press.

Sinnott-Armstrong, Walter and Timmons, Mark, eds. 1996. *Moral Knowledge? New Readings in Moral Epistemology*. New York: Oxford Press.

Skolnick, Joan, Dulberg, Nancy and Maestre, Thea. 2004. *Through Other Eyes: Developing Empathy and Multicultural Perspectives in the Social Studies*. Don Mills, Ontario: Pippin Publishing Corporation.

Skyrms, Brian. 1996. *Evolution of the Social Contract*. Cambridge: Cambridge University Press.

Slalavitz, Maia. 2010. "School Bullying Prevention: Teach Empathy at a Young Age," TIME Magazine, April 17, 2010.

Slote, Michael. 2007. *The Ethics of Care and Empathy*. London: Routledge Press.

Smith, Adam. 1759/2002. *A Theory of Moral Sentiments*. Cambridge: Cambridge University Press.

Snow, Nancy. 2000. "Empathy," *American Philosophical Quarterly*, 37(1): 65–78.

Sorensen, Roy A. 1998. "Self-Strengthening Empathy," *Philosophy and Phenomenological Research*, 58: 75–98.

Sober, Elliot and Wilson, David Sloan. 1998. *Unto Others: The Evolution and Psychology of Unselfish Behavior*. Cambridge: Harvard University Press.

Solomon, Robert C. 2003. *What is an Emotion?: Classic and Contemporary Readings*. New York: Oxford University Press.

Stark, Cynthia. 1997. "Decision Procedures, Standards of Rightness, and Impartiality," *Nous*, 31(4): 478–495.

——. 2000. "Hypothetical Consent and Justification," *Journal of Philosophy*, 97(6): 313–332.

Stocker, Michael and Elizabeth Hegemon. 1996. *Valuing Emotions*. Cambridge: Cambridge University Press.

Stotland, E., Matthews, K., Sherman, S., Hansson, R. and Richardson, B. 1978. *Empathy, Fantasy, and Helping*. Beverly Hills, CA: Sage Publications.

Strauss, Claudia. 2004. "Is Empathy Gendered and, If So, Why? An Approach from Feminist Psychological Anthropology," *Ethos*, 32(4): 432–457.

Stueber, Karsten. 2006. *Rediscovering Empathy*. Cambridge: MIT Press.

Sudgen, Robert. 2002. "Beyond Sympathy and Empathy: Adam Smith's Concept of Fellow-Feeling," *Economics and Philosophy*, 18(1): 63–87.

Thomas, Laurence. 1998. "Rationality and Affectivity," *Social Philosophy and Policy* 5(2): 154–172.

Thompson, Ross A. 1987. "Empathy and Emotional Understanding: The Early Development of Empathy," in *Empathy and Its Development*, Eisenberg, Nancy and Strayer, Janet, eds. Cambridge: Cambridge University Press.

Tong, Rosemarie. 1997. "Feminist Perspectives on Empathy as an Epistemic Skill and Caring as a Moral Virtue," *Journal of Medical Humanities*, 18(3): 153–168.

Tsoudis, Olga. 2002. "The Influence of Empathy in Mock Jury Criminal Cases: Adding to the Affect Control Model," *Western Criminology Review*, 4(1): 55–67.

Vallentyne, Peter, ed. 1991. *Contractarianism and Rational Choice*. Cambridge: Cambridge University Press.

Vignemont, Frederique de and Frith, Uta. 2008. "Autism, Morality, and Empathy," in *The Neuroscience of Morality: Emotion, Brain Disorders, and Development, Volume 3*, edited by Walter Sinnott-Armstrong.

Ward, Cynthia V. 1994. "A Kinder, Gentler Liberalism? Visions of Empathy in Feminist and Communitarian Literature," *The University of Chicago Law Review*, 61(3): 929–955.

Weymark, John. 1991. "A Reconsideration of the Harsanyi-Sen Debate on Utilitarianism," in Jon Elster and John Roemer, eds. *Interpersonal Comparisons of Wellbeing*. Cambridge: Cambridge University Press.

Wispe, Lauren. 1987. "History of the Concept of Empathy," in *Empathy and Its Development*, Eisenberg, Nancy, and Strayer, Janet, eds. Cambridge: Cambridge University Press.

Yang, C.Y., Decety, J., Lee, S., Chen, G. and Cheng, Y. 2009. "Gender Differences in the Mu Rhythm during Empathy for Pain: An Electroencephalographic Study," *Brain Research*, 1251: 176–184.

Index